Chi's Sweet Home

チーズ スイートホーム

3

Konami Kanata

contents
homemade 39~56

homemade 39: a cat mimics

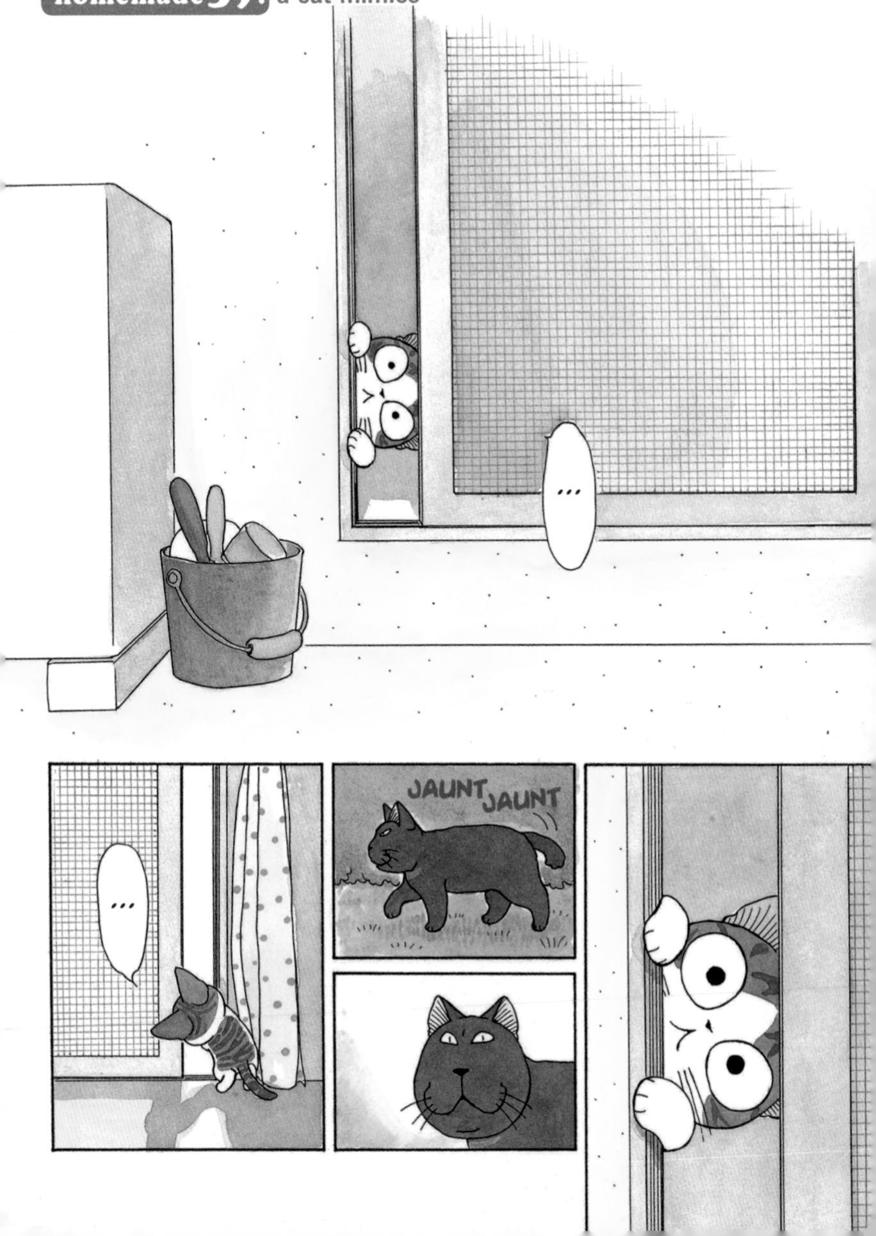
...
...
JAUNT JAUNT

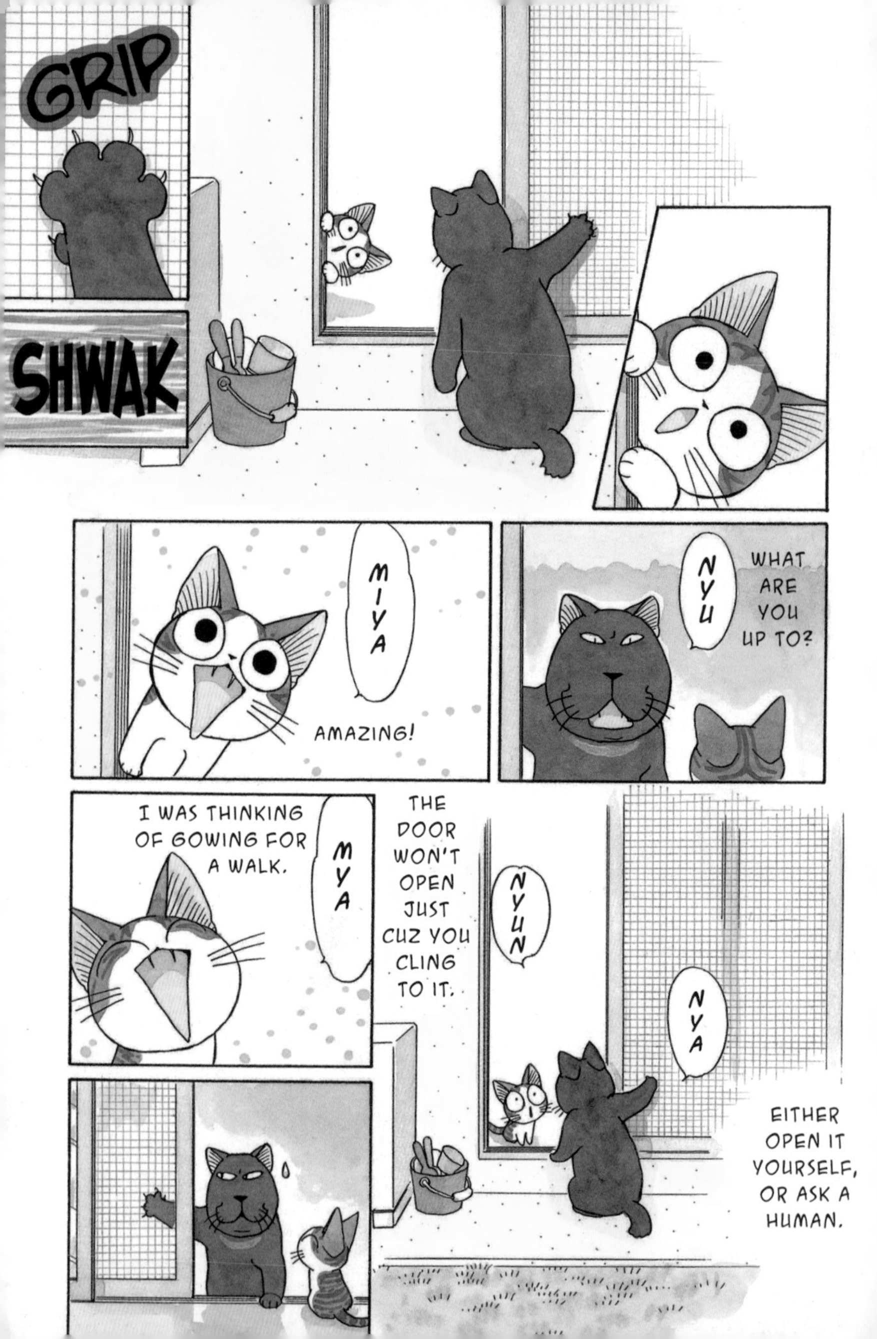
GRIP
SHWAK
MIYA
AMAZING!
NYU
WHAT ARE YOU UP TO?
I WAS THINKING OF GOWING FOR A WALK.
MYA
THE DOOR WON'T OPEN JUST CUZ YOU CLING TO IT.
NYUN
NYA
EITHER OPEN IT YOURSELF, OR ASK A HUMAN.

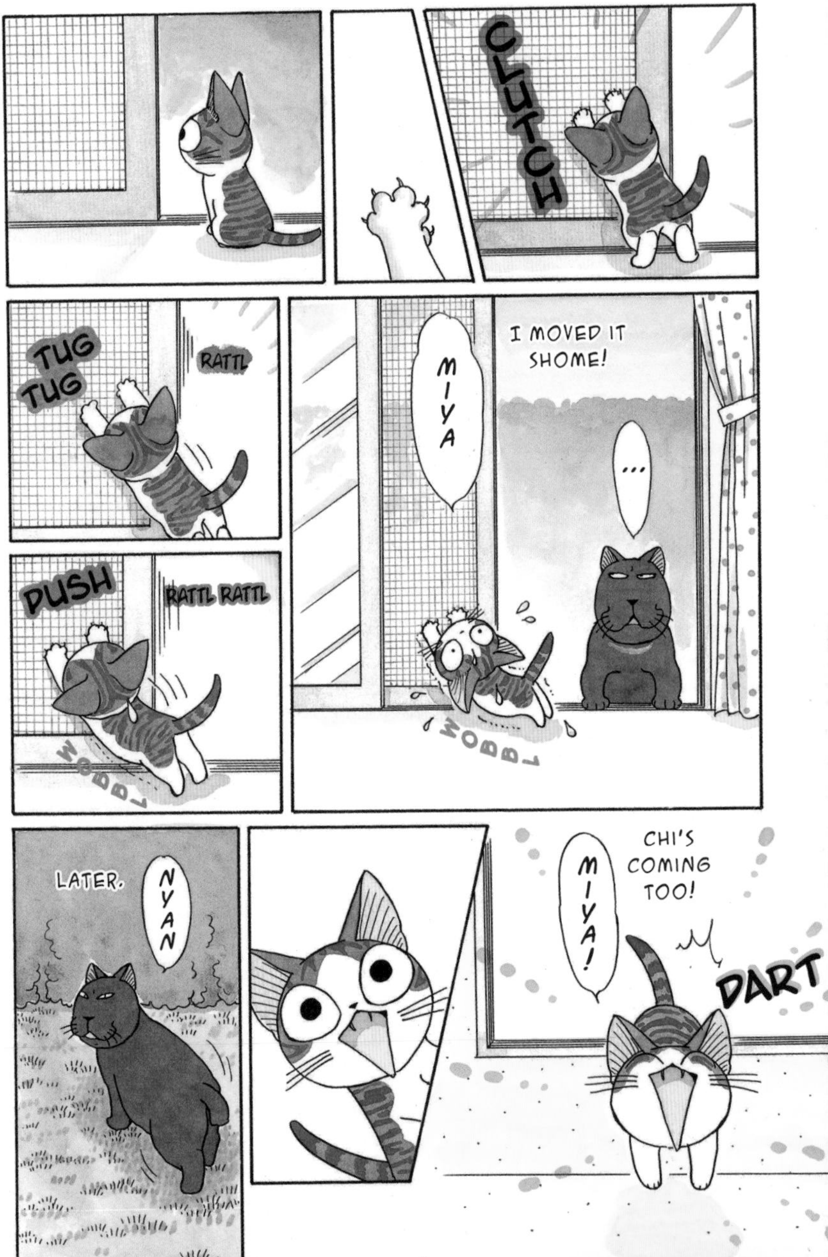
CLUTCH
TUG TUG
RATTL
PUSH
RATTL RATTL
WOBBL
MIYA
I MOVED IT SHOME!
...
WOBBL
LATER.
NYAN
MIYA!
CHI'S COMING TOO!
DART

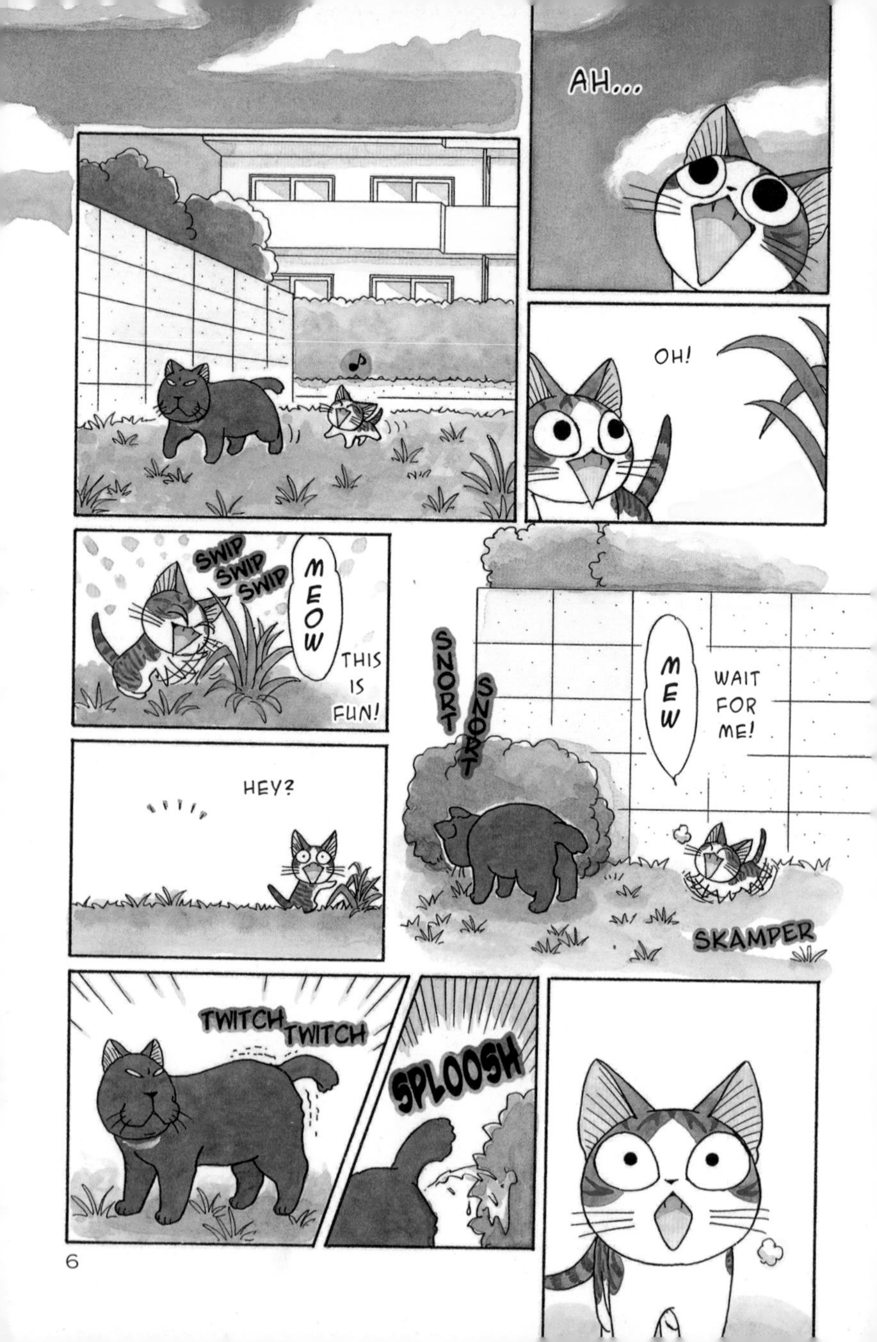
AH...
OH!
SWIP SWIP SWIP
MEOW
THIS IS FUN!
HEY?
SNORT SNORT
MEW
WAIT FOR ME!
SKAMPER
TWITCH TWITCH
SPLOOSH

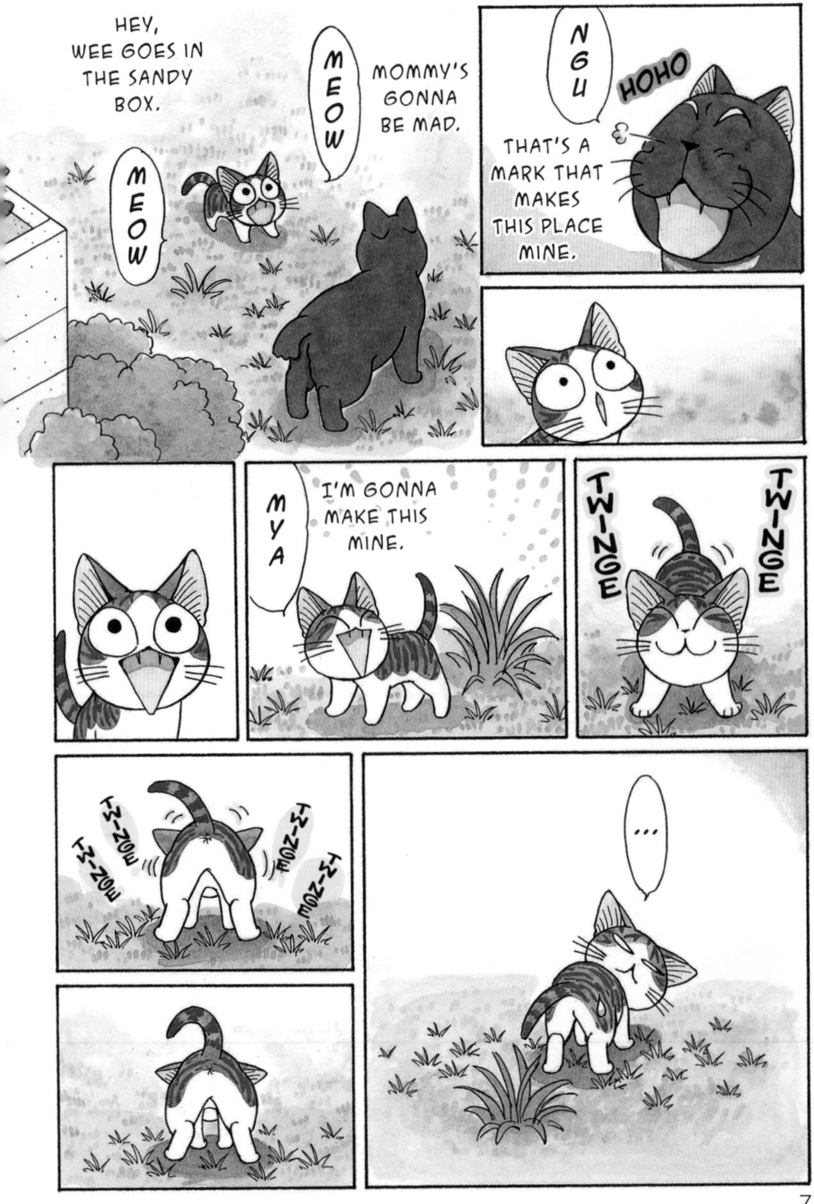
HEY, WEE GOES IN THE SANDY BOX.
MEOW
MEOW
MOMMY'S GONNA BE MAD.
NGU
HOHO
THAT'S A MARK THAT MAKES THIS PLACE MINE.
MYA
I'M GONNA MAKE THIS MINE.
TWINGE
TWINGE
TWINGE
TWINGE
TWINGE
TWINGE
...

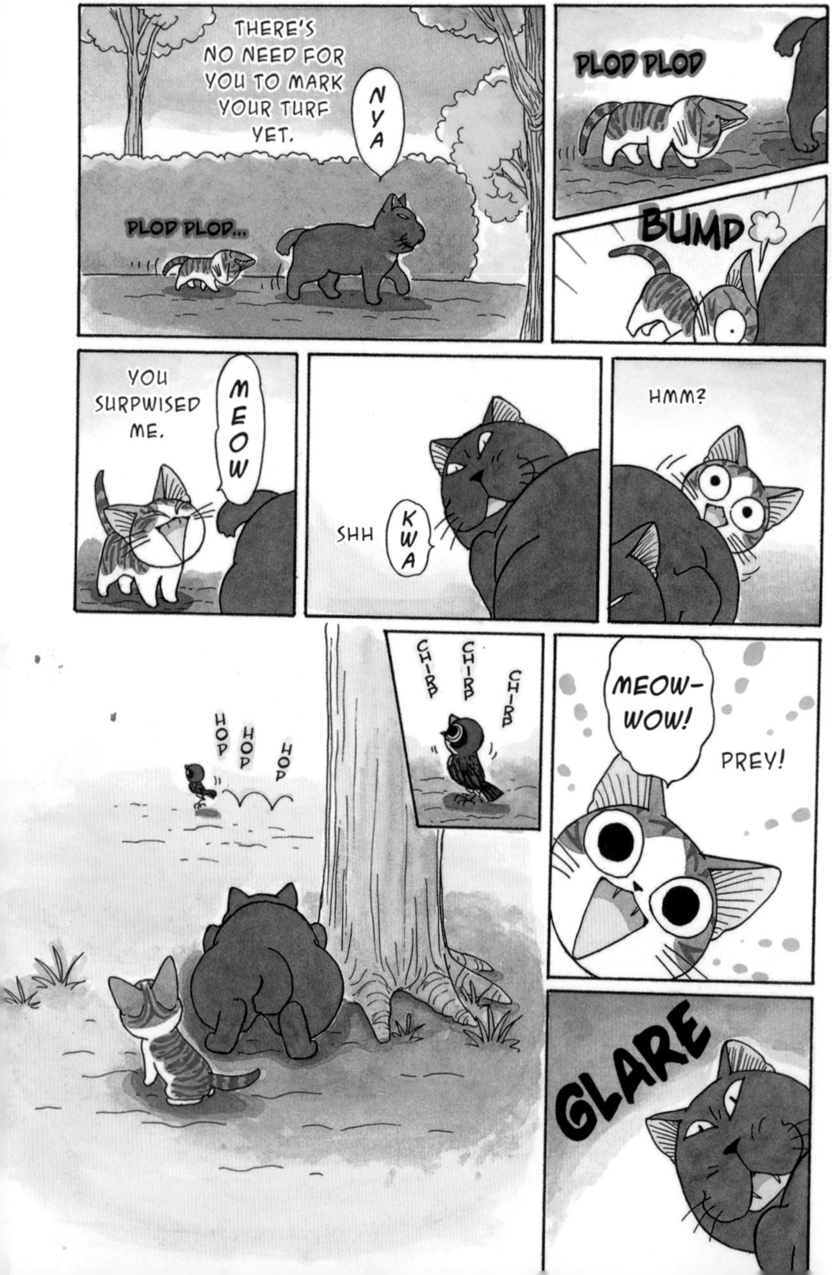
THERE'S NO NEED FOR YOU TO MARK YOUR TURF YET.
NYA
PLOD PLOD...
PLOD PLOD
BUMP
YOU SURPWISED ME.
MEOW
SHH
KWA
HMM?
HOP HOP HOP
CHIRP CHIRP CHIRP
MEOW-WOW!
PREY!
GLARE

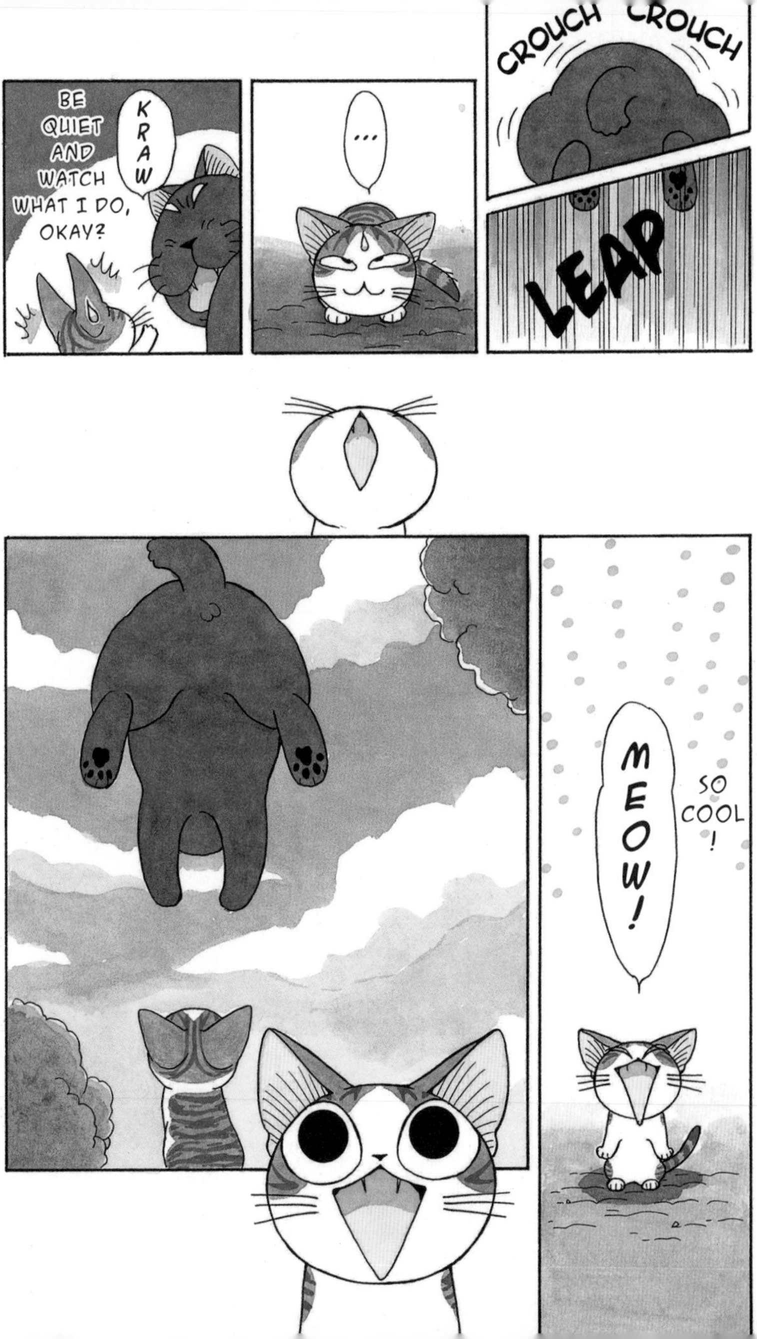
BE QUIET AND WATCH WHAT I DO, OKAY?
KRAW
...
CROUCH CROUCH
LEAP
MEOW!
SO COOL!

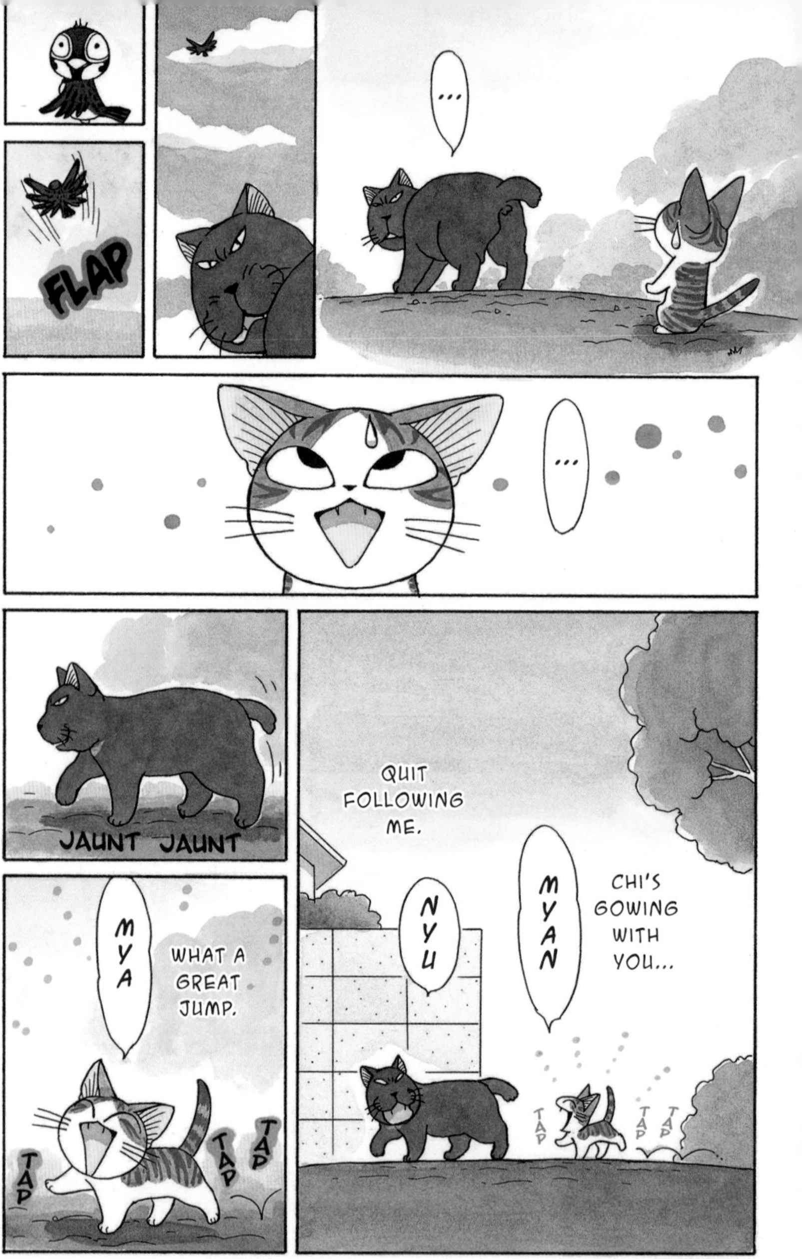
FLAP
...
...
JAUNT JAUNT
MYA
WHAT A GREAT JUMP.
TAP TAP TAP
QUIT FOLLOWING ME.
NYU
MYAN
CHI'S GOWING WITH YOU...
TAP TAP TAP

the end

homemade 40: a cat is photographed

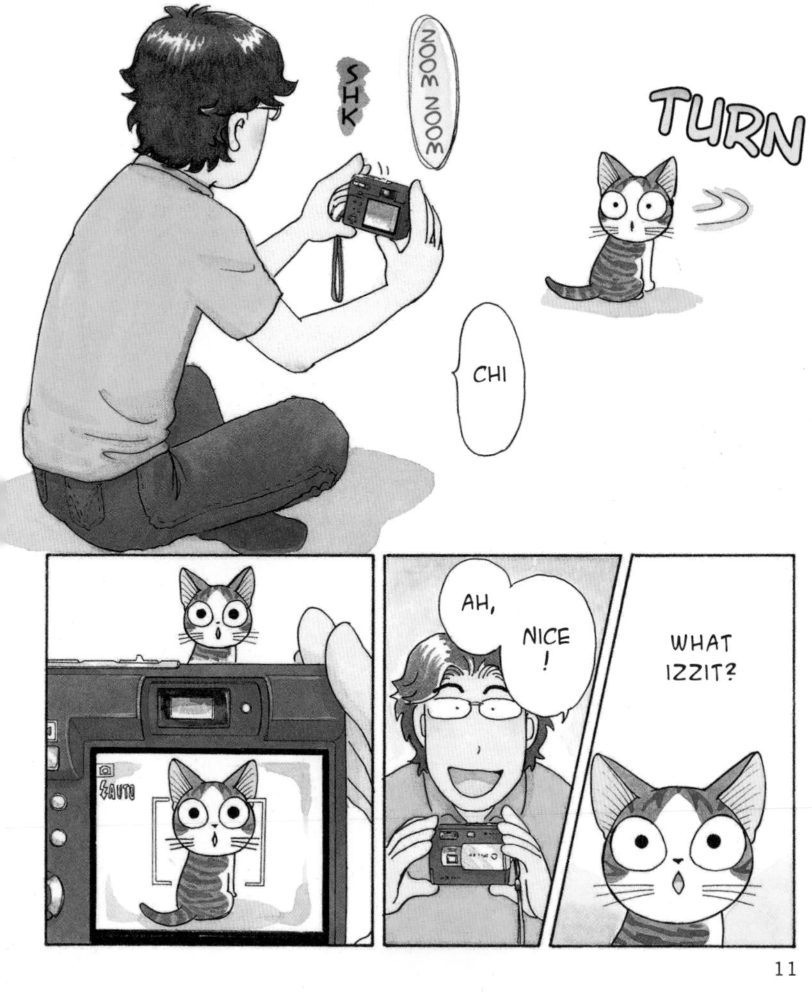
SHK
ZOOM ZOOM
TURN
CHI
AUTO
AH,
NICE!
WHAT IZZIT?

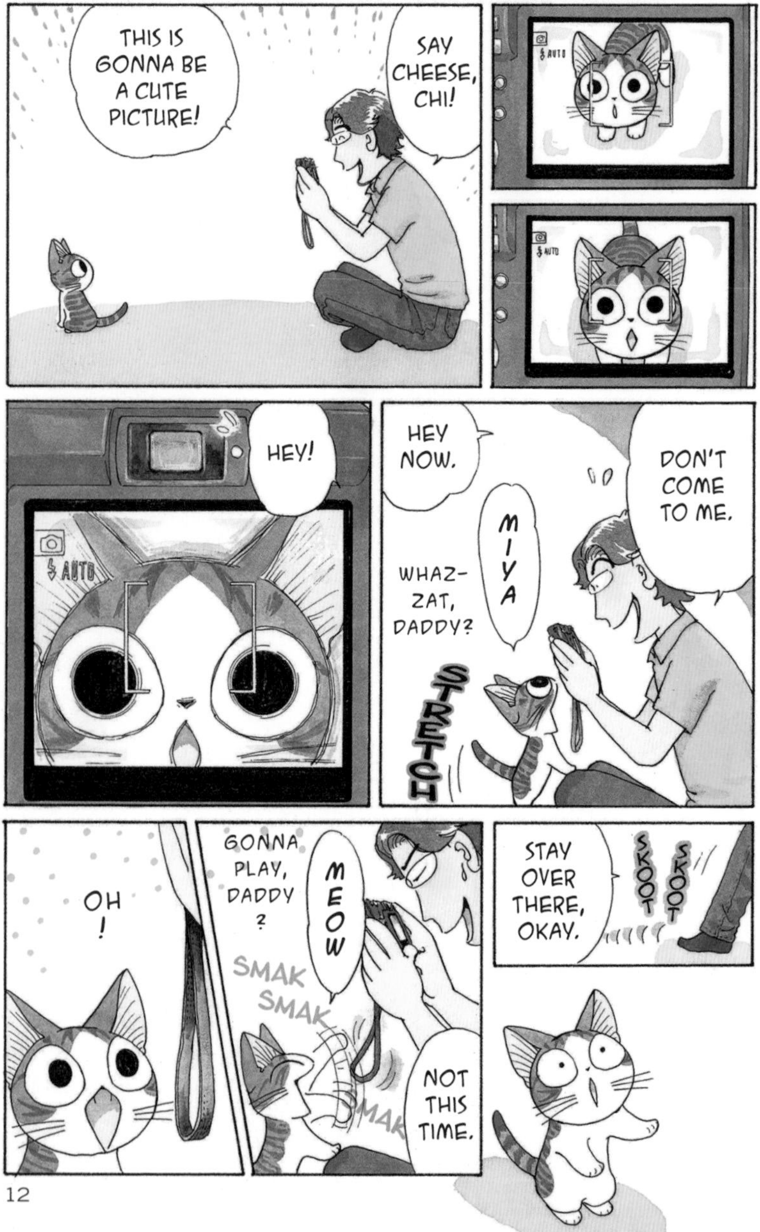
THIS IS GONNA BE A CUTE PICTURE!
SAY CHEESE, CHI!
AUTO
AUTO
HEY!
AUTO
HEY NOW.
MIYA
WHAZ-ZAT, DADDY?
DON'T COME TO ME.
STRETCH
OH!
GONNA PLAY, DADDY?
MEOW
SMAK SMAK
SMAK
NOT THIS TIME.
STAY OVER THERE, OKAY.
SKOOT SKOOT

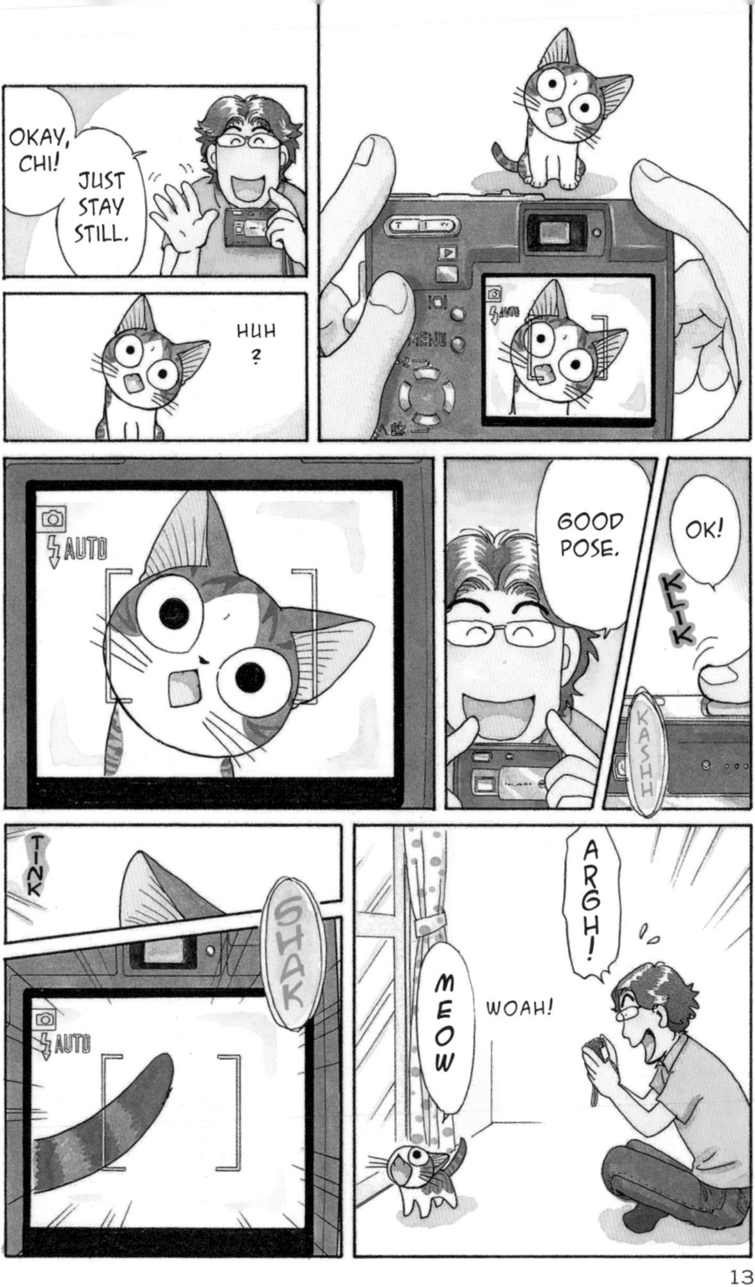
OKAY, CHI!
JUST STAY STILL.
HUH ?
GOOD POSE.
OK!
KLIK
KASHH
TINK
SHAK
ARGH!
MEOW
WOAH!

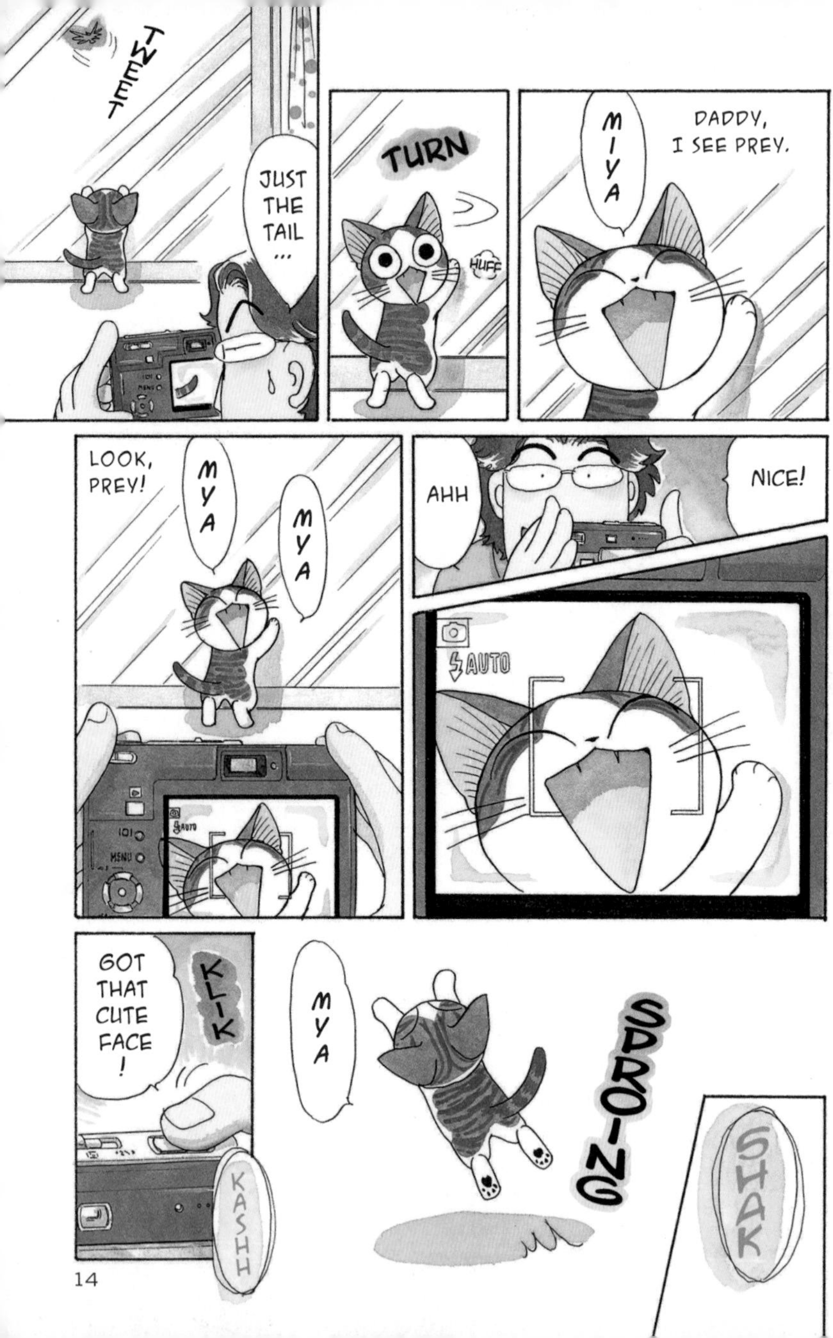
TWEET
JUST THE TAIL ...
TURN
HUFF
MIYA
DADDY, I SEE PREY.
LOOK, PREY!
MYA
MYA
AHH
NICE!
AUTO
GOT THAT CUTE FACE !
KLIK
KASHH
MYA
SPROING
SHAK

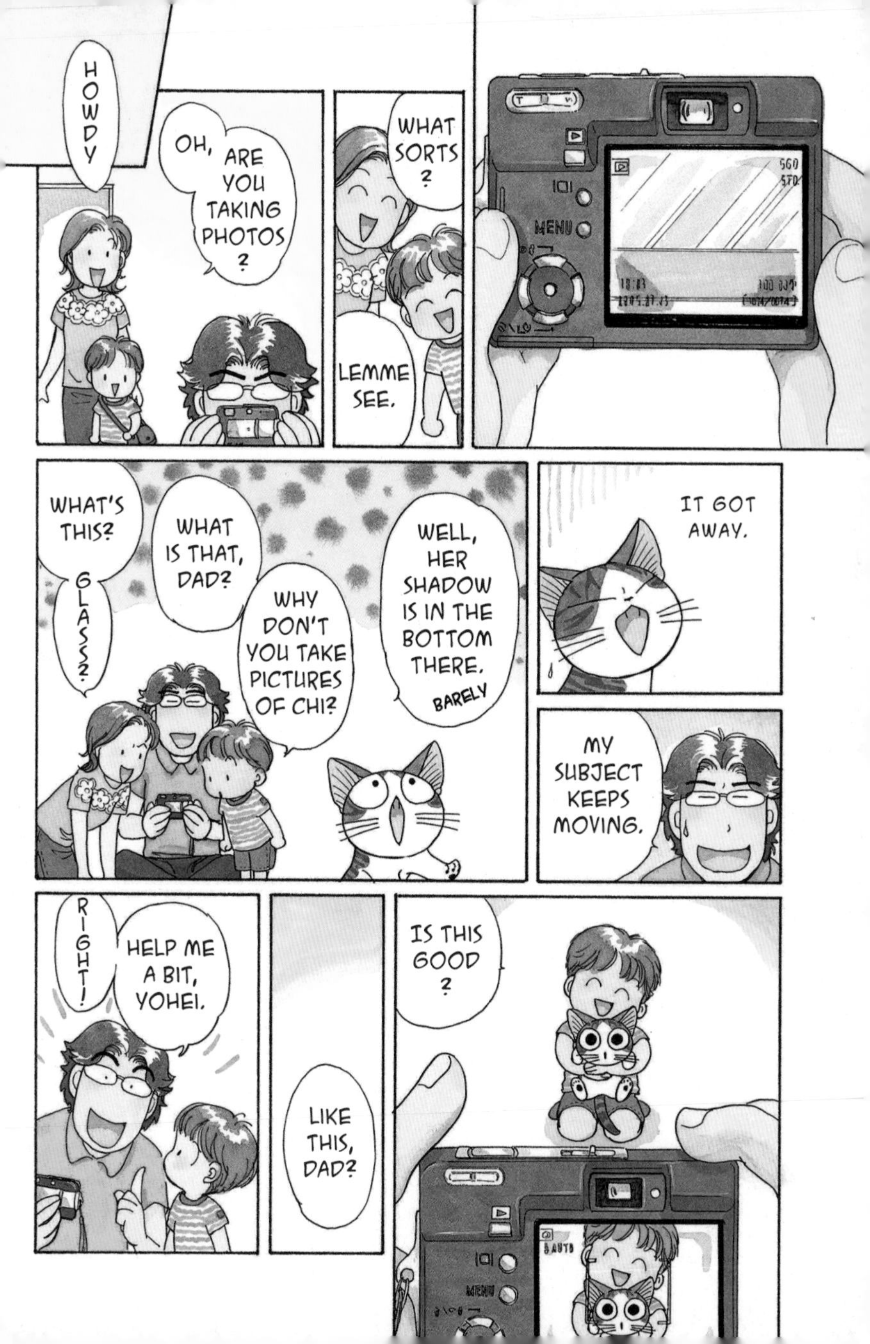
HOWDY
OH, ARE YOU TAKING PHOTOS?
WHAT SORTS?
LEMME SEE.
WHAT'S THIS?
GLASS?
WHAT IS THAT, DAD?
WHY DON'T YOU TAKE PICTURES OF CHI?
WELL, HER SHADOW IS IN THE BOTTOM THERE.
BARELY
IT GOT AWAY.
MY SUBJECT KEEPS MOVING.
HELP ME A BIT, YOHEI.
RIGHT!
LIKE THIS, DAD?
IS THIS GOOD?

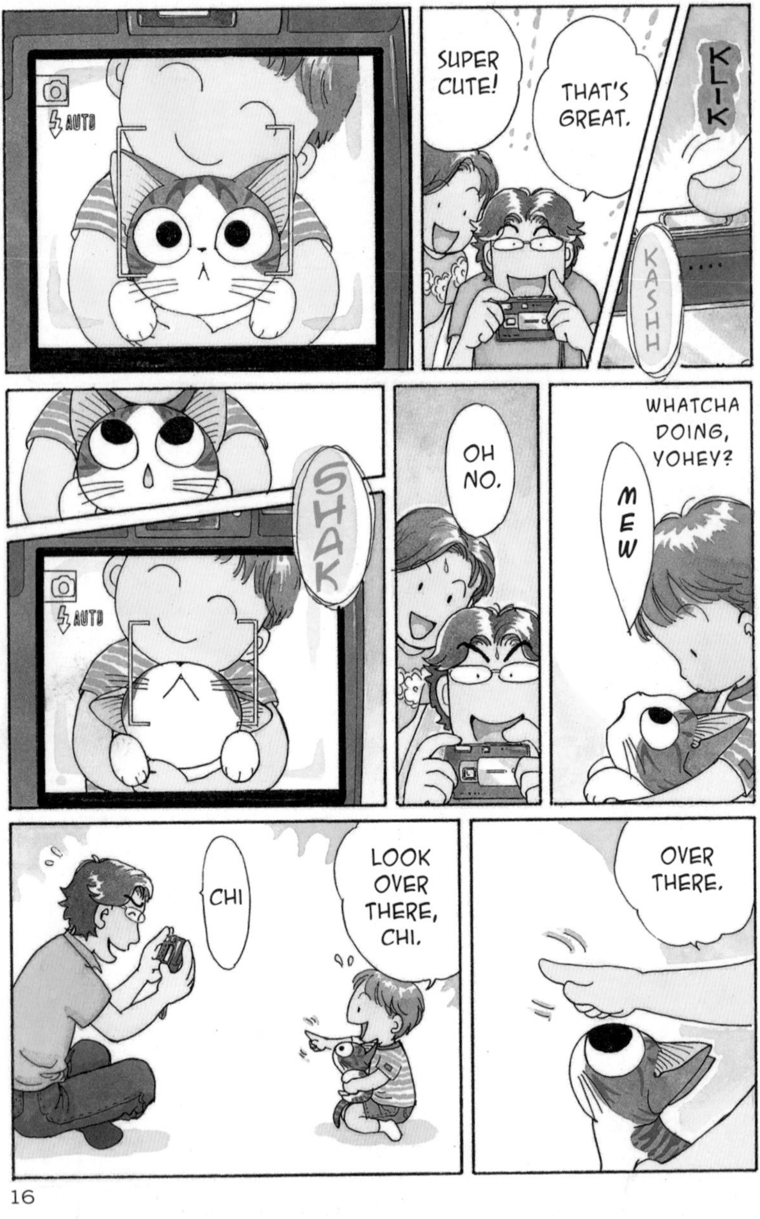
AUTO
SUPER CUTE!
THAT'S GREAT.
KLIK
KASHH
SHAK
AUTO
OH NO.
WHATCHA DOING, YOHEY?
MEW
CHI
LOOK OVER THERE, CHI.
OVER THERE.

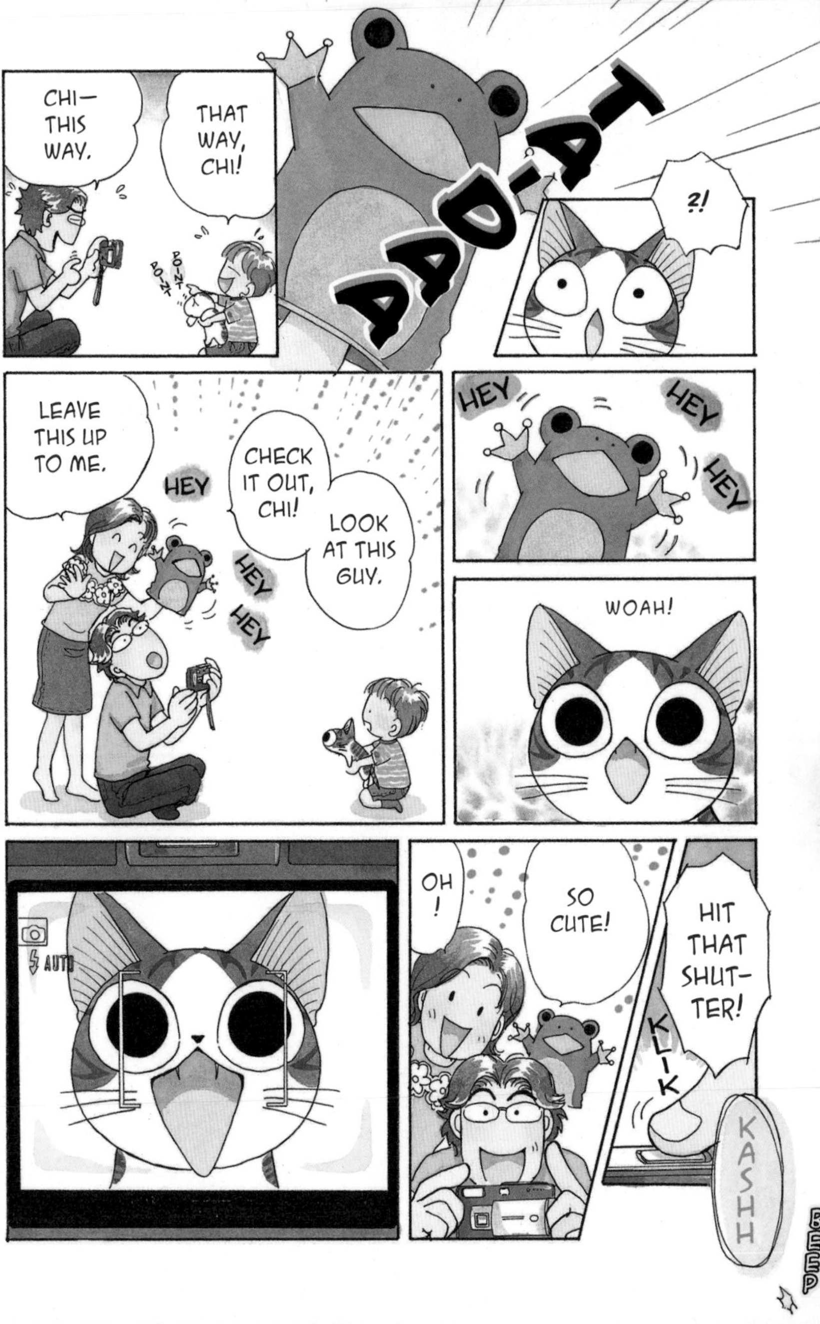
CHI— THIS WAY.
THAT WAY, CHI!
POINT POINT
AAD-AT
?!
LEAVE THIS UP TO ME.
HEY
CHECK IT OUT, CHI!
LOOK AT THIS GUY.
HEY
HEY
HEY
HEY
HEY
WOAH!
AUTO
OH!
SO CUTE!
HIT THAT SHUT-TER!
KLIK
KASHH
BEEP

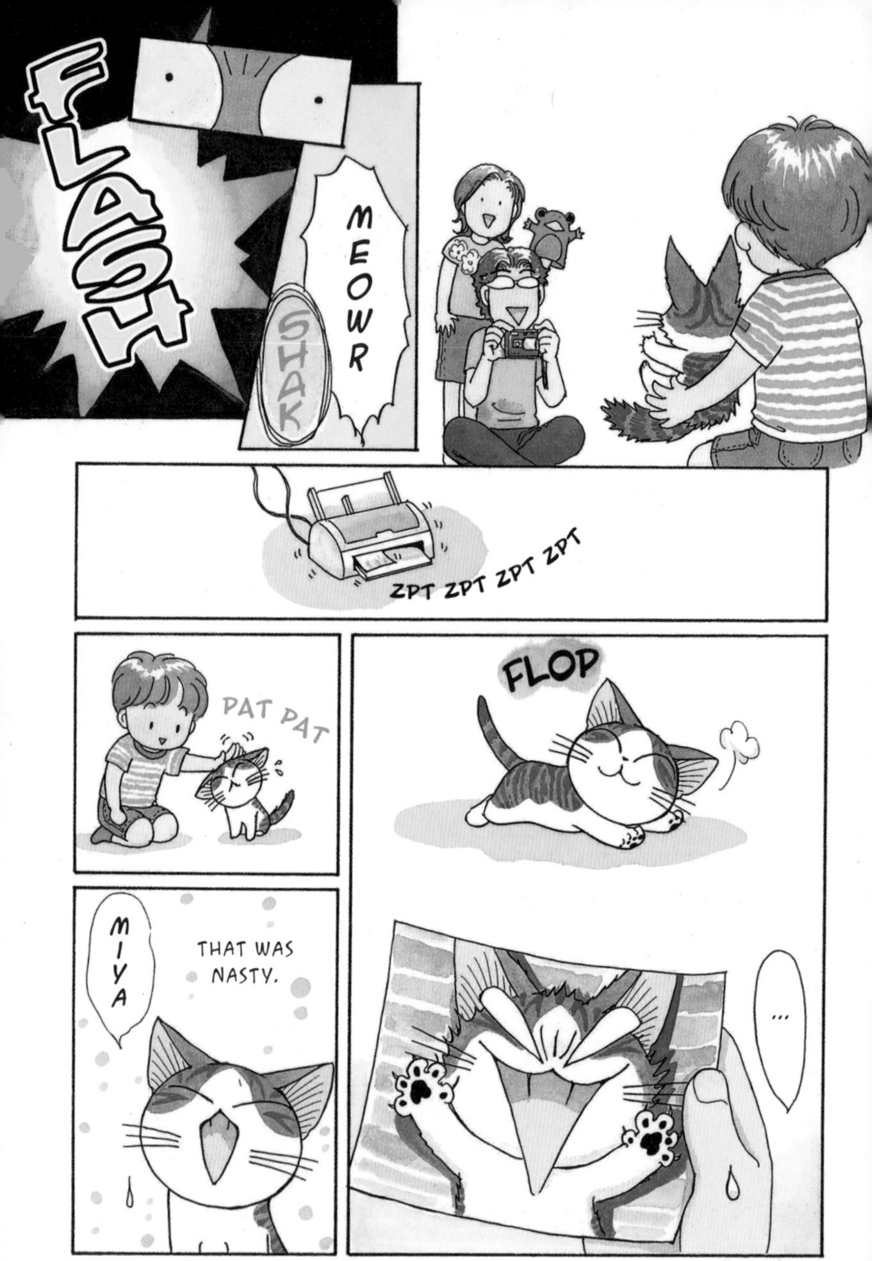
FLASH
MEOWR
SHAK
ZPT ZPT ZPT ZPT
PAT PAT
MIYA
THAT WAS NASTY.
FLOP
...

the end

homemade 41: a cat is taught

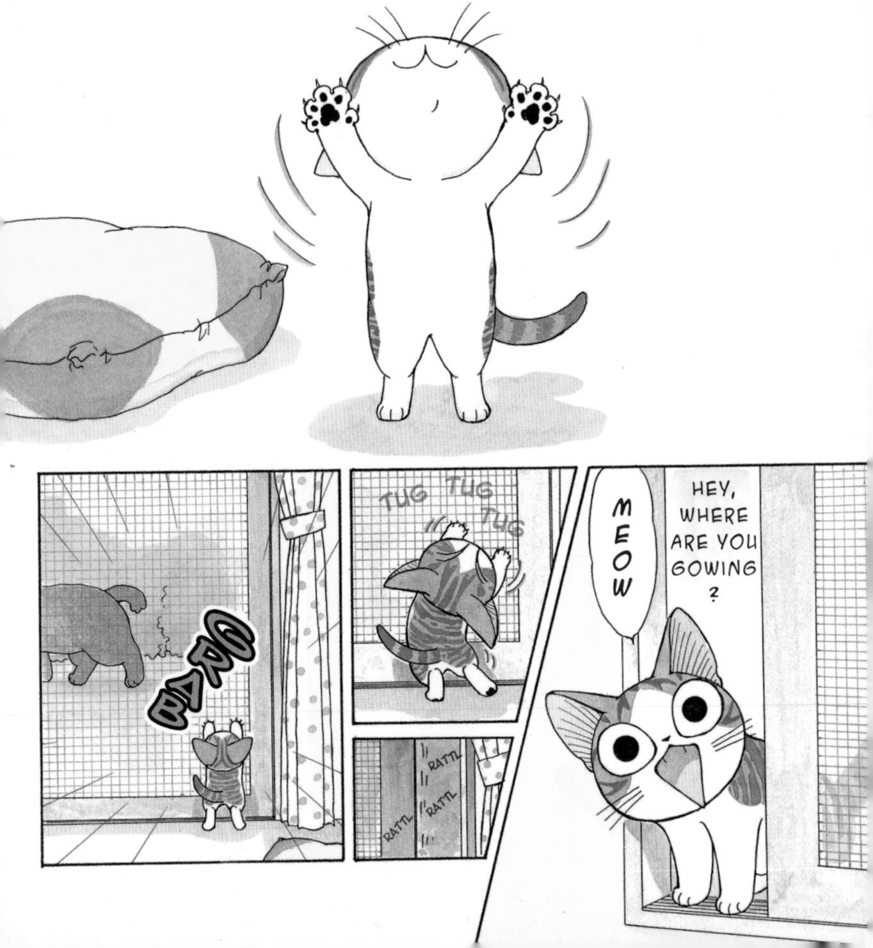

BANG
TUG TUG TUG
RATTL RATTL RATTL RATTL
MEOW
HEY, WHERE ARE YOU GOWING?

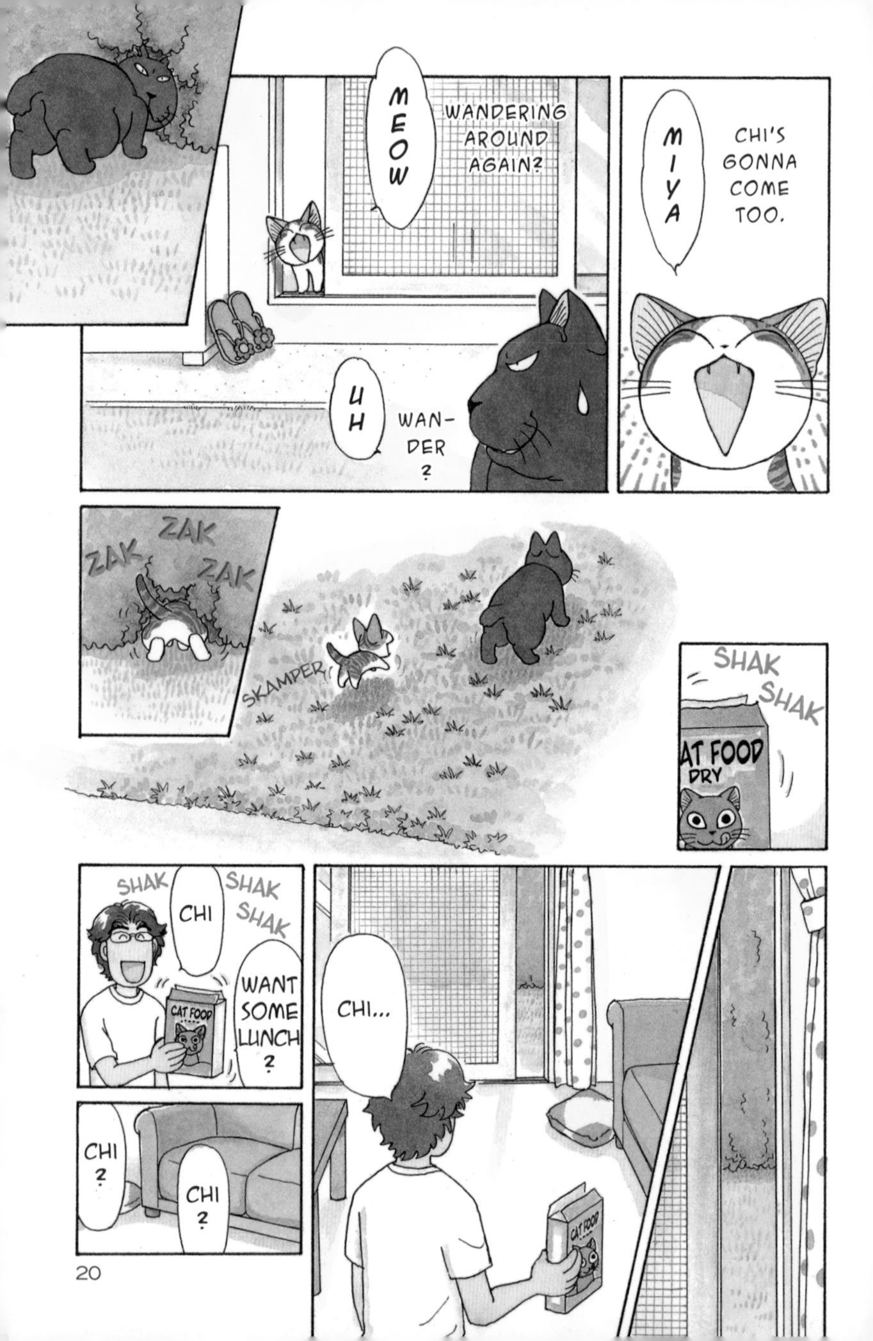
MEOW
WANDERING AROUND AGAIN?
UH
WAN-DER?
MIYA
CHI'S GONNA COME TOO.
ZAK
ZAK
ZAK
SKAMPER
SHAK
SHAK
AT FOOD
DRY
SHAK
CHI
SHAK
SHAK
WANT SOME LUNCH?
CAT FOOD
CHI?
CHI?
CHI...
CAT FOOD

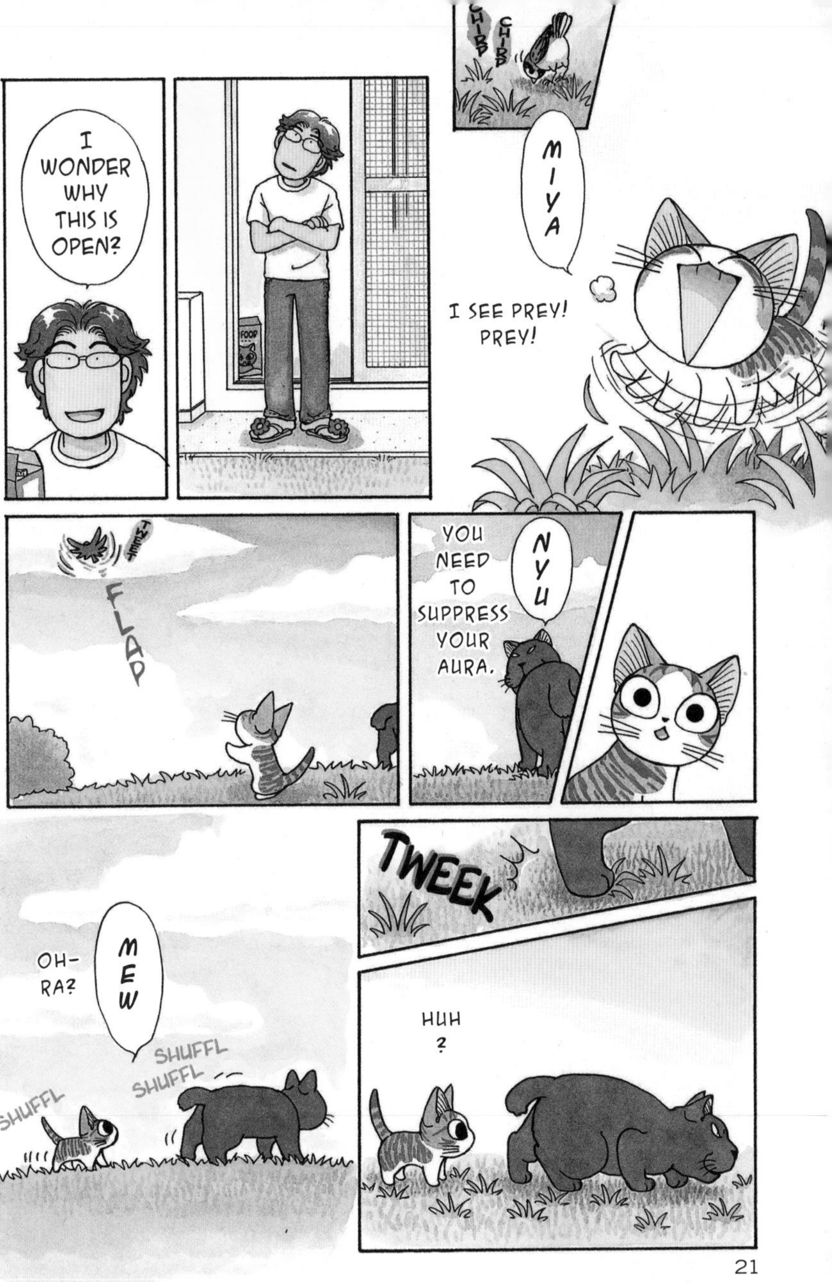
I WONDER WHY THIS IS OPEN?
FOOD
CHIRP
CHIRP
MIYA
I SEE PREY! PREY!
TWEET
FLAP
YOU NEED TO SUPPRESS YOUR AURA.
NYU
OH-RA?
MEW
SHUFFL
SHUFFL
SHUFFL
TWEEK
HUH ?

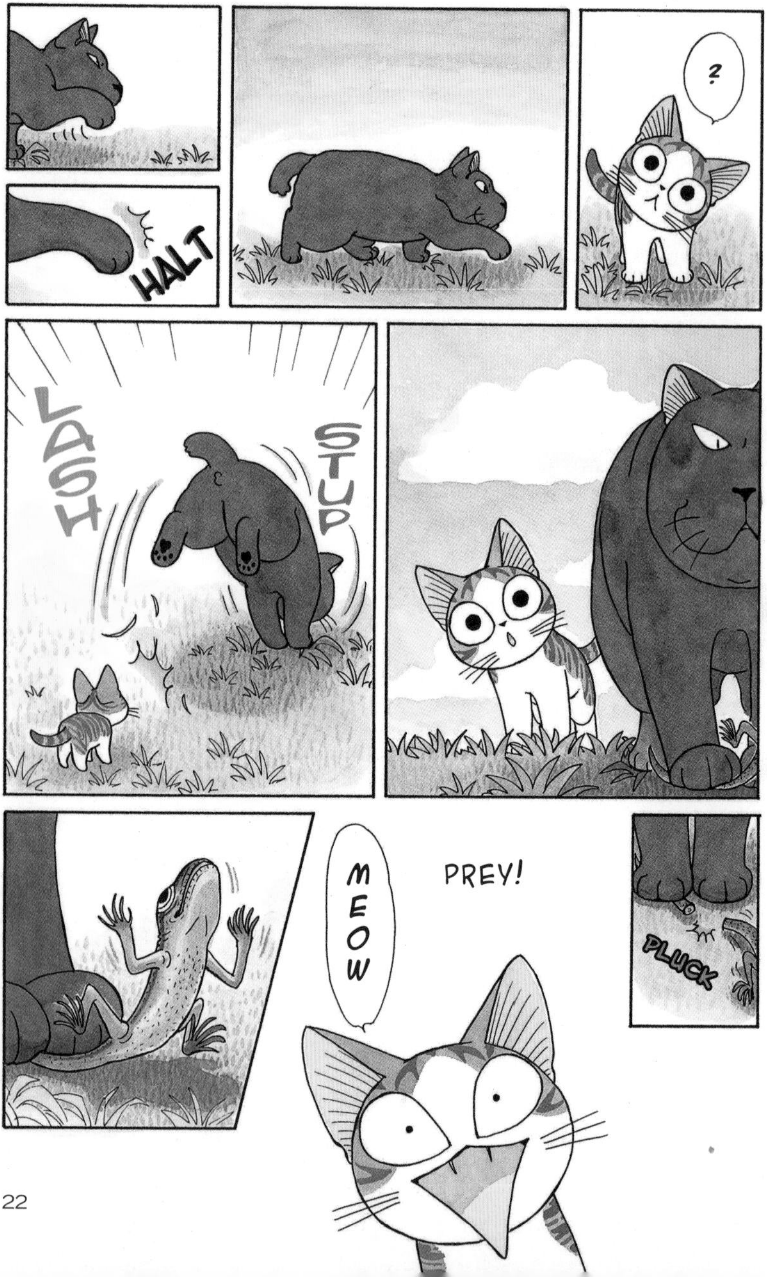
HALT
?
LASH
STUP
MEOW
PREY!
PLUCK

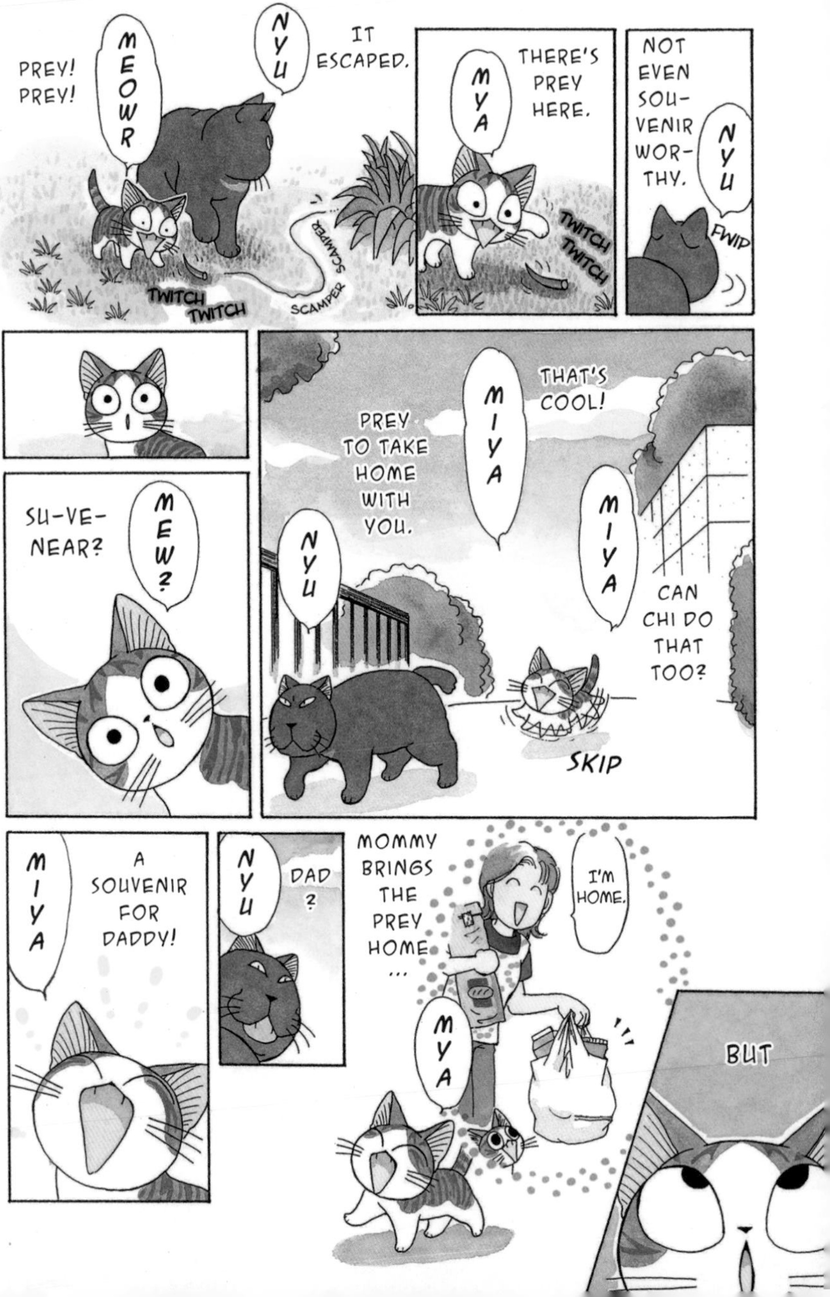
PREY! PREY!
MEOWR
NYU
IT ESCAPED.
TWITCH TWITCH
SCAMPER SCAMPER
MYA
THERE'S PREY HERE.
TWITCH TWITCH
NOT EVEN SOU-VENIR WOR-THY.
NYU
FWIP
SU-VE-NEAR?
MEW?
MIYA
THAT'S COOL!
PREY TO TAKE HOME WITH YOU.
NYU
MIYA
CAN CHI DO THAT TOO?
SKIP
MIYA
A SOUVENIR FOR DADDY!
NYU
DAD?
MOMMY BRINGS THE PREY HOME ...
I'M HOME.
MYA
BUT

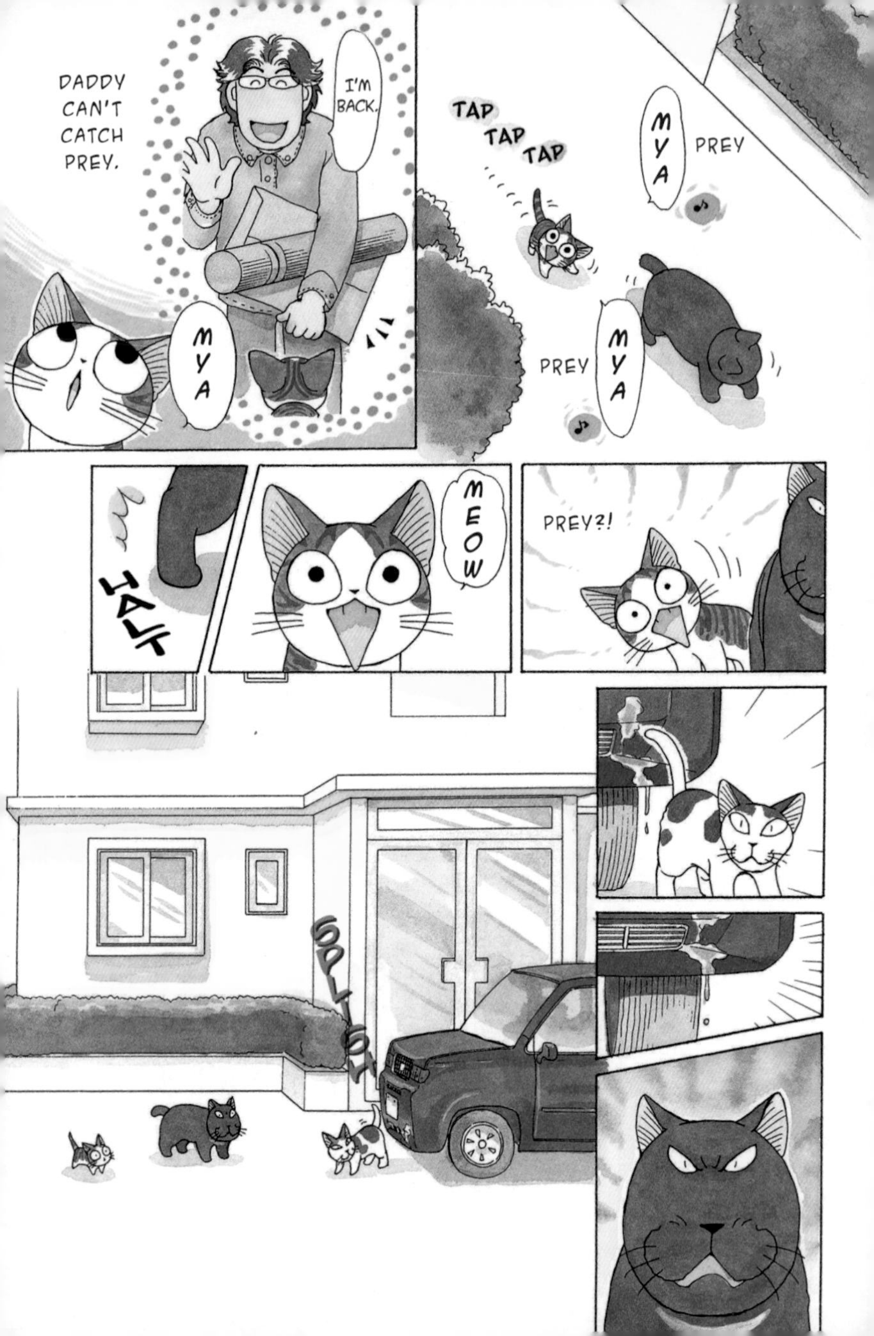
DADDY CAN'T CATCH PREY.
I'M BACK.
MYA
TAP TAP TAP
MYA
PREY
MYA
PREY
HALT
MEOW
PREY?!
SPLISH

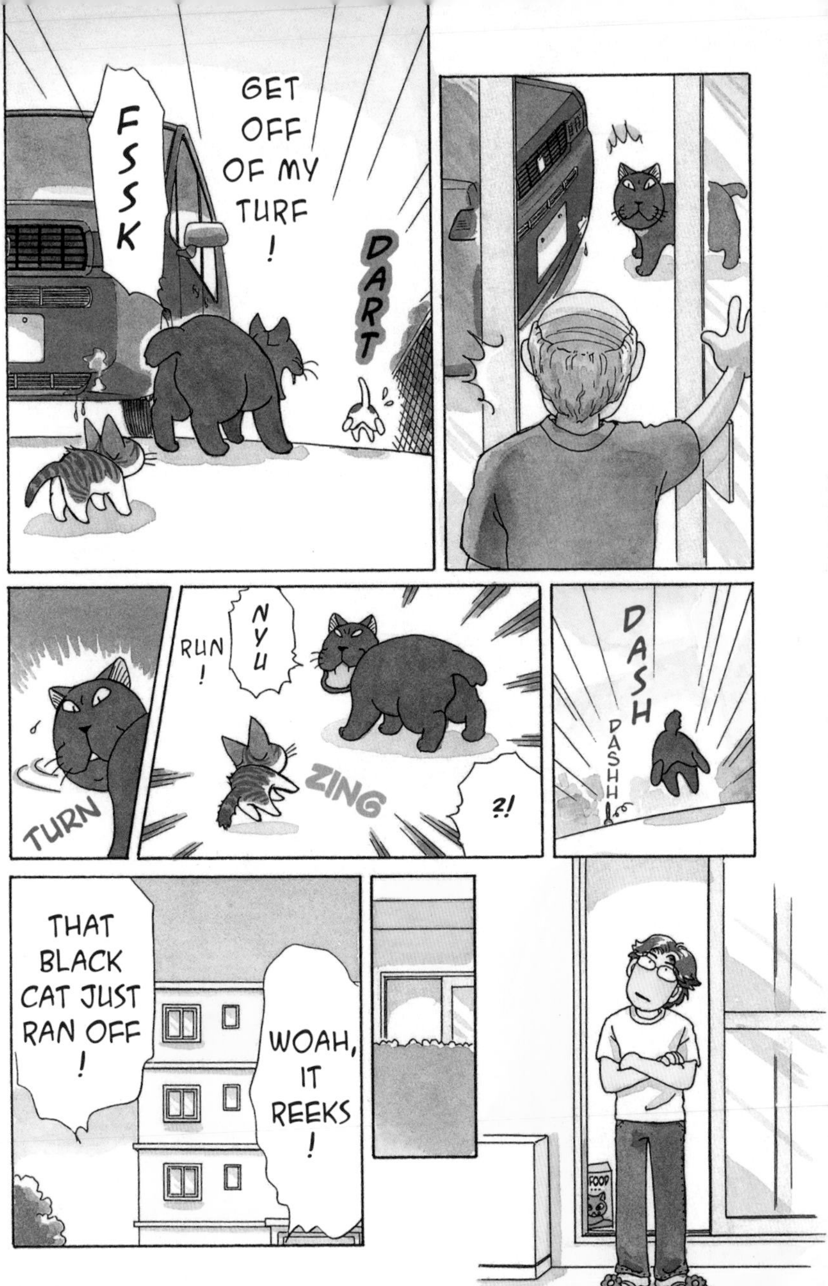
FSSK
GET OFF OF MY TURF !
DART
RUN !
NYU
ZING
TURN
?!
DASH
DASHH
THAT BLACK CAT JUST RAN OFF !
WOAH, IT REEKS !
FOOD

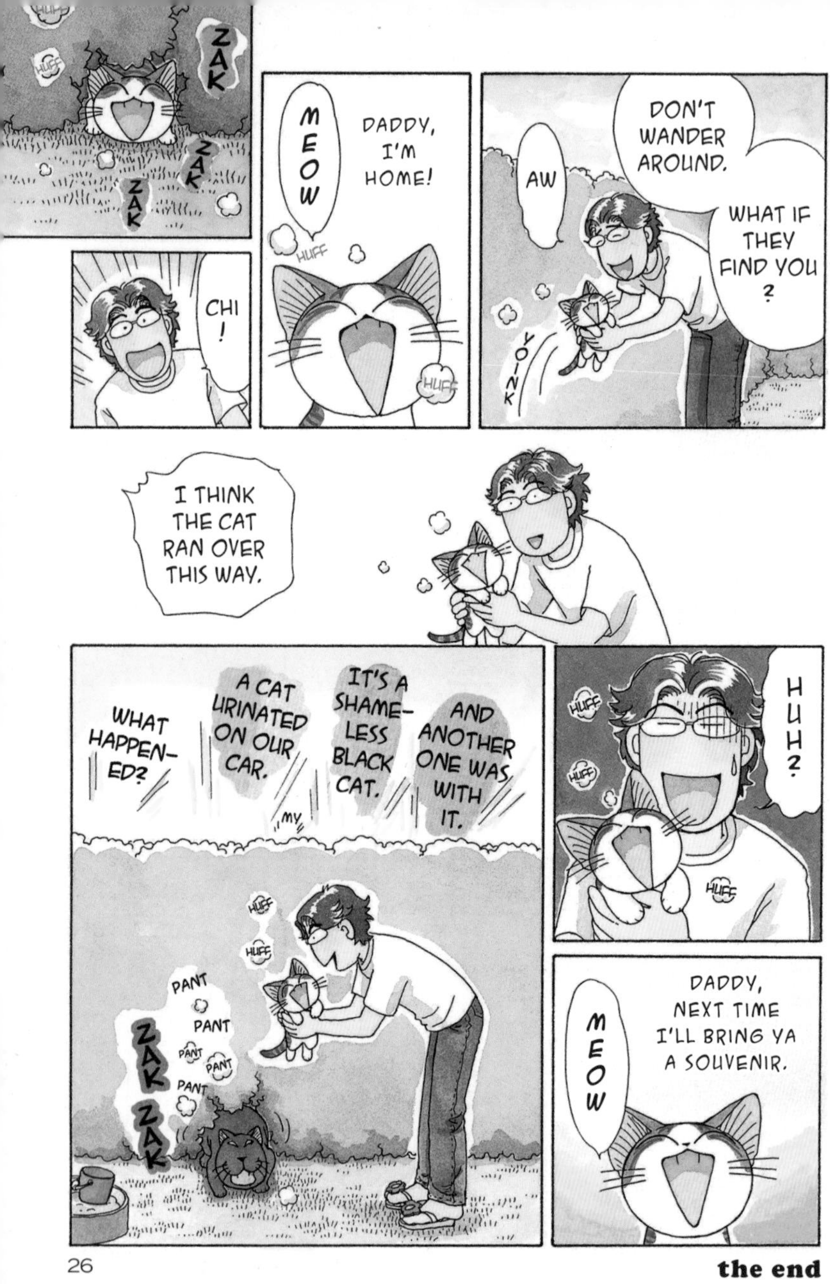
HUFF
HUFF
ZAK
ZAK
ZAK
CHI!
MEOW
DADDY, I'M HOME!
HUFF
HUFF
AW
DON'T WANDER AROUND.
WHAT IF THEY FIND YOU?
YOINK
I THINK THE CAT RAN OVER THIS WAY.
WHAT HAPPENED?
A CAT URINATED ON OUR CAR.
IT'S A SHAMELESS BLACK CAT.
AND ANOTHER ONE WAS WITH IT.
MY
HUFF
HUFF
PANT
PANT
PANT
PANT
PANT
ZAK
ZAK
ZAK
HUH?
HUFF
HUFF
HUFF
MEOW
DADDY, NEXT TIME I'LL BRING YA A SOUVENIR.

the end

homemade 42: a cat hides

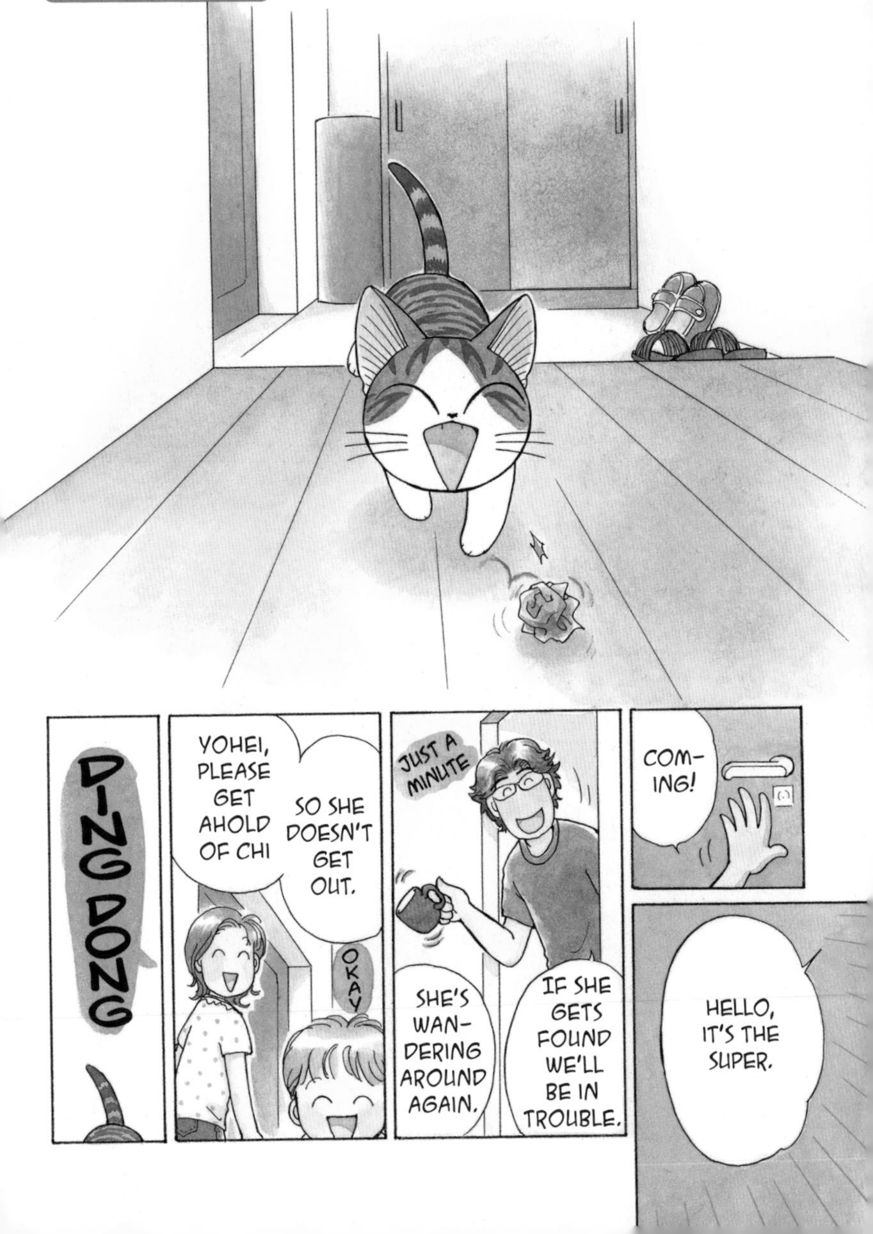

DING DONG
YOHEI, PLEASE GET AHOLD OF CHI
SO SHE DOESN'T GET OUT.
OKAY
JUST A MINUTE
SHE'S WANDERING AROUND AGAIN.
IF SHE GETS FOUND WE'LL BE IN TROUBLE.
COMING!
HELLO, IT'S THE SUPER.

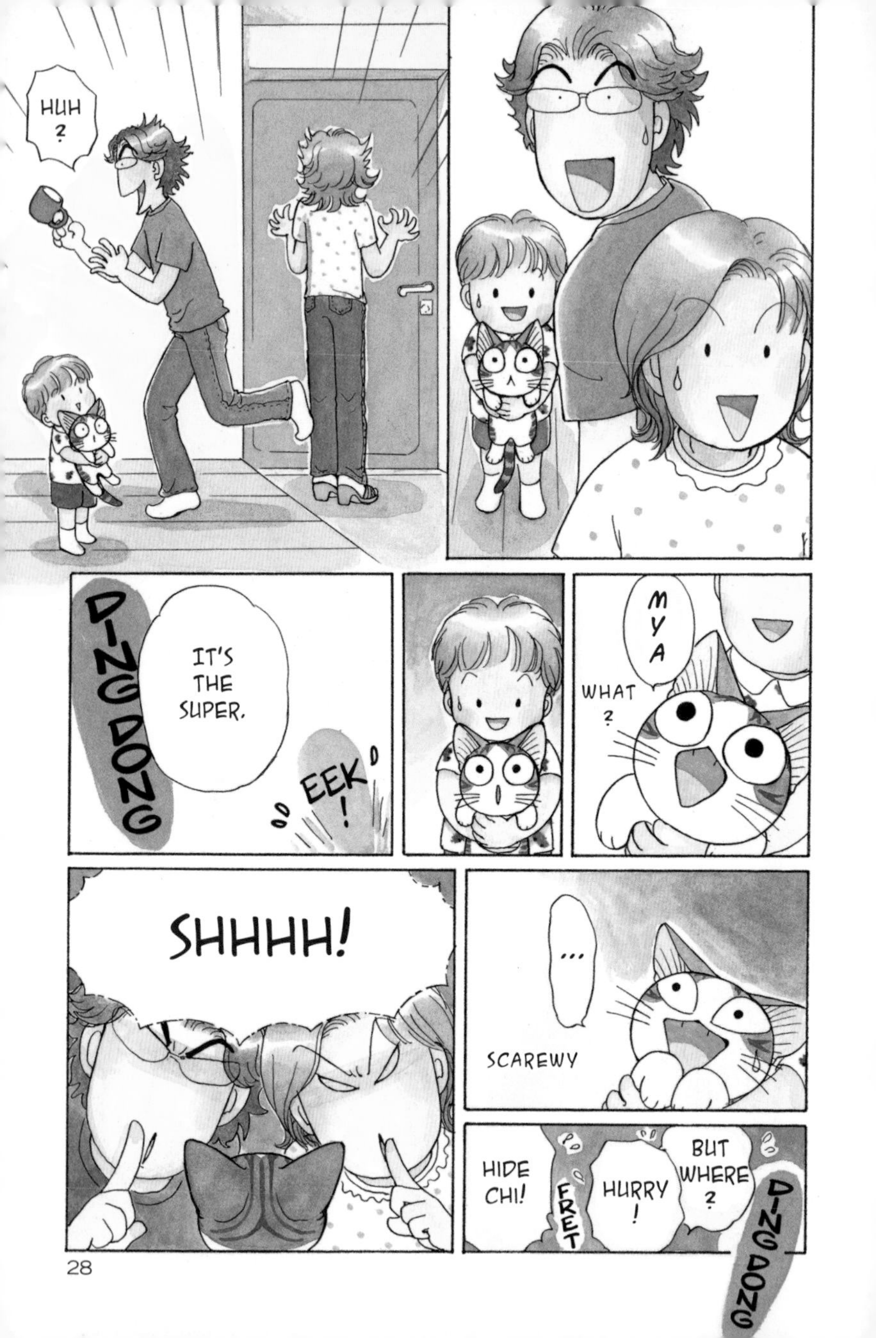
HUH?
IT'S THE SUPER.
DING DONG
EEK!
MYA
WHAT?
SHHHH!
...
SCAREWY
HIDE CHI!
FRET
HURRY!
BUT WHERE?
DING DONG

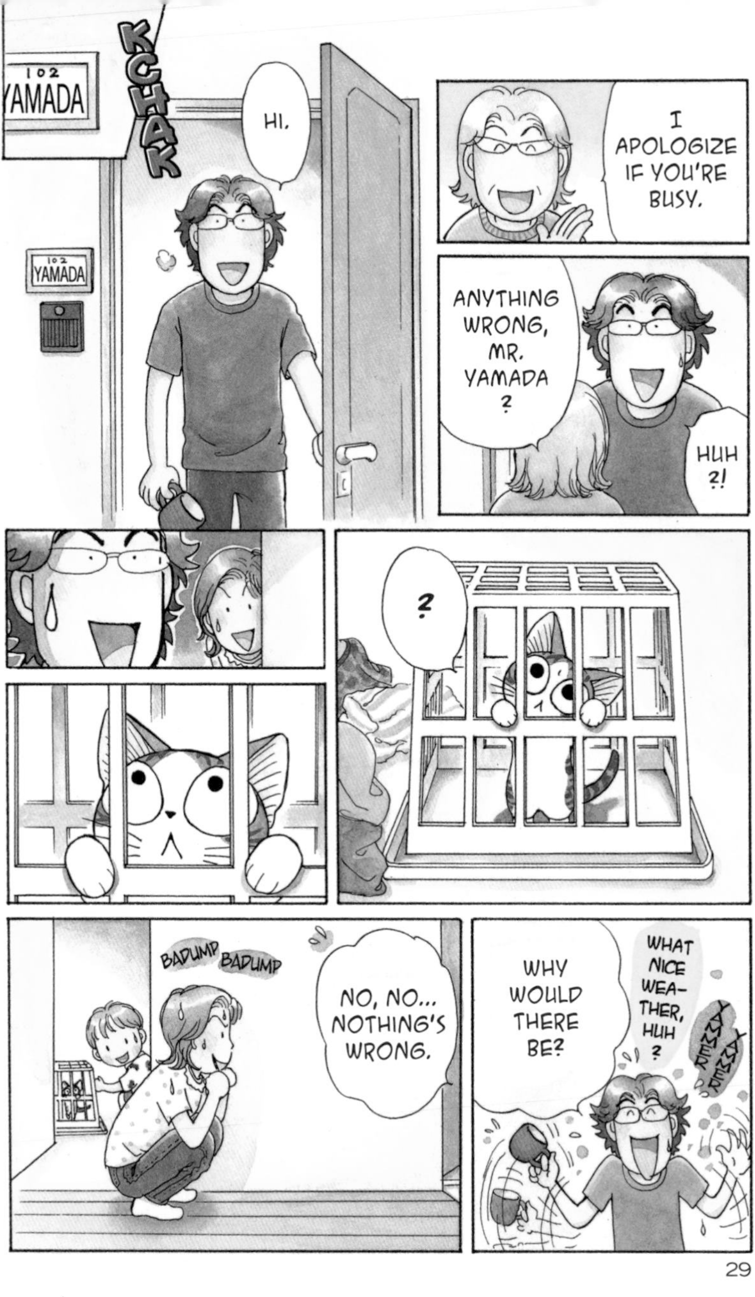
102
YAMADA
KCHAK
HI.
I APOLOGIZE IF YOU'RE BUSY.
102
YAMADA
ANYTHING WRONG, MR. YAMADA?
HUH?!
?
BADUMP BADUMP
NO, NO... NOTHING'S WRONG.
WHY WOULD THERE BE?
WHAT NICE WEATHER, HUH?
YAMMER YAMMER

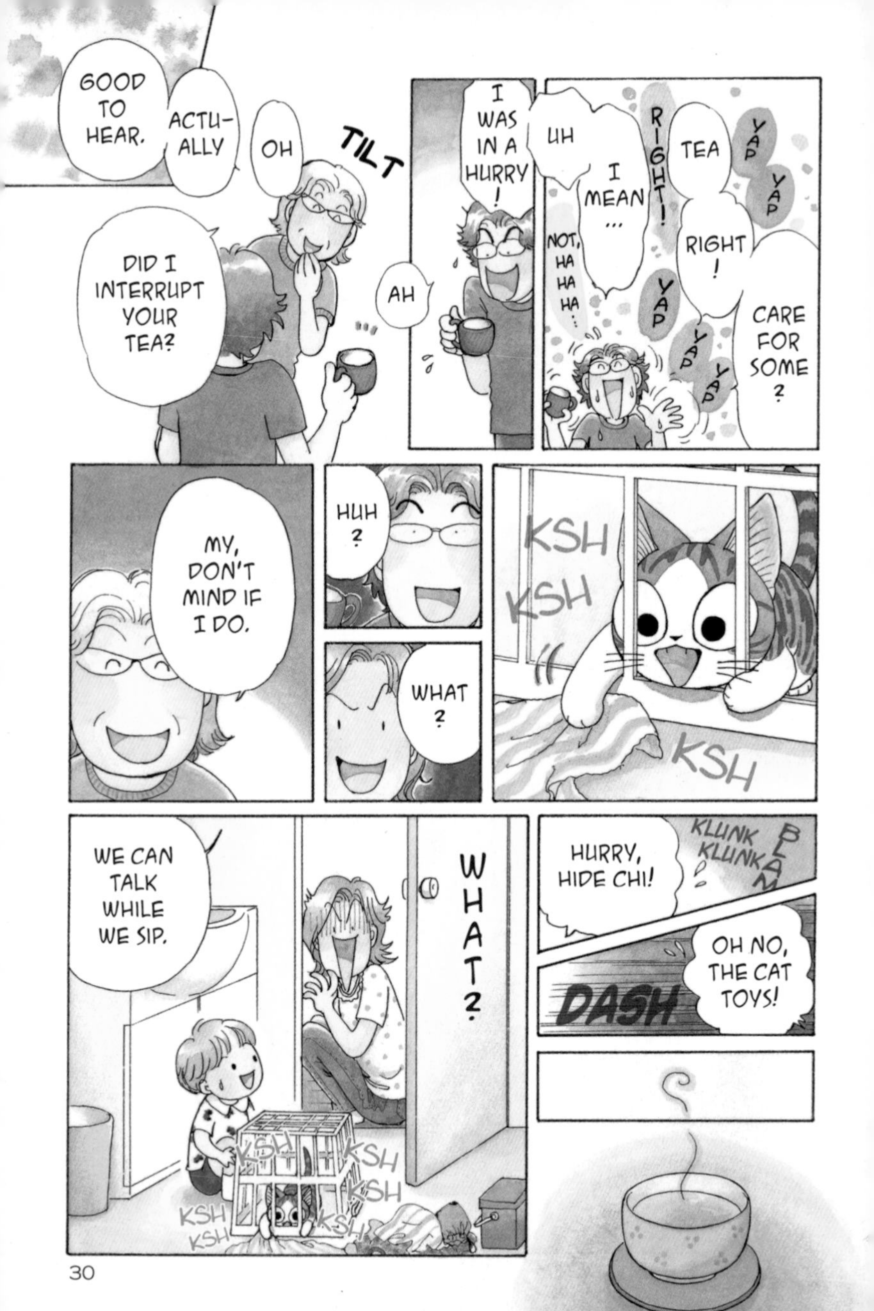
GOOD TO HEAR.
ACTU-ALLY
OH
TILT
DID I INTERRUPT YOUR TEA?
AH
I WAS IN A HURRY!
UH
I MEAN...
NOT, HA HA HA HA...
RIGHT!
TEA
RIGHT!
YAP YAP YAP YAP YAP YAP
CARE FOR SOME?
MY, DON'T MIND IF I DO.
HUH?
WHAT?
KSH
KSH
KSH
WE CAN TALK WHILE WE SIP.
WHAT?
KSH KSH KSH KSH KSH KSH
HURRY, HIDE CHI!
KLUNK KLUNK
BLAM
DASH
OH NO, THE CAT TOYS!

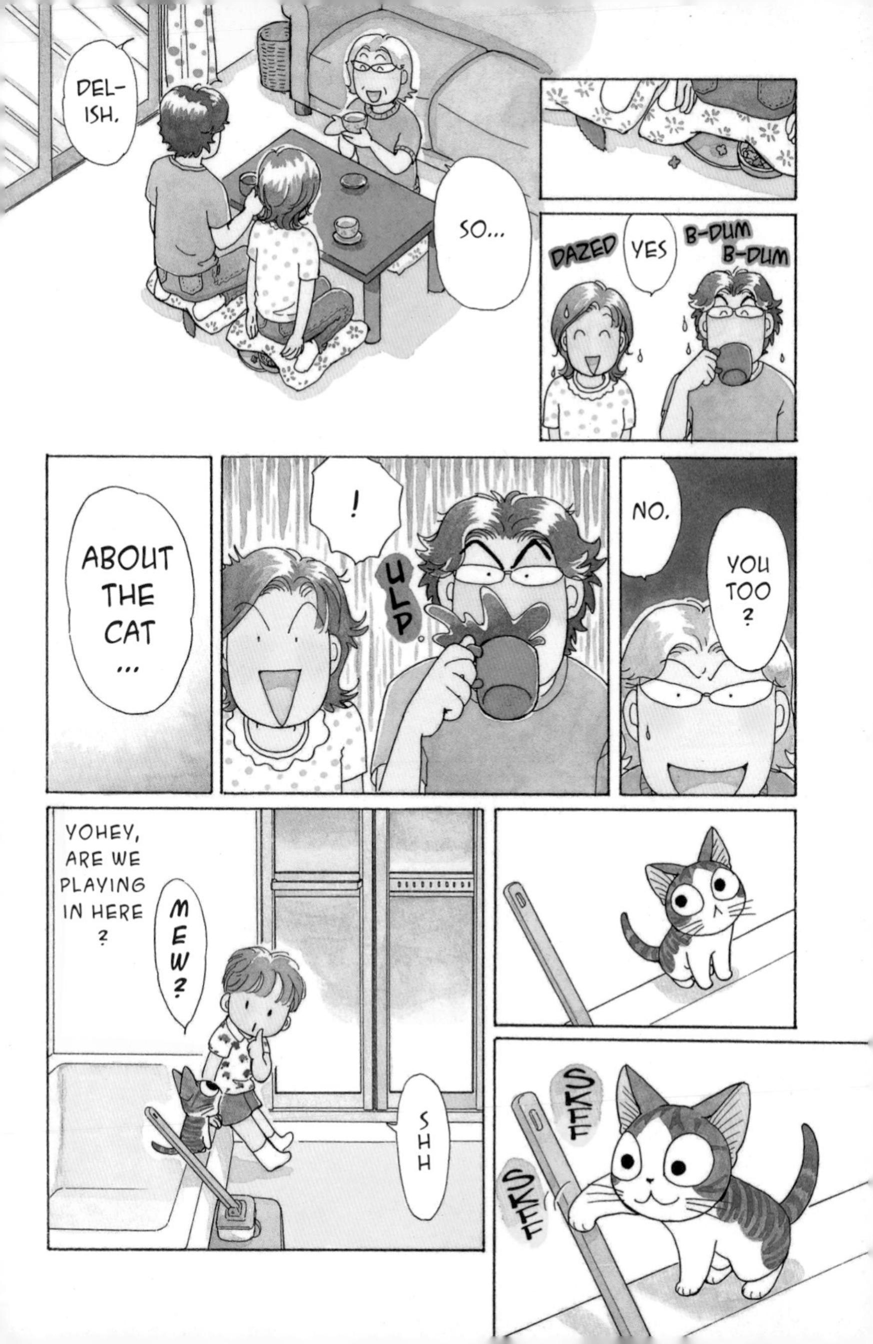
DEL-ISH.
SO...
DAZED
YES
B-DUM B-DUM
ABOUT THE CAT ...
!
ULP
NO.
YOU TOO?
YOHEY, ARE WE PLAYING IN HERE?
MEW?
SHH
SKFF
SKFF

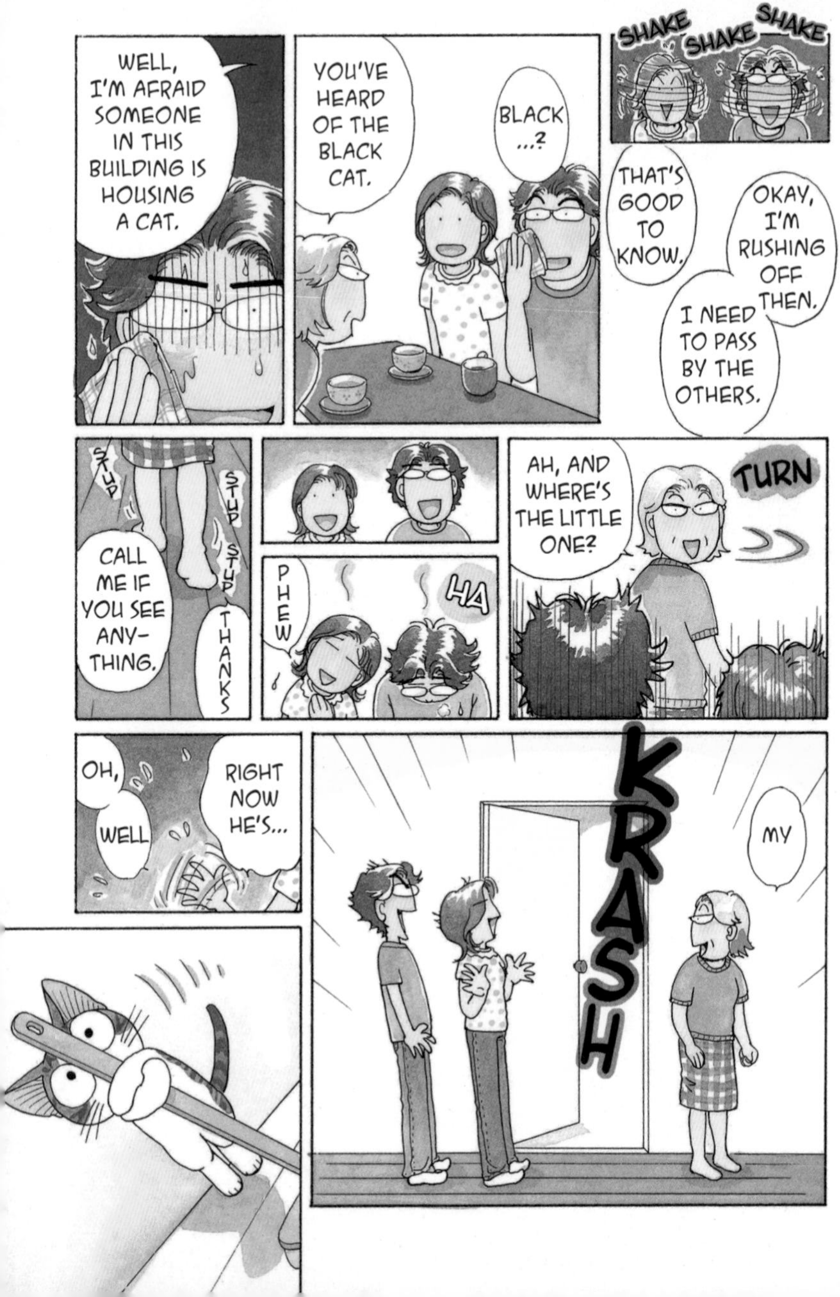
WELL, I'M AFRAID SOMEONE IN THIS BUILDING IS HOUSING A CAT.
YOU'VE HEARD OF THE BLACK CAT.
BLACK ...?
SHAKE SHAKE SHAKE
THAT'S GOOD TO KNOW.
OKAY, I'M RUSHING OFF THEN.
I NEED TO PASS BY THE OTHERS.
STUP
STUP
STUP
CALL ME IF YOU SEE ANYTHING.
THANKS
PHEW
HA
AH, AND WHERE'S THE LITTLE ONE?
TURN
OH,
WELL
RIGHT NOW HE'S...
KRASH
MY

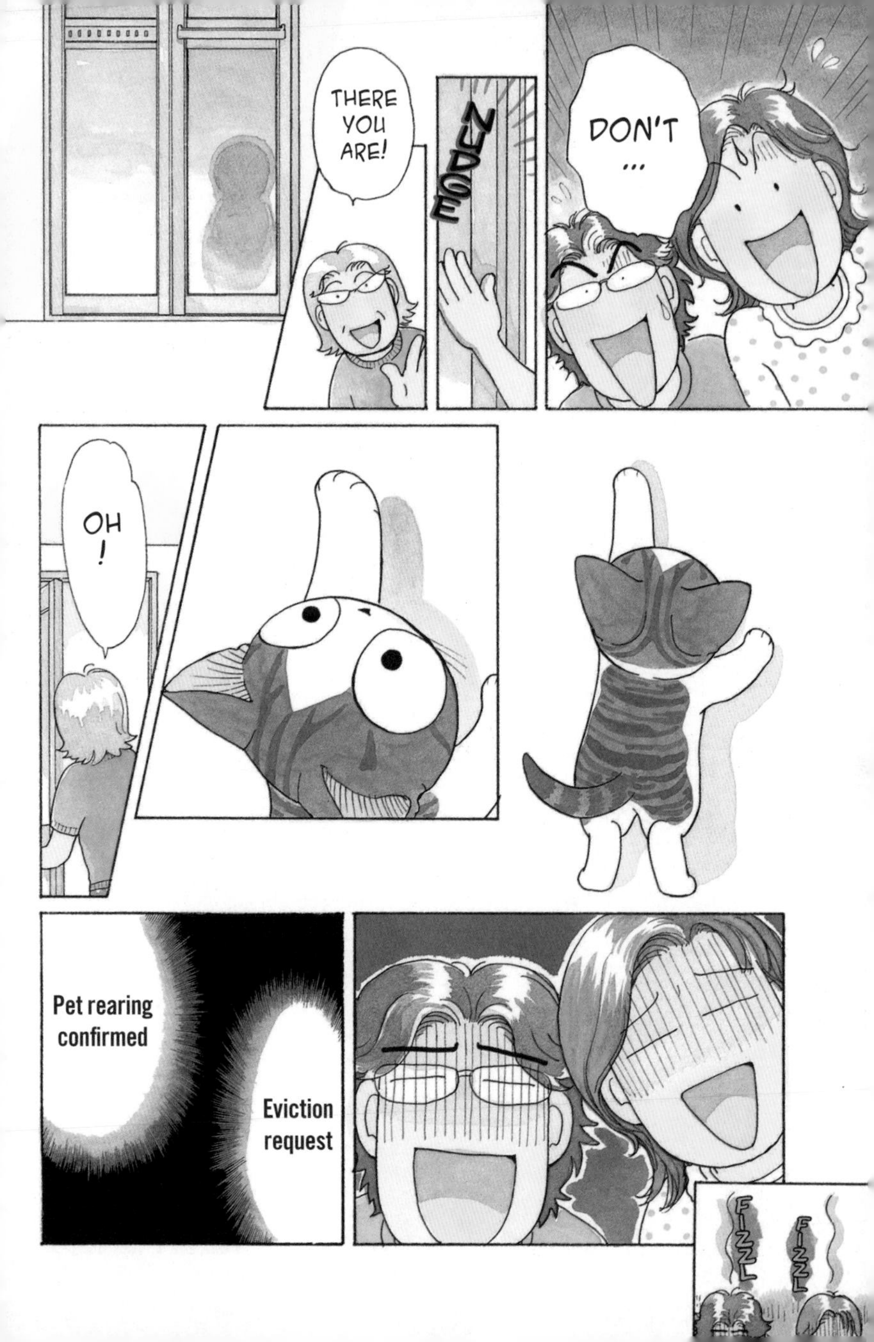
THERE YOU ARE!
NUDGE
DON'T ...
OH!
Pet rearing confirmed
Eviction request
FIZZL
FIZZL

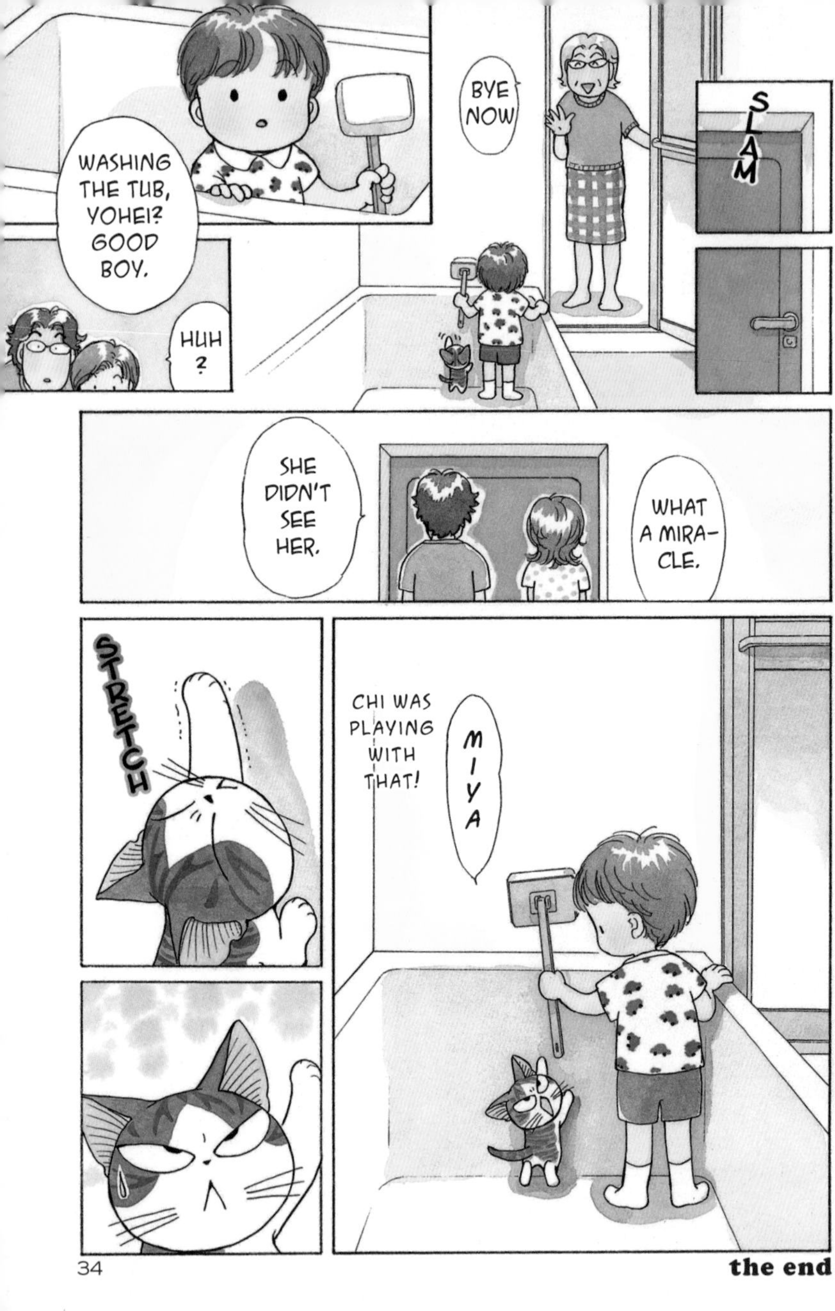
WASHING THE TUB, YOHEI? GOOD BOY.
HUH?
BYE NOW
SLAM
SHE DIDN'T SEE HER.
WHAT A MIRA-CLE.
STRETCH
CHI WAS PLAYING WITH THAT!
MIYA

the end

homemade 43: a cat mediates

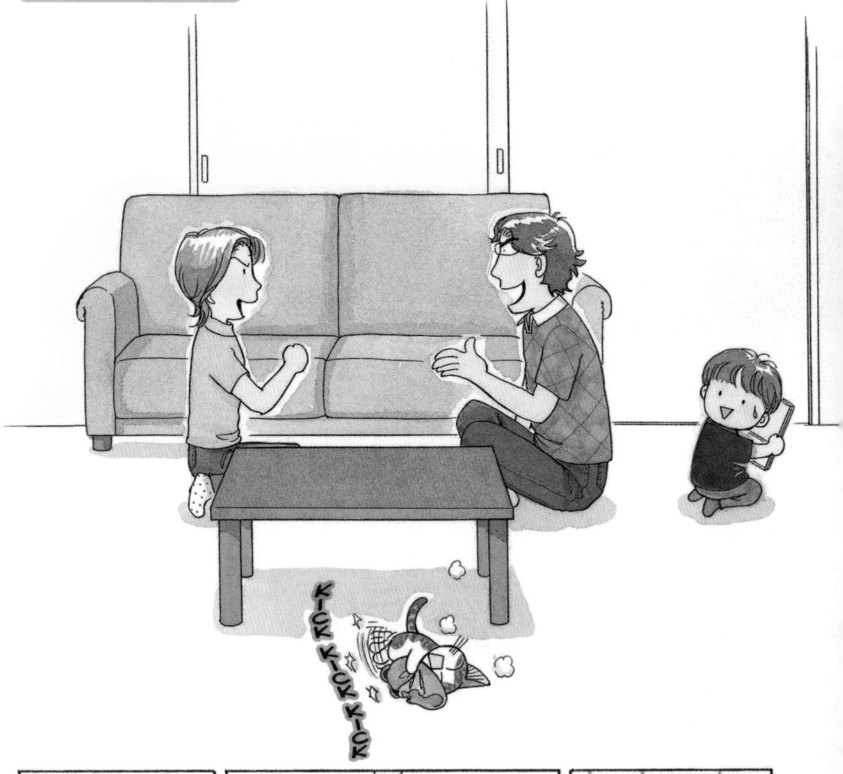
KICK KICK KICK

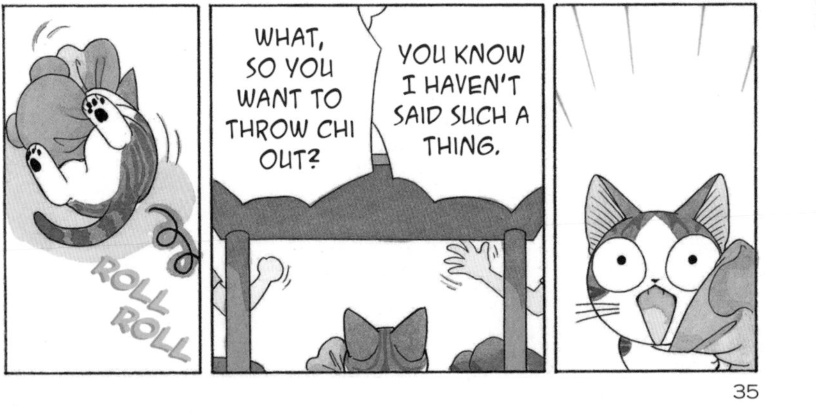
ROLL ROLL
WHAT, SO YOU WANT TO THROW CHI OUT?
YOU KNOW I HAVEN'T SAID SUCH A THING.

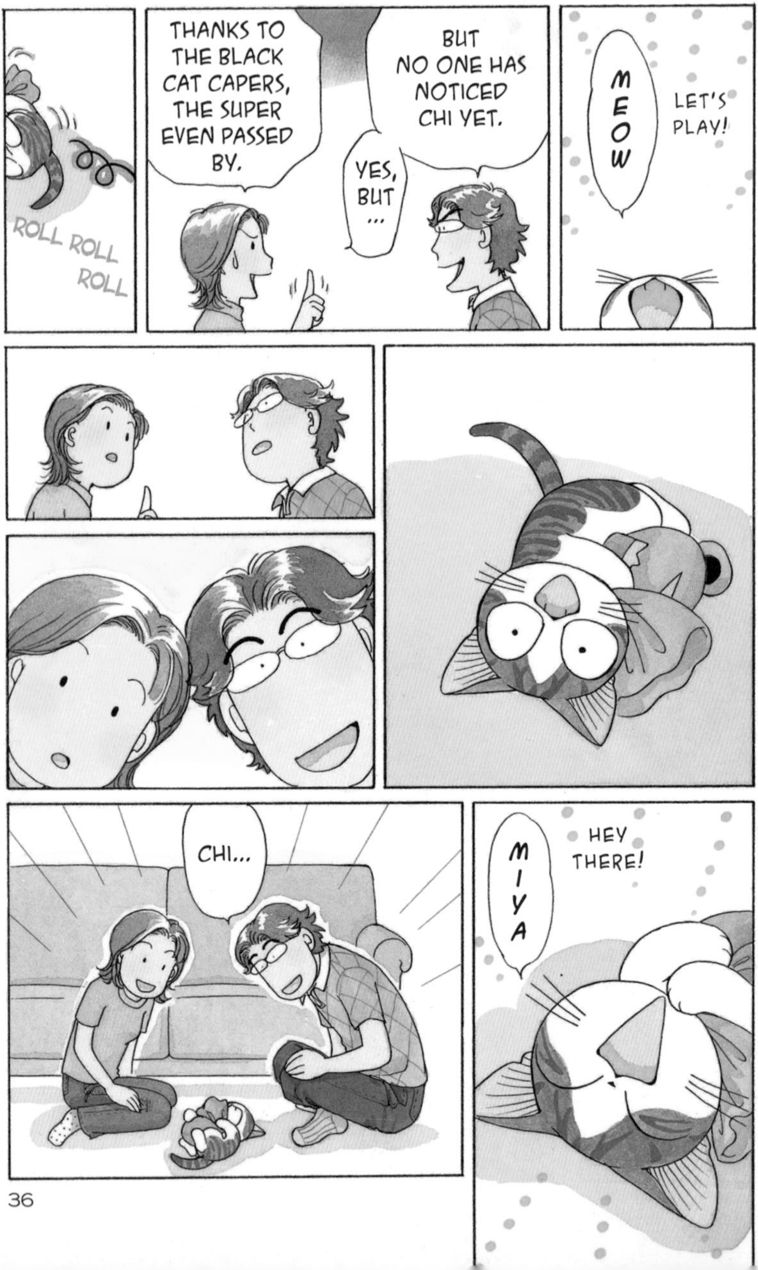
ROLL ROLL ROLL
THANKS TO THE BLACK CAT CAPERS, THE SUPER EVEN PASSED BY.
YES, BUT ...
BUT NO ONE HAS NOTICED CHI YET.
MEOW
LET'S PLAY!
CHI...
MIYA
HEY THERE!

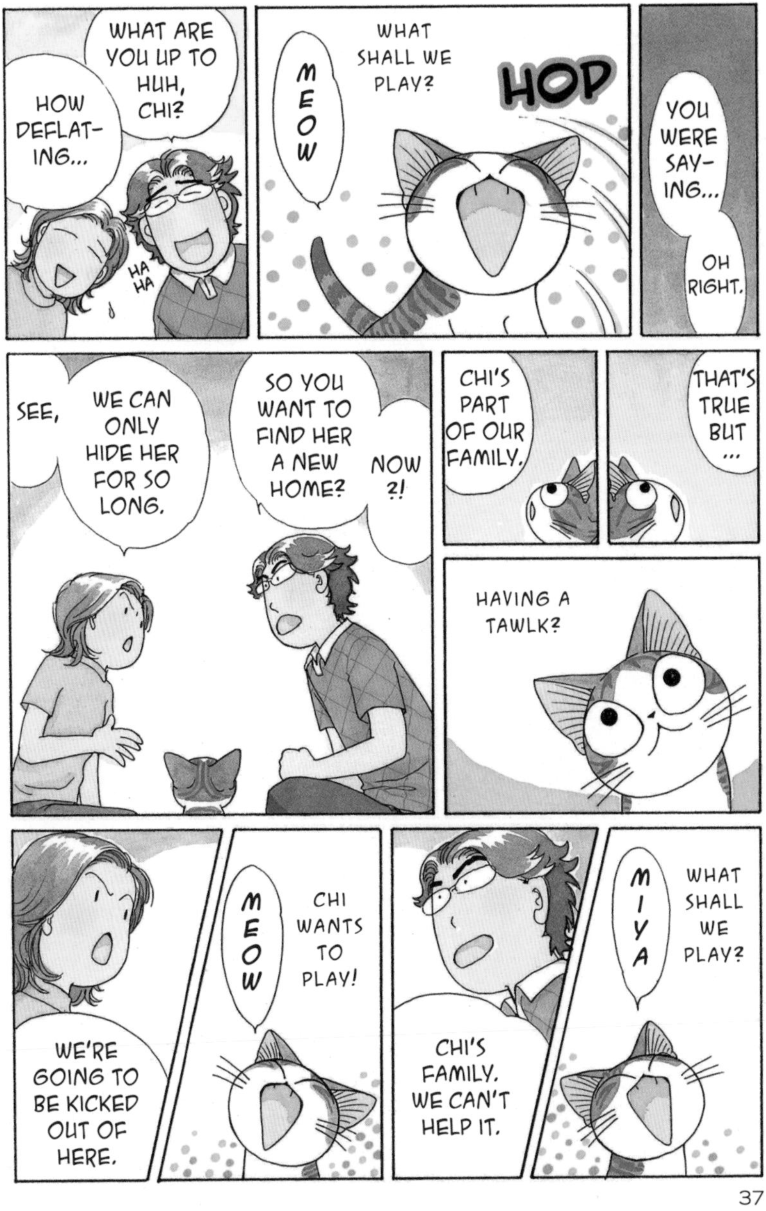
WHAT ARE YOU UP TO HUH, CHI?
HOW DEFLAT-ING...
HA HA
MEOW
WHAT SHALL WE PLAY?
HOP
YOU WERE SAY-ING...
OH RIGHT.
SEE,
WE CAN ONLY HIDE HER FOR SO LONG.
SO YOU WANT TO FIND HER A NEW HOME?
NOW ?!
CHI'S PART OF OUR FAMILY.
THAT'S TRUE BUT ...
HAVING A TAWLK?
WE'RE GOING TO BE KICKED OUT OF HERE.
MEOW
CHI WANTS TO PLAY!
CHI'S FAMILY. WE CAN'T HELP IT.
MIYA
WHAT SHALL WE PLAY?

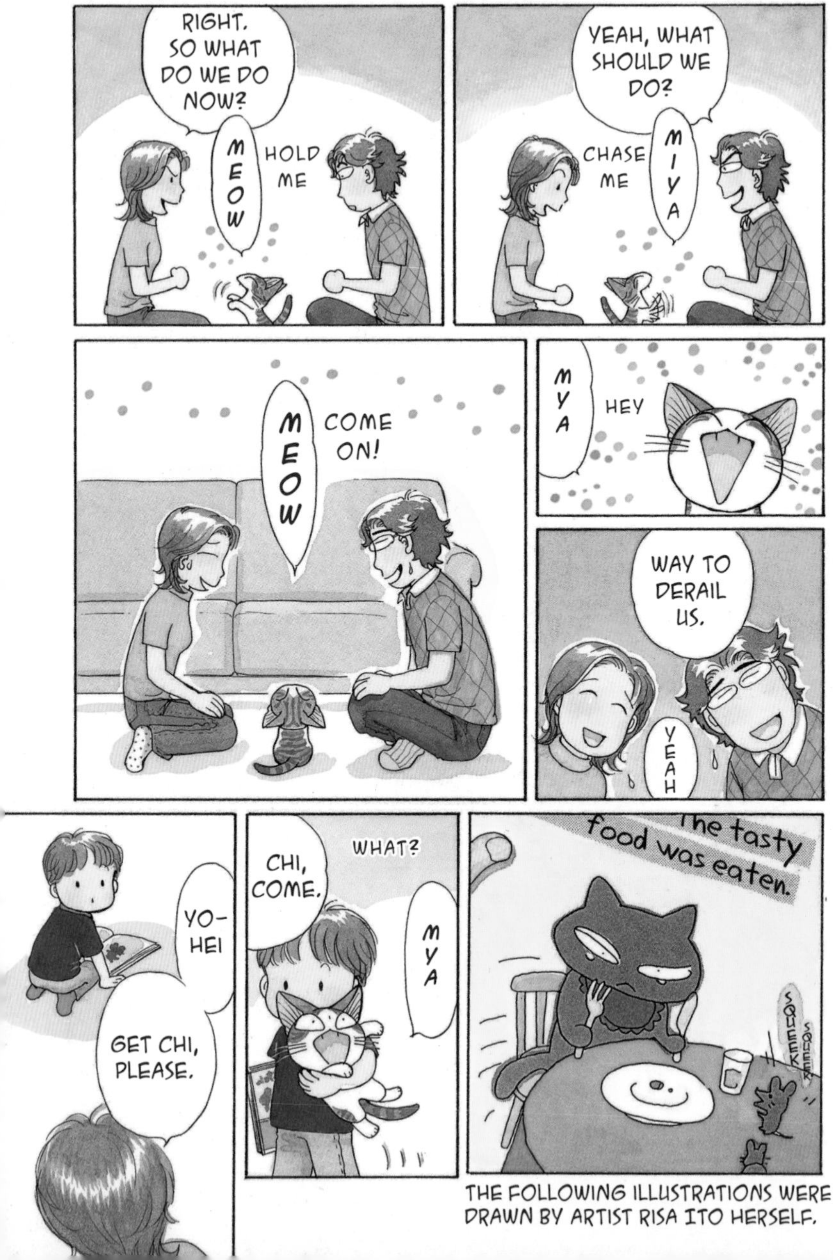

RIGHT. SO WHAT DO WE DO NOW?
MEOW
HOLD ME
YEAH, WHAT SHOULD WE DO?
CHASE ME
MIYA
MEOW
COME ON!
MYA
HEY
WAY TO DERAIL US.
YEAH
YO-HEI
GET CHI, PLEASE.
CHI, COME.
WHAT?
MYA
The tasty food was eaten.
SQUEEK
SQUEEK

THE FOLLOWING ILLUSTRATIONS WERE DRAWN BY ARTIST RISA ITO HERSELF.

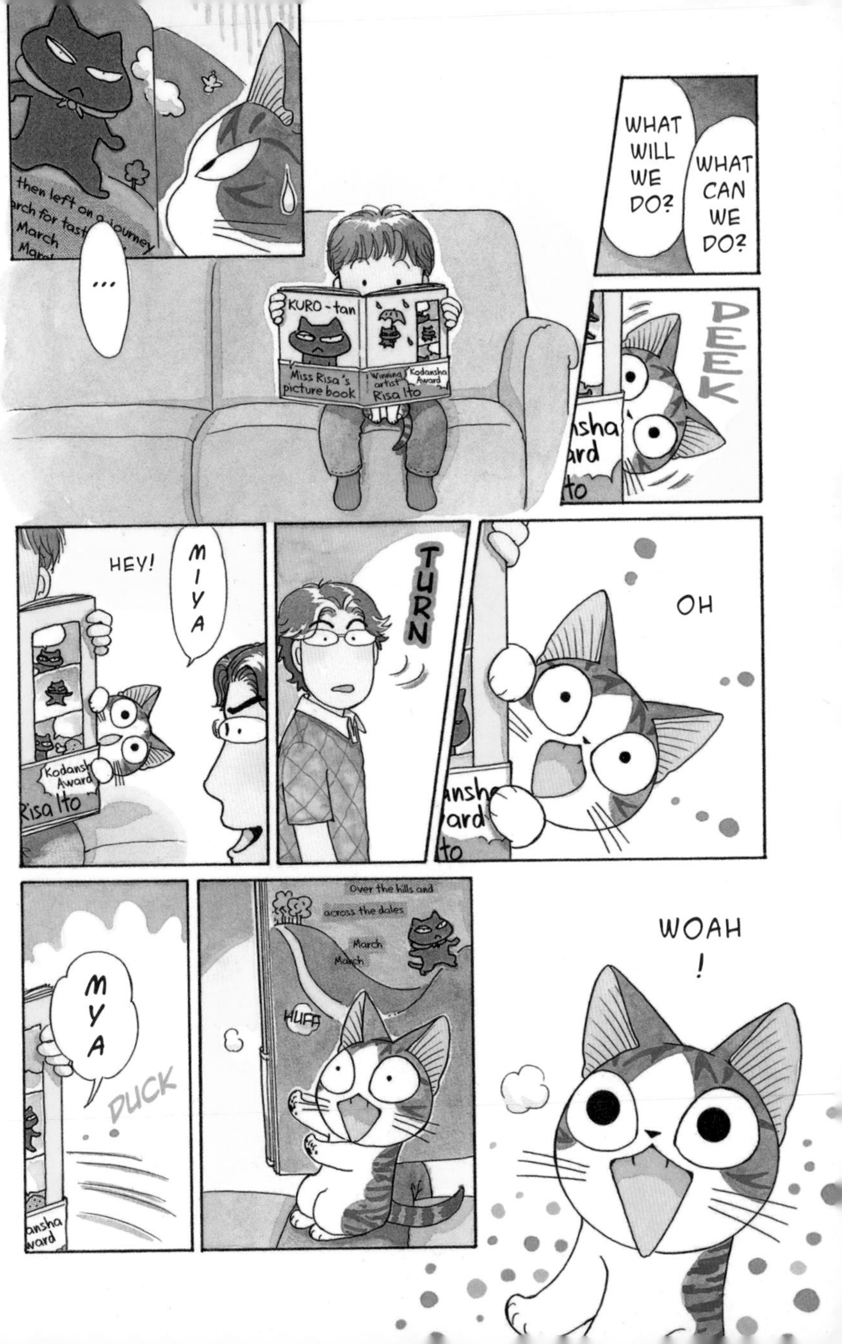
then left on a journey
March
...
KURO-tan
Miss Risa's picture book
Winning artist Risa Ito
Kodansha Award
WHAT WILL WE DO?
WHAT CAN WE DO?
PEEK
HEY!
MIYA
Kodansha Award
Risa Ito
TURN
OH
MYA
DUCK
Over the hills and
across the dales
March
March
HUFF
WOAH!

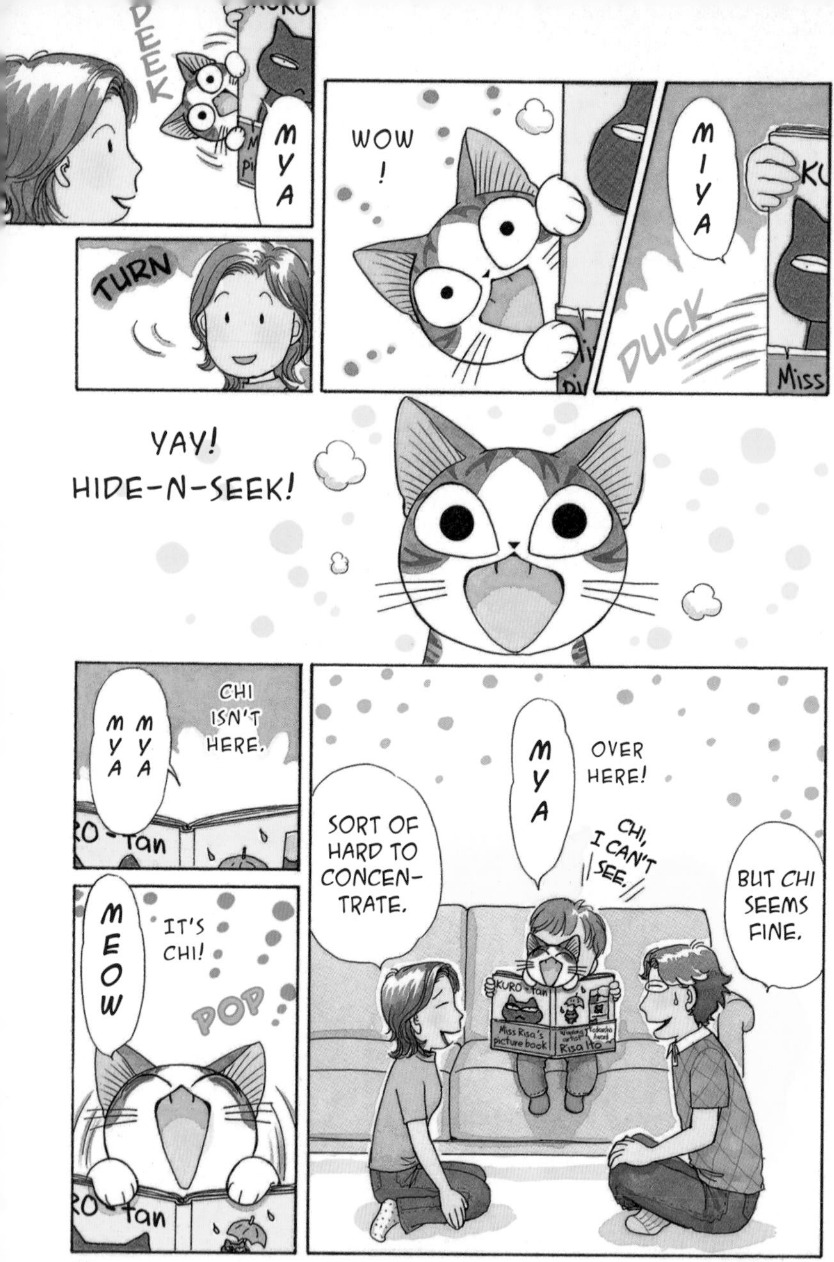
PEEK
MYA
TURN
WOW!
MIYA
DUCK
YAY! HIDE-N-SEEK!
MYA MYA
CHI ISN'T HERE.
MEOW
IT'S CHI!
POP
SORT OF HARD TO CONCENTRATE.
MYA
OVER HERE!
CHI, I CAN'T SEE.
BUT CHI SEEMS FINE.
KURO-tan
Miss Risa's picture book
Risa Ito

the end

homemade 44: a cat is attacked

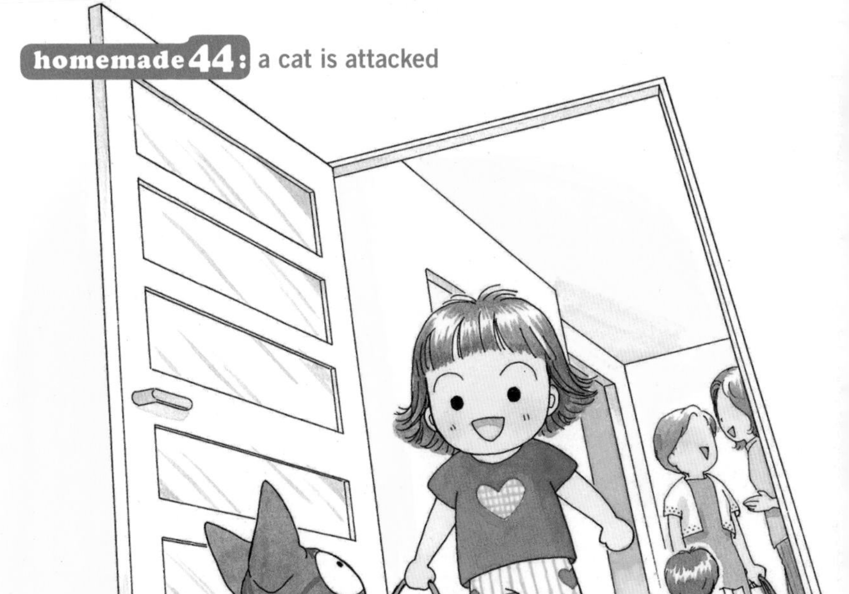

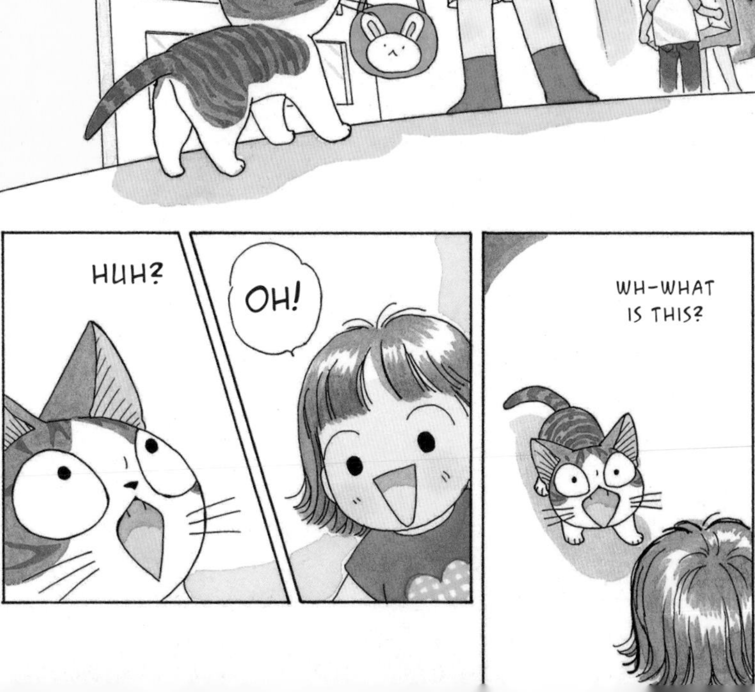
HUH?
OH!
WH-WHAT IS THIS?

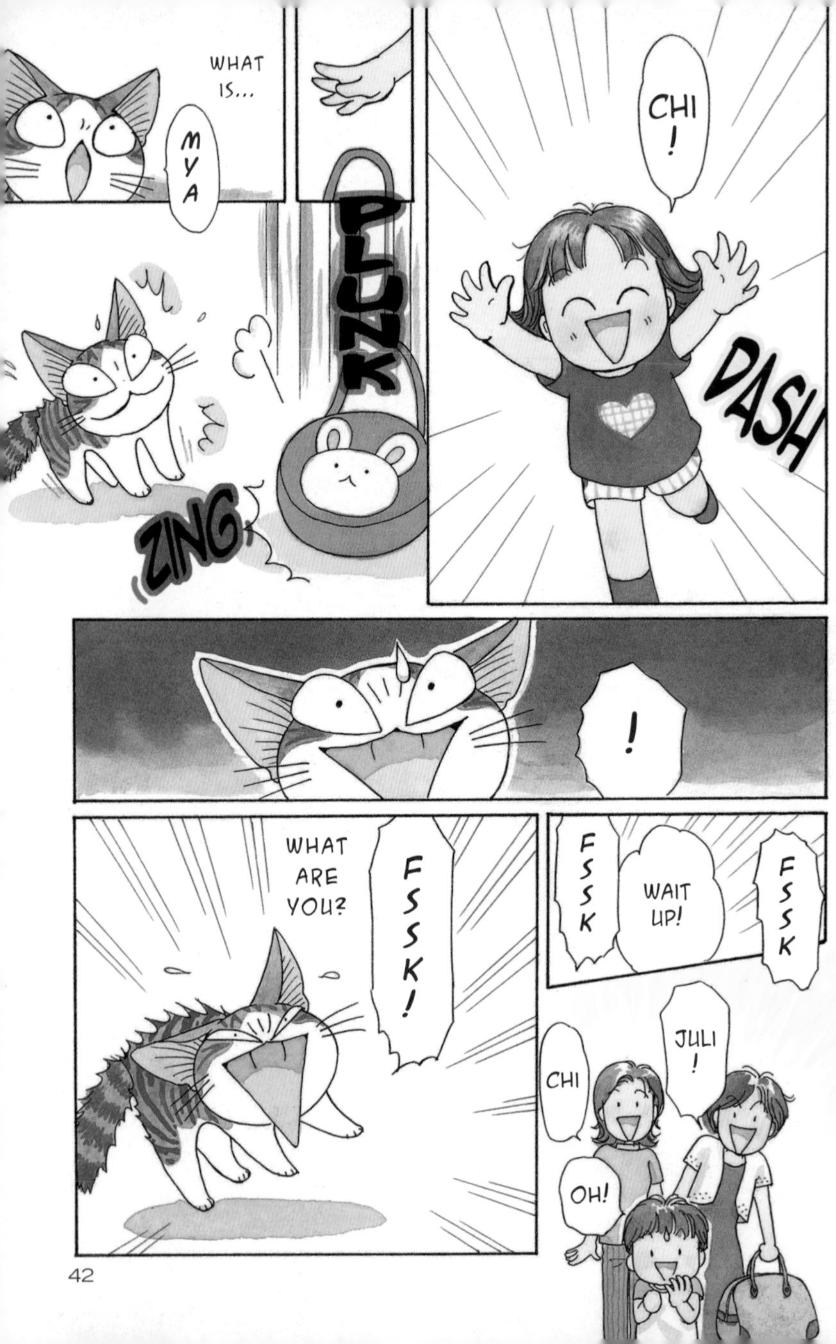
WHAT IS...
MYA
PLUNK
ZING
CHI!
DASH
!
WHAT ARE YOU?
FSSK!
FSSK
WAIT UP!
FSSK
CHI
JULI!
OH!

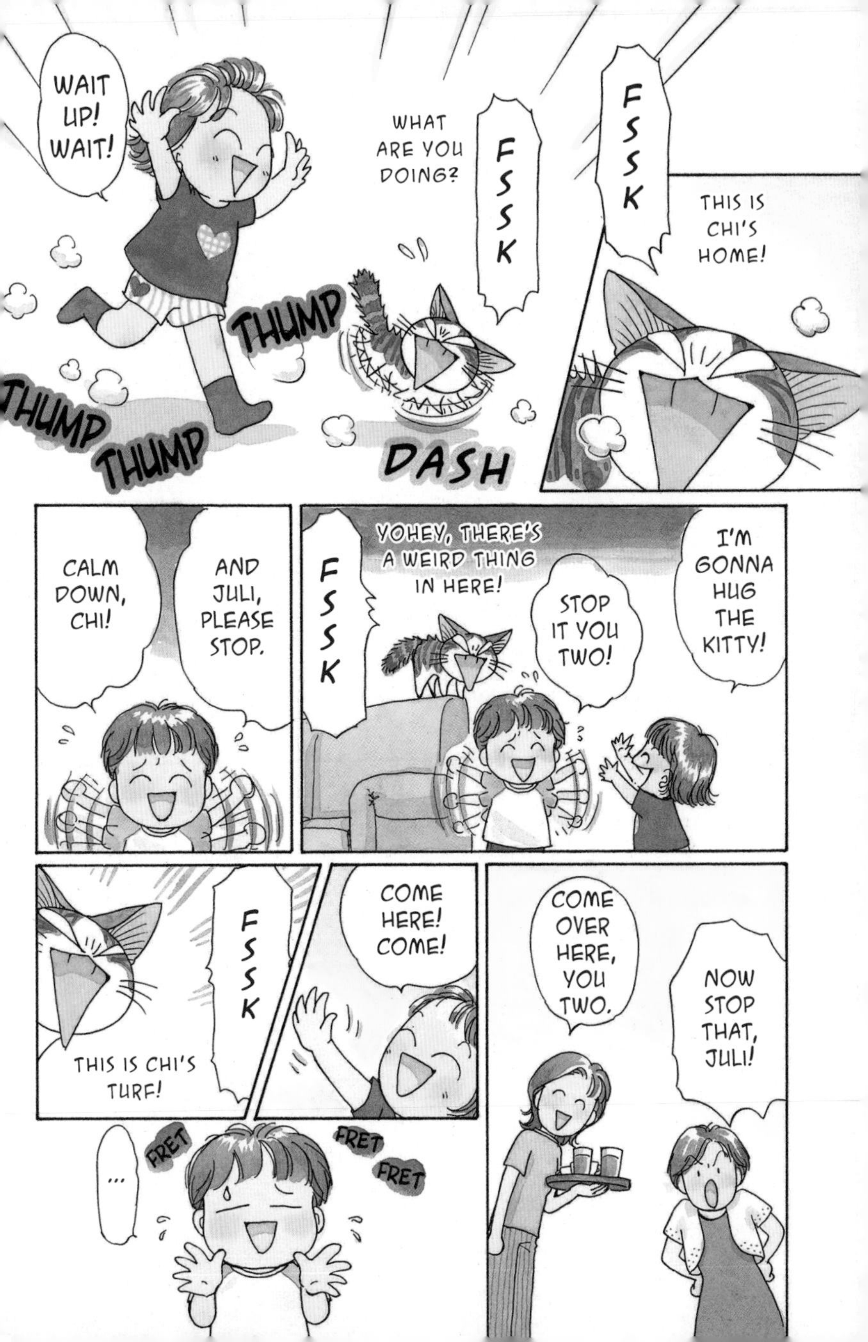
WAIT UP! WAIT!
THUMP
THUMP
THUMP
WHAT ARE YOU DOING?
FSSK
DASH
FSSK
THIS IS CHI'S HOME!
CALM DOWN, CHI!
AND JULI, PLEASE STOP.
FSSK
YOHEY, THERE'S A WEIRD THING IN HERE!
STOP IT YOU TWO!
I'M GONNA HUG THE KITTY!
FSSK
THIS IS CHI'S TURF!
COME HERE! COME!
...
FRET
FRET
FRET
COME OVER HERE, YOU TWO.
NOW STOP THAT, JULI!

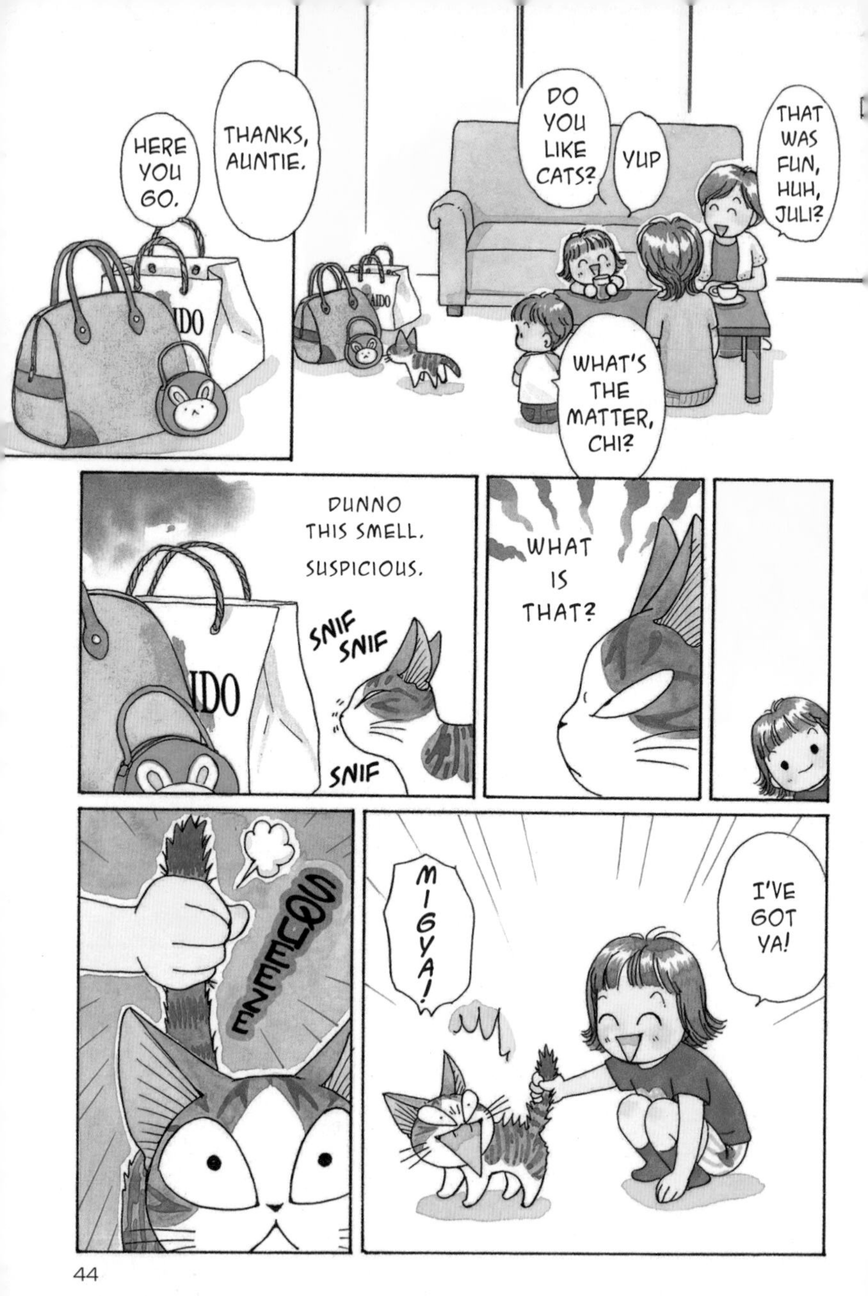
HERE YOU GO.
THANKS, AUNTIE.
DO YOU LIKE CATS?
YUP
THAT WAS FUN, HUH, JULI?
WHAT'S THE MATTER, CHI?
DUNNO THIS SMELL.
SUSPICIOUS.
SNIF SNIF
SNIF
WHAT IS THAT?
SQUEEEZE
MIGYA!
I'VE GOT YA!

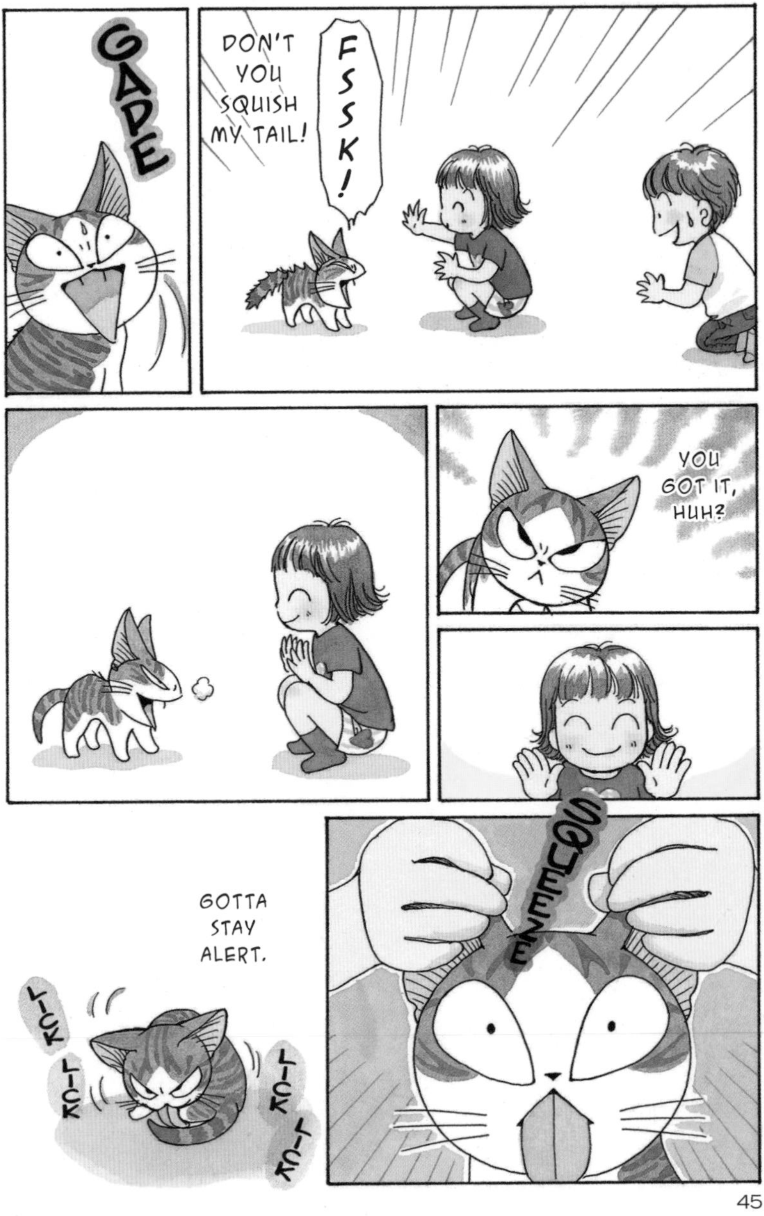

GAPE
DON'T YOU SQUISH MY TAIL!
FSSK!
YOU GOT IT, HUH?
GOTTA STAY ALERT.
LICK LICK
LICK LICK
SQUEEEEE

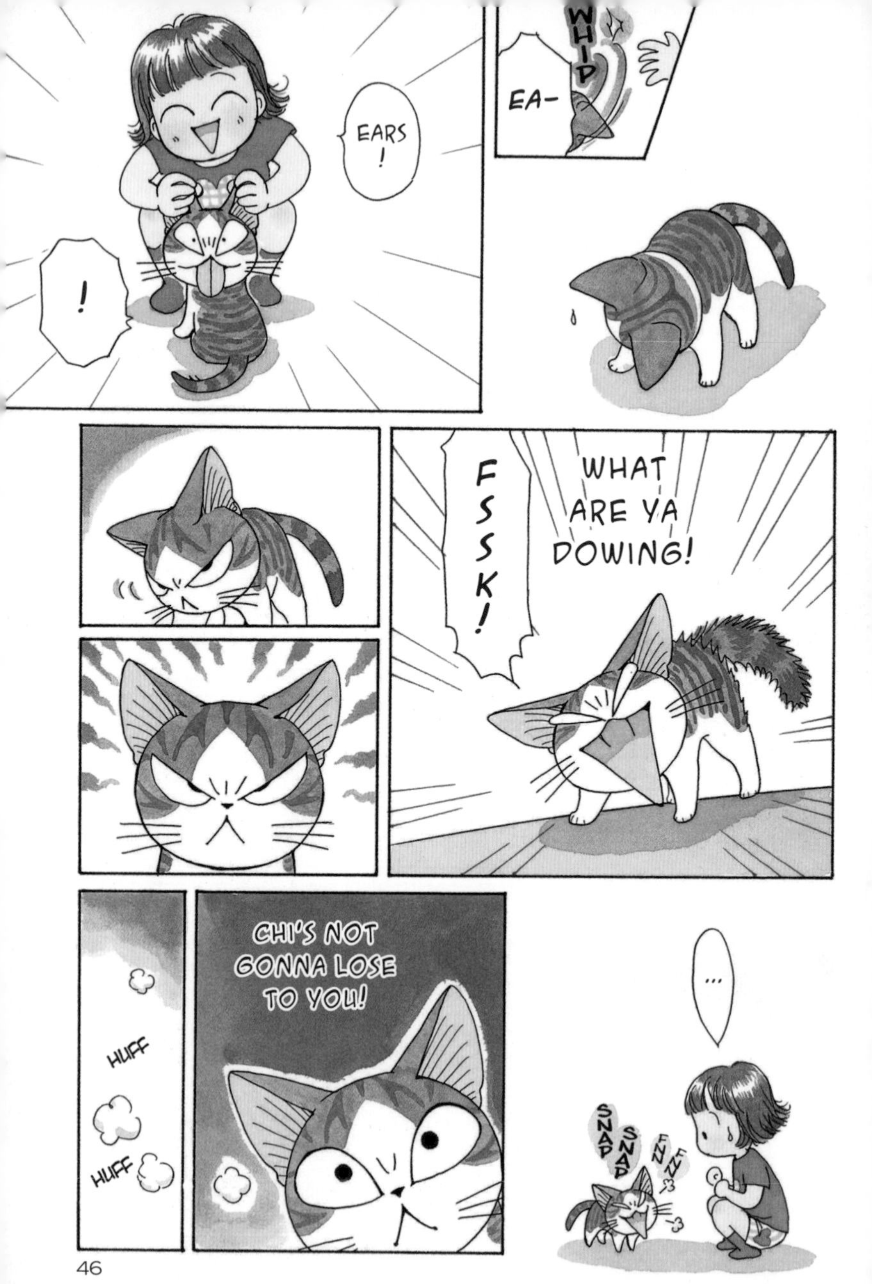

EARS!
!
WHIP
EA-
FSSK!
WHAT ARE YA DOWING!
HUFF
HUFF
CHI'S NOT GONNA LOSE TO YOU!
...
SNAP
SNAP
FNN
FNN

CHI'S TINY BUT SHE'S PRETTY SPUNKY.

YEAH,

YOU'RE A GOOD MATCH.

LET'S OPEN UP THE SOUVENIR, YES?

RIGHT

HOKKAIDO

WOAH, AWE-SOME!

YAMMER

OOH

AH

I'M TOO SCARED TO TOUCH IT.

WOW

WHEE

WHAT NOW?

KYAA!

SKAMPER

PEEK

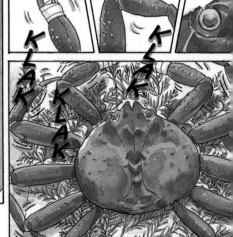

KLAK

KLAK

KLAK

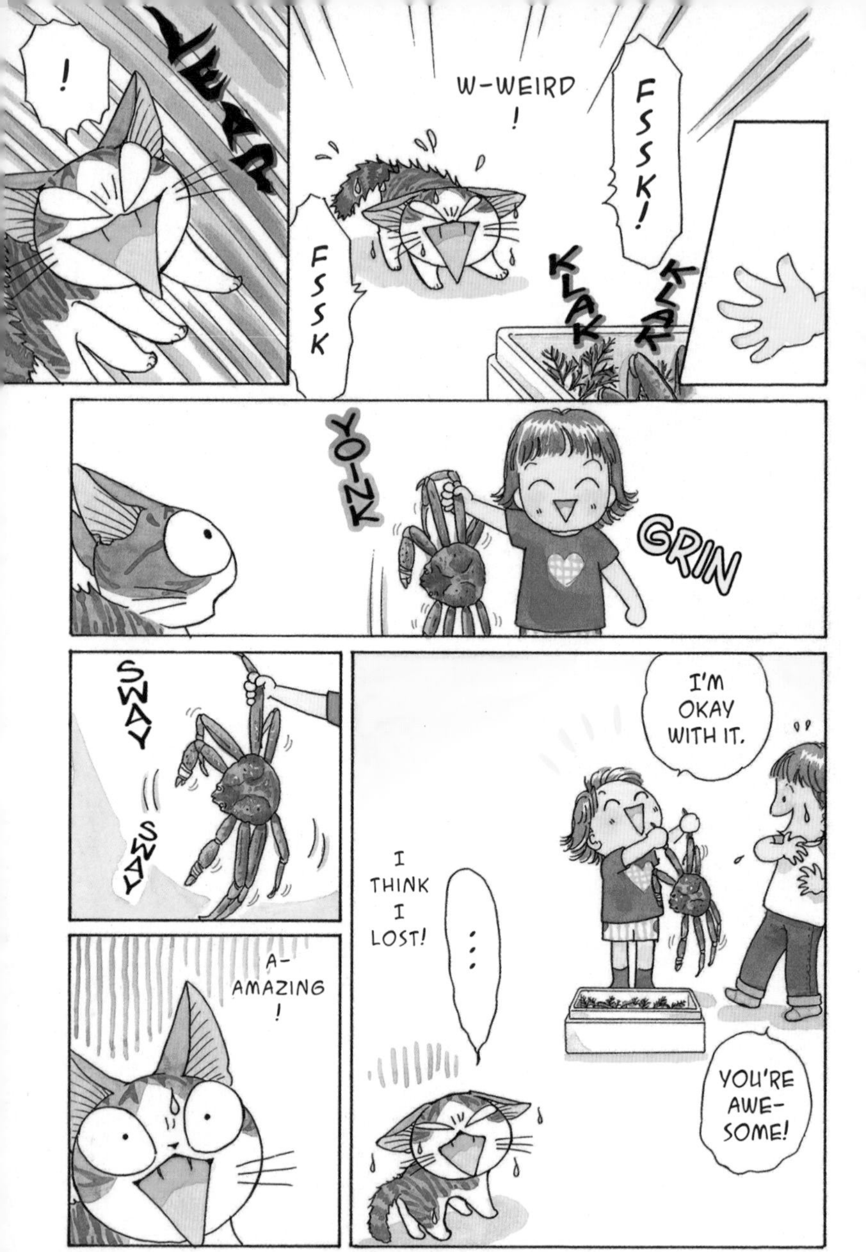
!
YEAR
W-WEIRD!
FSSK
FSSK!
KLAK
KLAK
YOINK
GRIN
SWAY
SWAY
A-AMAZING!
I'M OKAY WITH IT.
I THINK I LOST!
...
YOU'RE AWESOME!

the end

homemade 45: a cat gets along

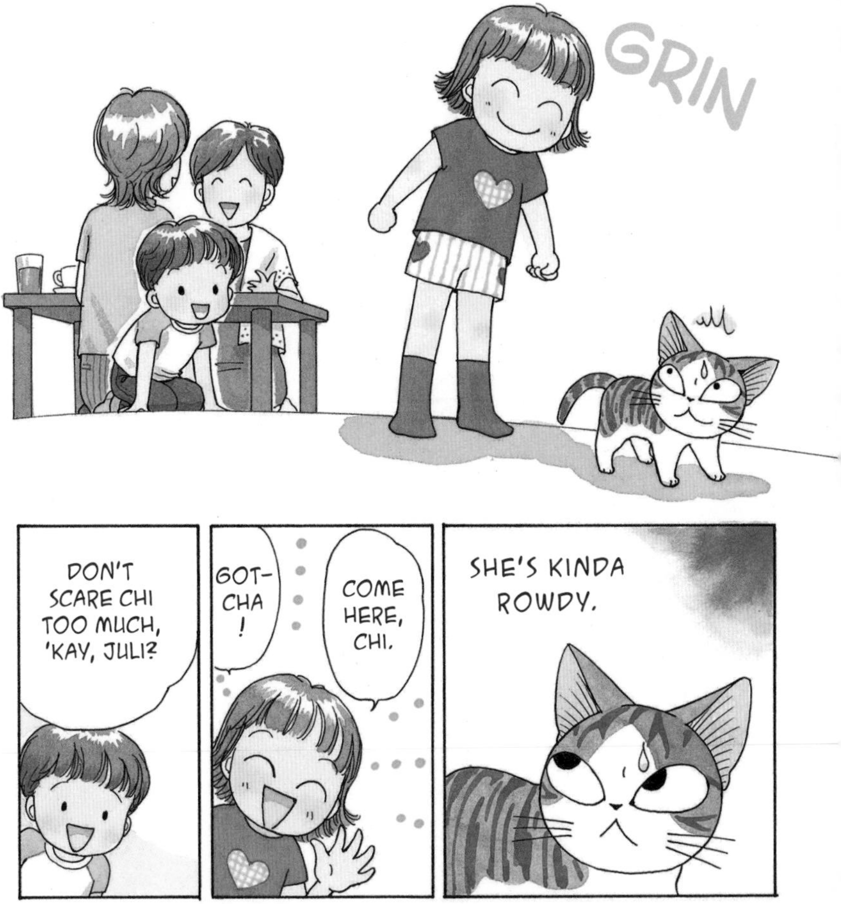
GRIN
DON'T SCARE CHI TOO MUCH, 'KAY, JULI?
GOT-CHA!
COME HERE, CHI.
SHE'S KINDA ROWDY.

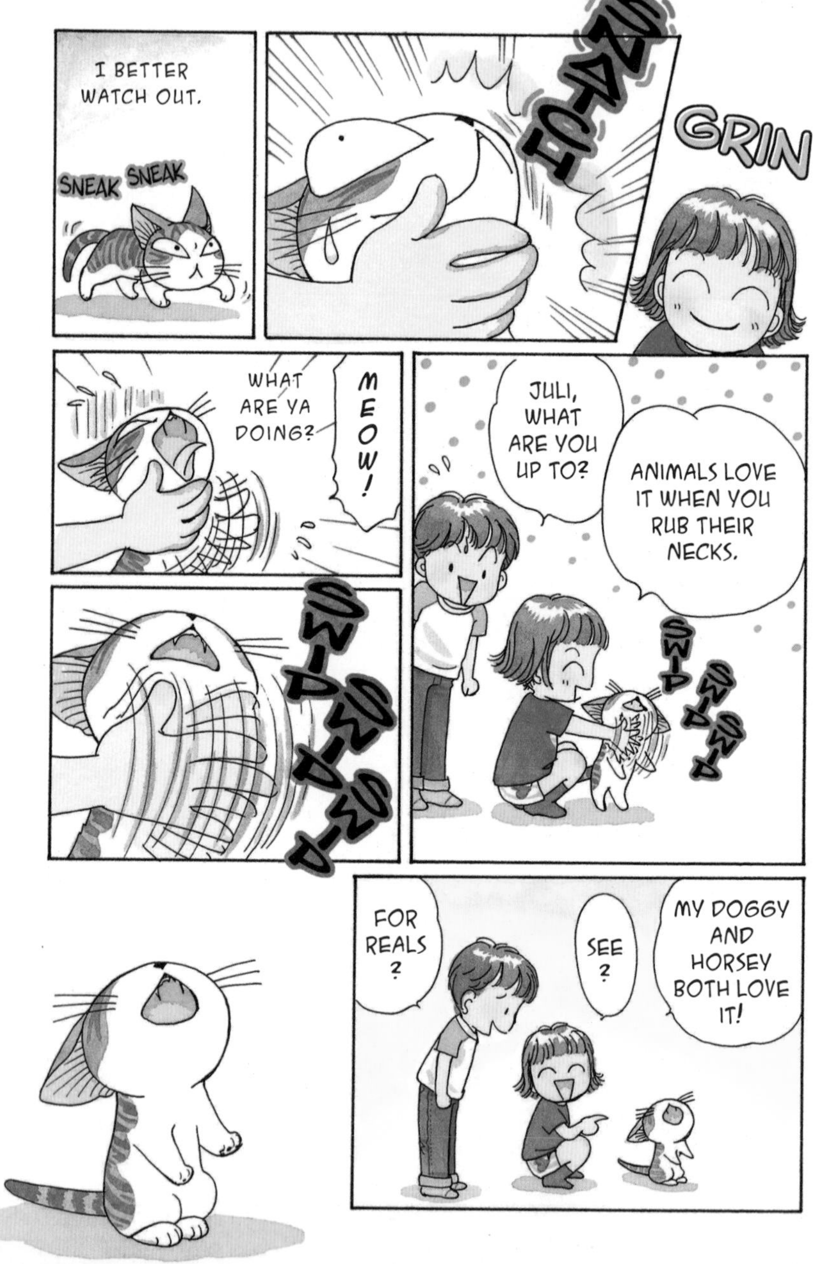
I BETTER WATCH OUT.
SNEAK SNEAK
SNATCH
GRIN
WHAT ARE YA DOING?
MEOW!
SWIP SWIP SWIP
JULI, WHAT ARE YOU UP TO?
ANIMALS LOVE IT WHEN YOU RUB THEIR NECKS.
SWIP SWIP SWIP
FOR REALS?
SEE?
MY DOGGY AND HORSEY BOTH LOVE IT!

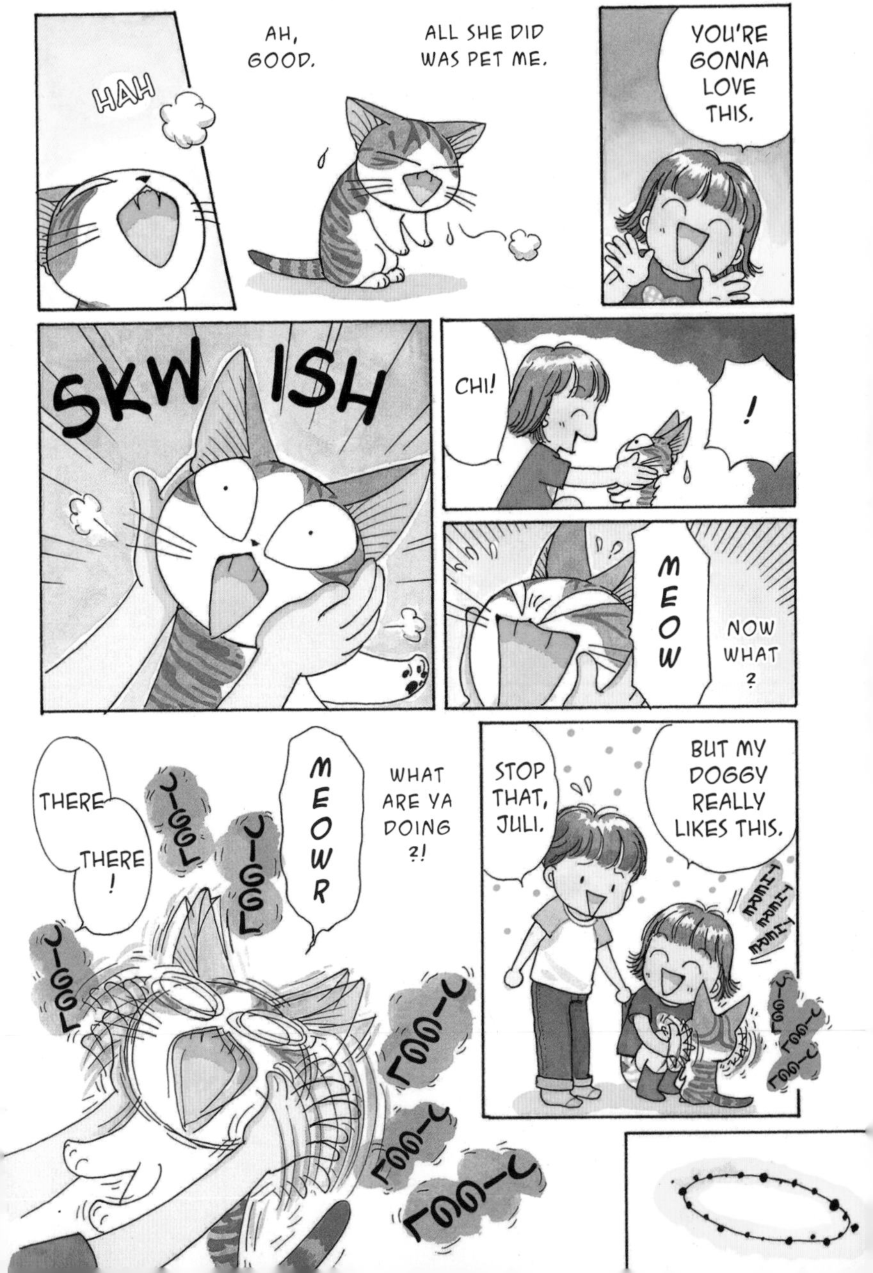
HAH
AH, GOOD.
ALL SHE DID WAS PET ME.
YOU'RE GONNA LOVE THIS.
SKW ISH
CHI!
!
MEOW
NOW WHAT?
THERE THERE!
JIGGL
JIGGL
JIGGL
MEOWR
WHAT ARE YA DOING?!
JIGGL
JIGGL
JIGGL
STOP THAT, JULI.
BUT MY DOGGY REALLY LIKES THIS.
JIGGL JIGGL

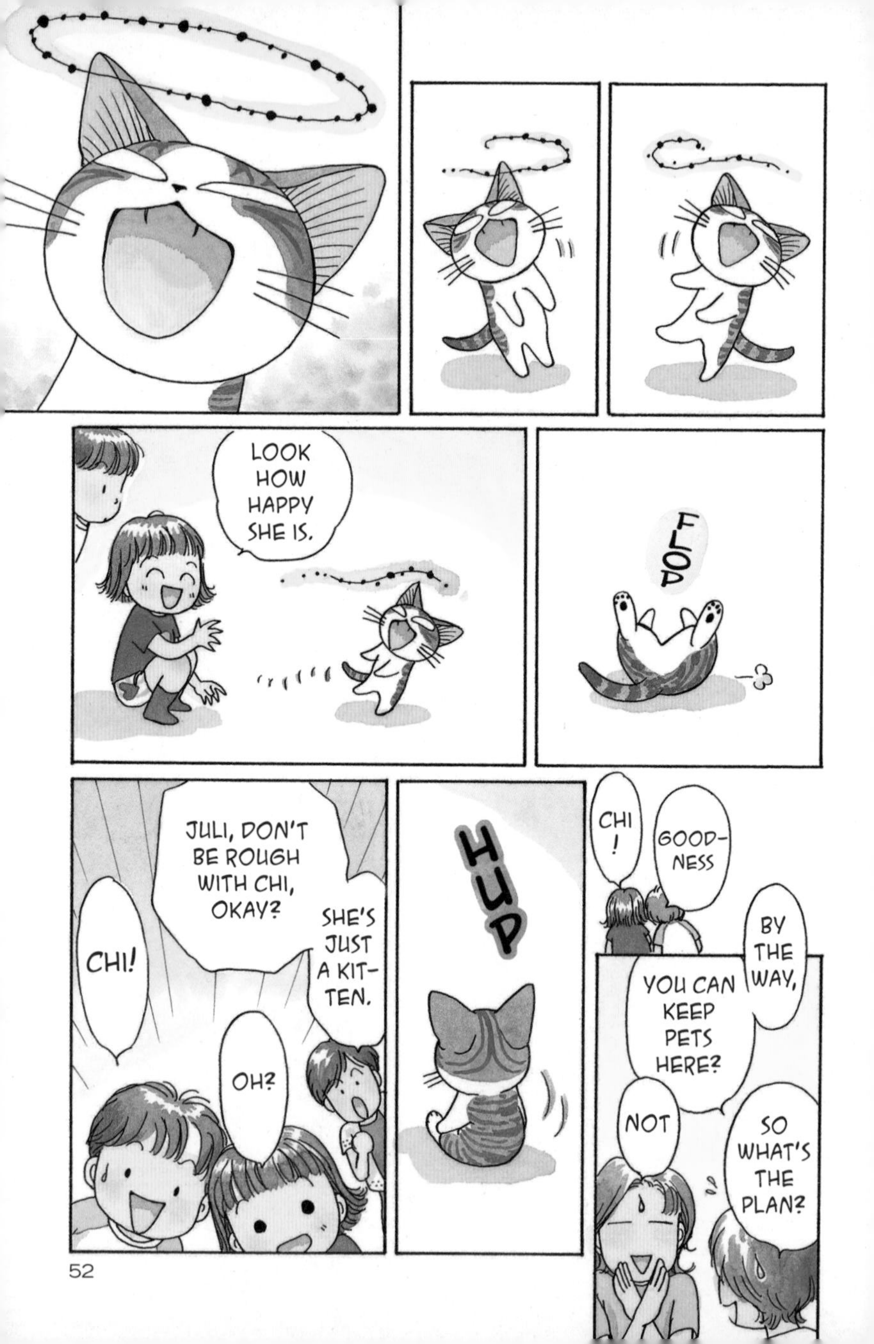
LOOK HOW HAPPY SHE IS.
FLOP
JULI, DON'T BE ROUGH WITH CHI, OKAY?
SHE'S JUST A KIT-TEN.
CHI!
OH?
HUP
CHI!
GOOD-NESS
BY THE WAY,
YOU CAN KEEP PETS HERE?
NOT
SO WHAT'S THE PLAN?

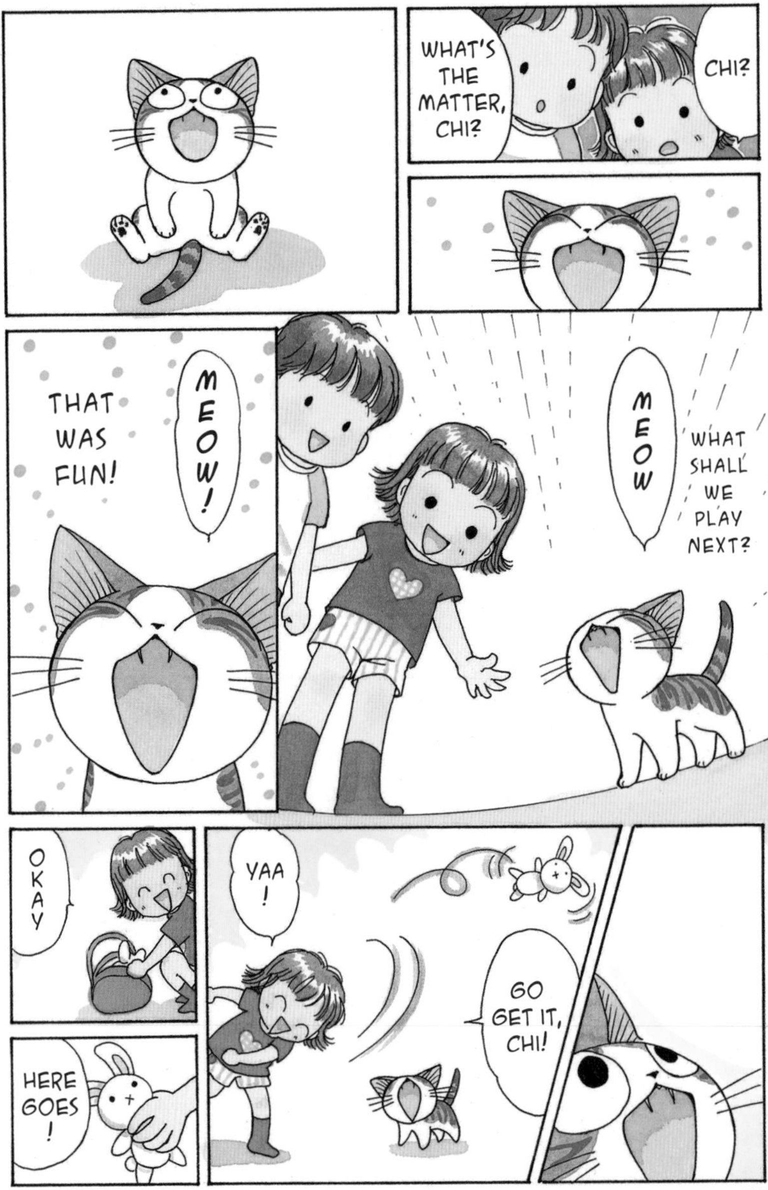
WHAT'S THE MATTER, CHI?
CHI?
THAT WAS FUN!
MEOW!
MEOW
WHAT SHALL WE PLAY NEXT?
OKAY
HERE GOES!
YAA!
GO GET IT, CHI!

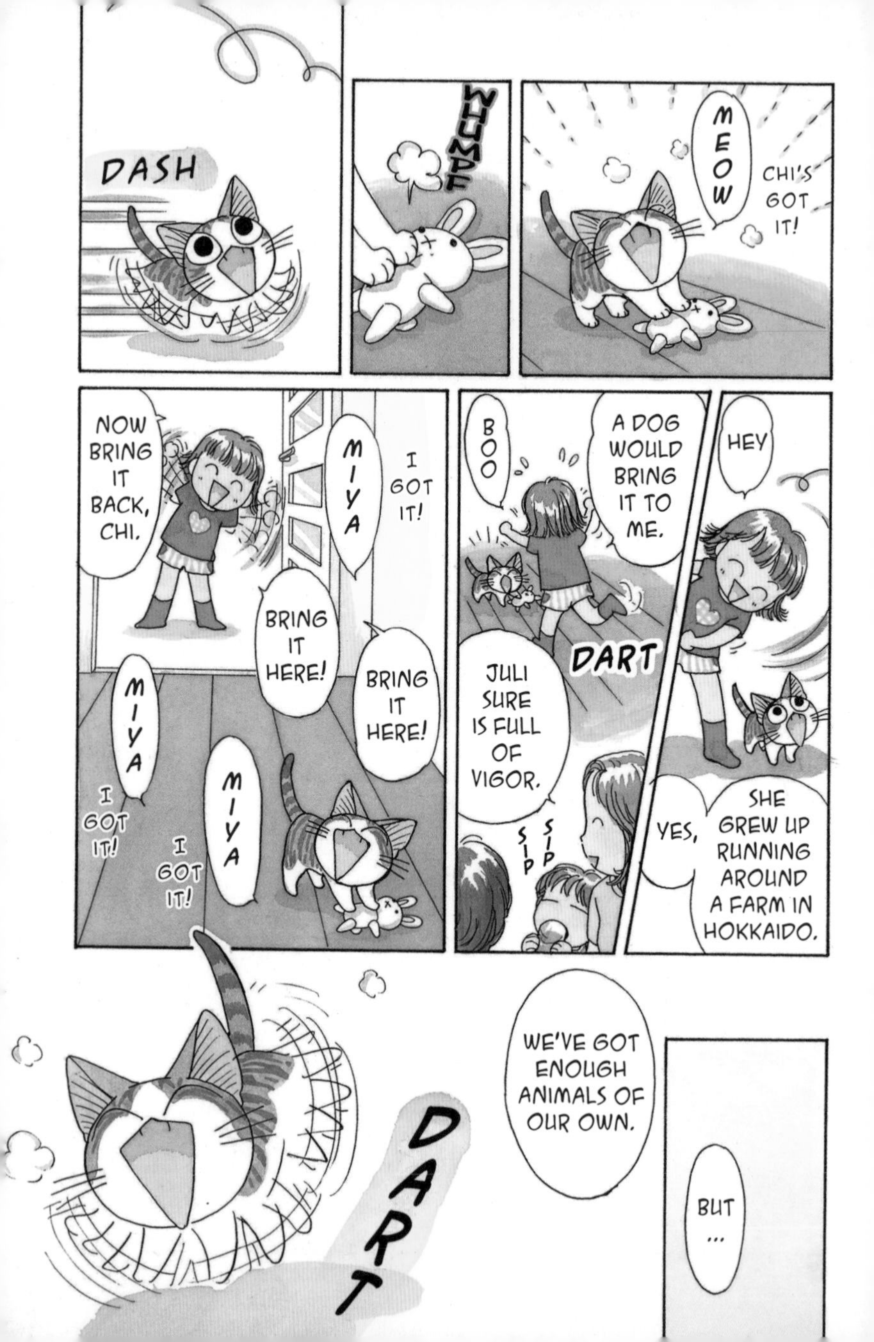
DASH
WHUMPF
MEOW
CHI'S GOT IT!
NOW BRING IT BACK, CHI.
MIYA
I GOT IT!
BRING IT HERE!
BRING IT HERE!
MIYA
I GOT IT!
MIYA
I GOT IT!
BOO
A DOG WOULD BRING IT TO ME.
DART
JULI SURE IS FULL OF VIGOR.
SIP SIP
HEY
YES, SHE GREW UP RUNNING AROUND A FARM IN HOKKAIDO.
DART
WE'VE GOT ENOUGH ANIMALS OF OUR OWN.
BUT ...

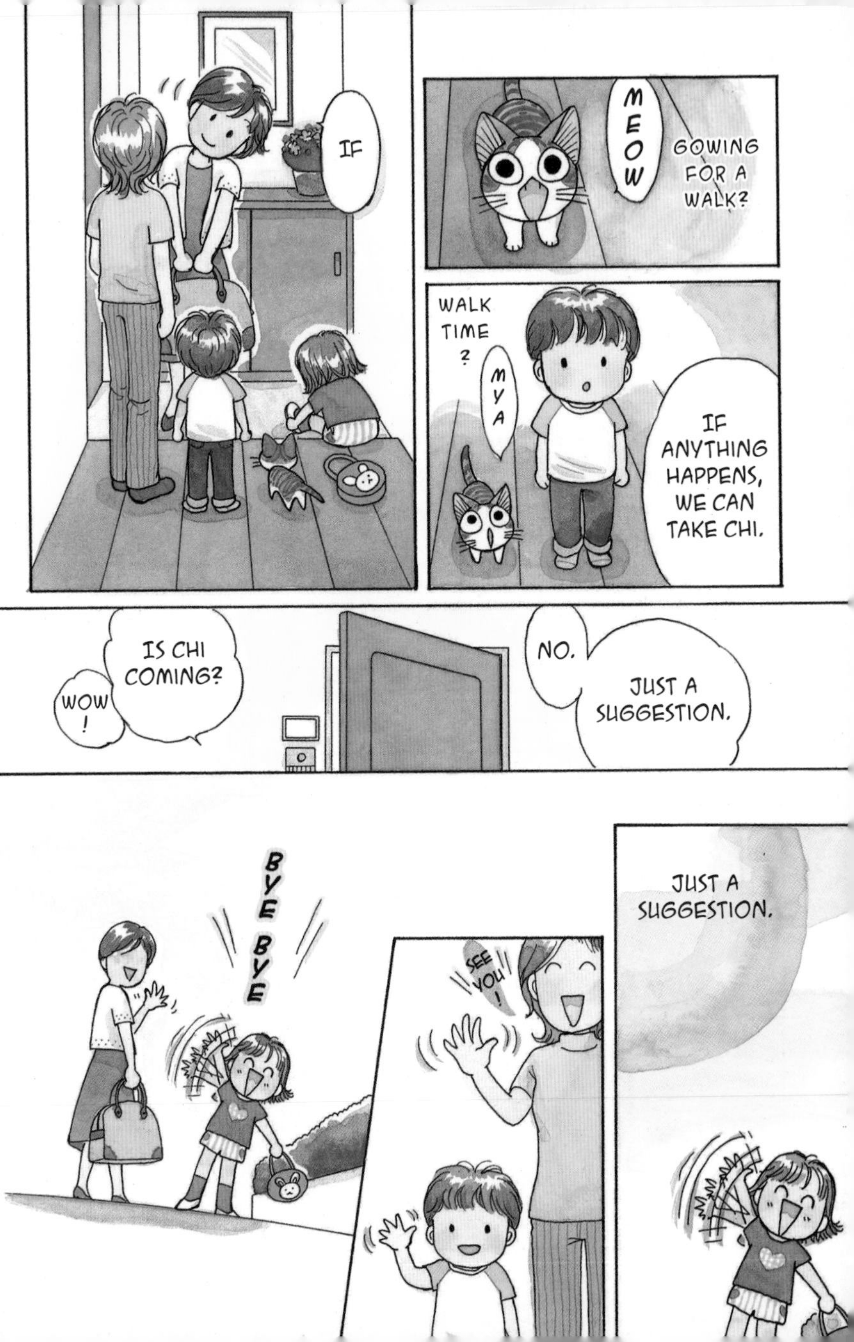
IF
MEOW
GOWING FOR A WALK?
WALK TIME?
MYA
IF ANYTHING HAPPENS, WE CAN TAKE CHI.
WOW!
IS CHI COMING?
NO.
JUST A SUGGESTION.
BYE BYE
SEE YOU!
JUST A SUGGESTION.

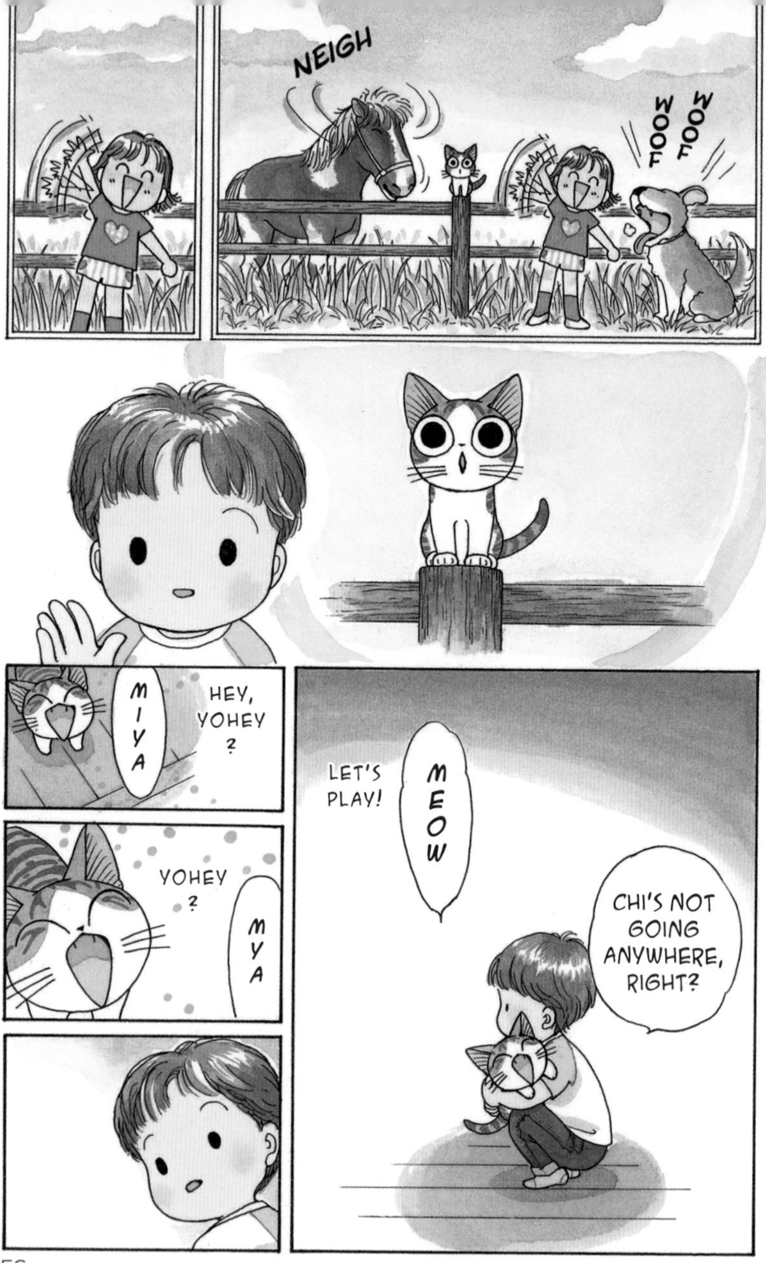
NEIGH
WOOF WOOF
MIYA
HEY, YOHEY?
YOHEY?
MYA
LET'S PLAY!
MEOW
CHI'S NOT GOING ANYWHERE, RIGHT?

the end

homemade 46: a cat learns

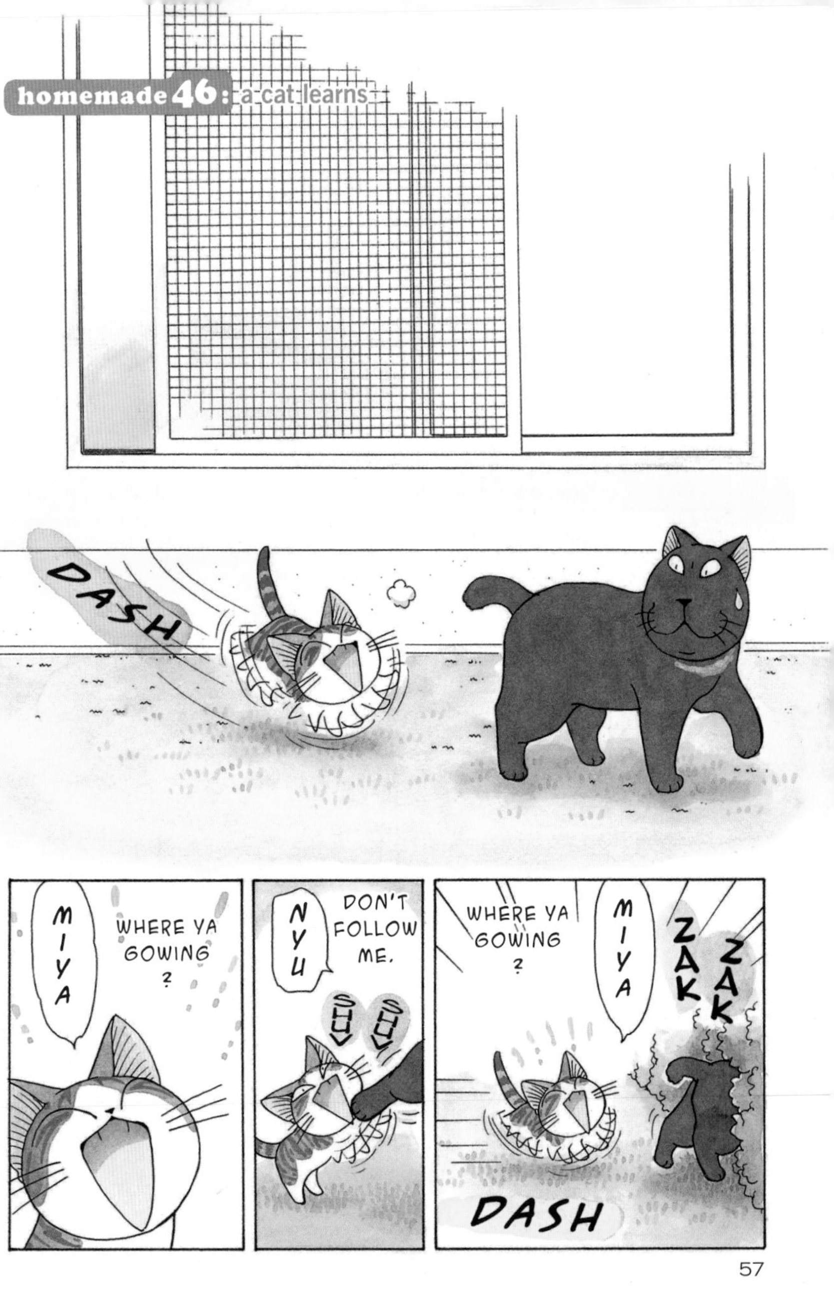
DASH
MIYA
WHERE YA GOWING ?
NYU
DON'T FOLLOW ME.
SHU SHU
WHERE YA GOWING ?
MIYA
ZAK ZAK
DASH

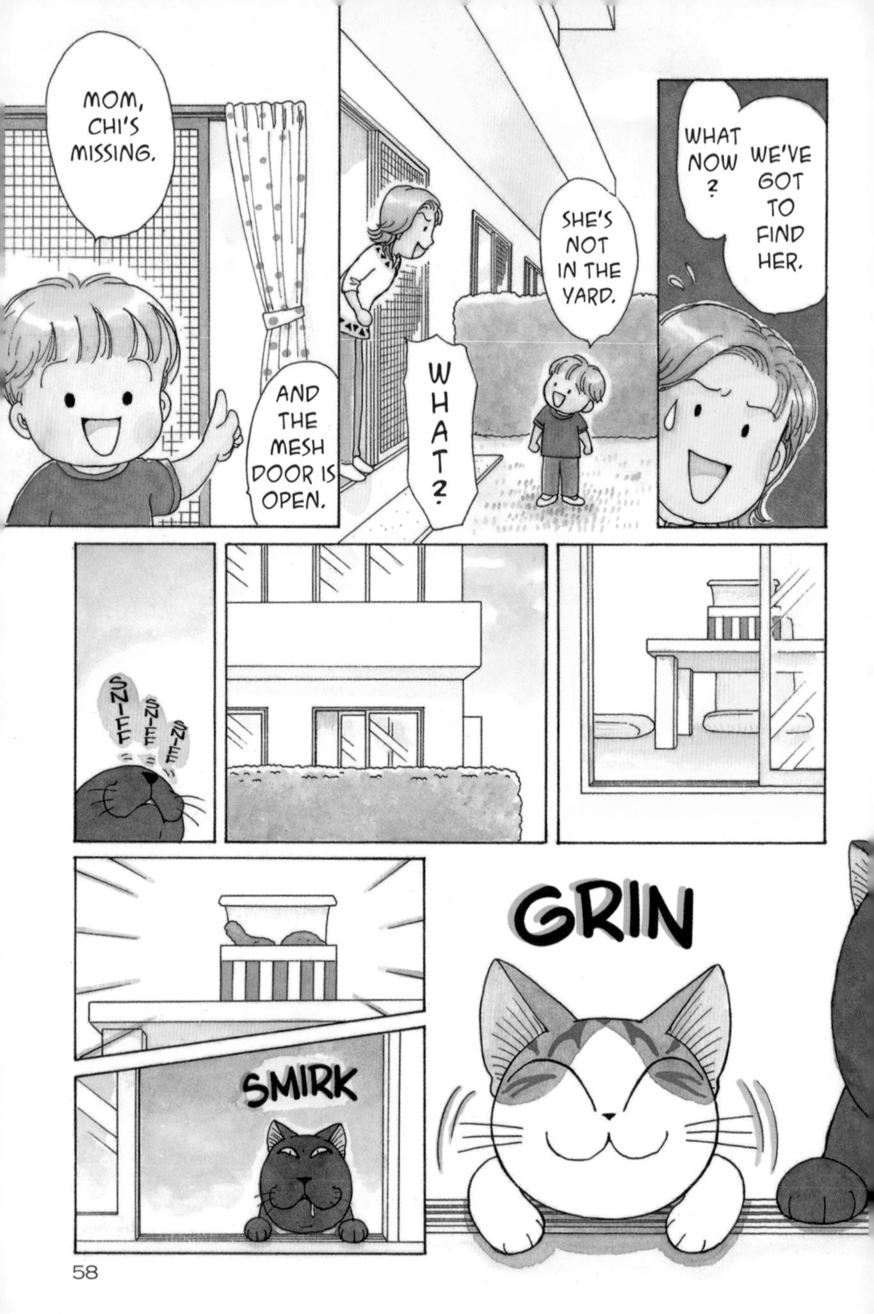
MOM, CHI'S MISSING.
AND THE MESH DOOR IS OPEN.
WHAT?
SHE'S NOT IN THE YARD.
WHAT NOW?
WE'VE GOT TO FIND HER.
SNIFF SNIFF SNIFF
SMIRK
GRIN

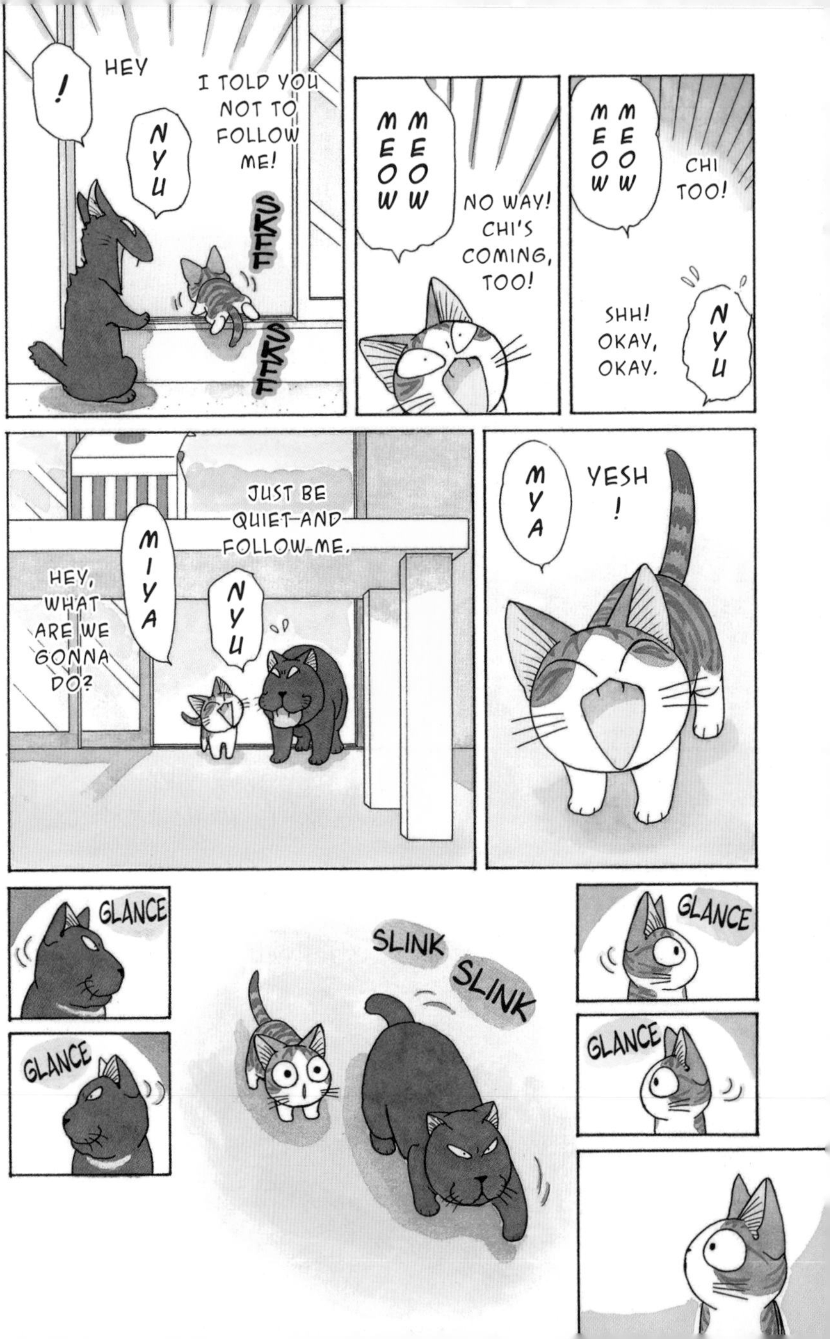
!
HEY
NYU
I TOLD YOU NOT TO FOLLOW ME!
SKFF
SKFF
MEOW MEOW
NO WAY! CHI'S COMING, TOO!
MEOW MEOW
CHI TOO!
SHH! OKAY, OKAY.
NYU
HEY, WHAT ARE WE GONNA DO?
MIYA
JUST BE QUIET AND FOLLOW ME.
NYU
MYA
YESH!
GLANCE
GLANCE
SLINK
SLINK
GLANCE
GLANCE

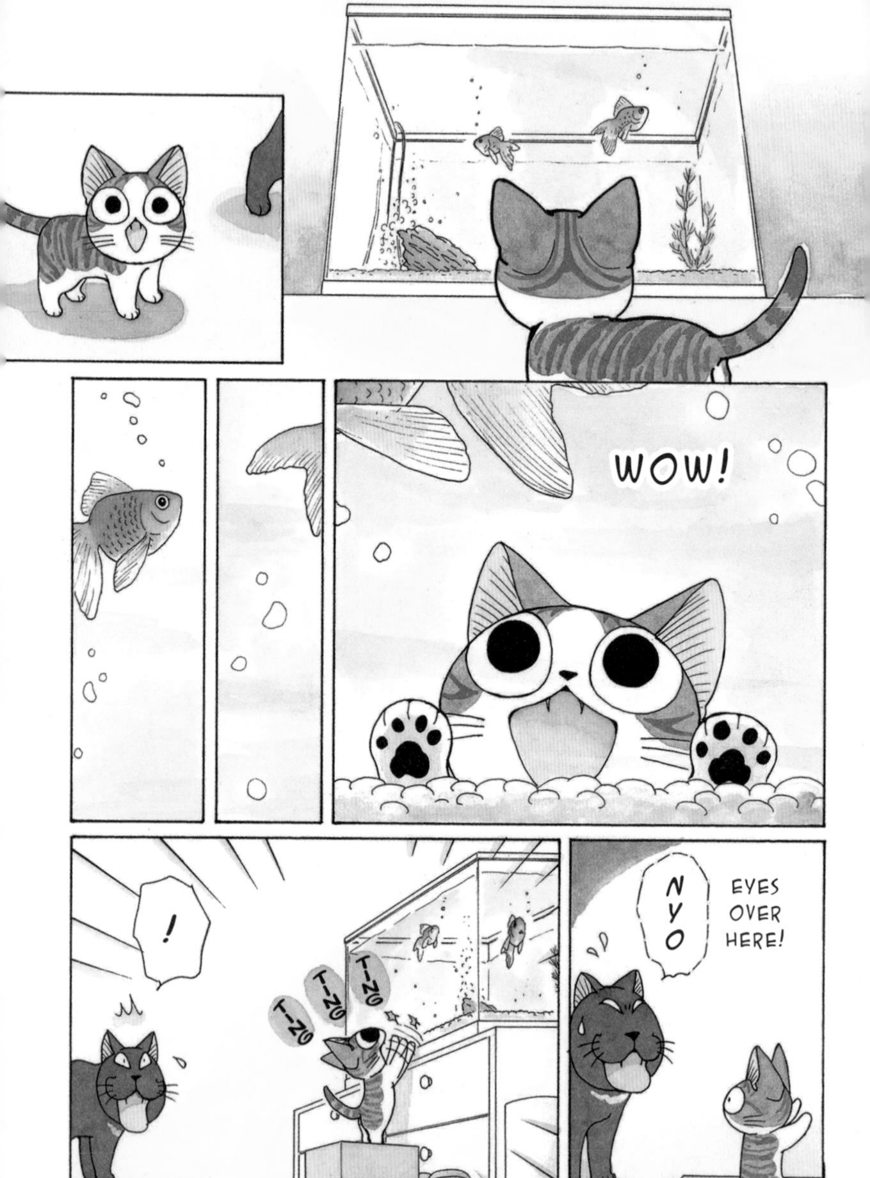
WOW!
!
T-ZO
TING
TING
NYO
EYES OVER HERE!

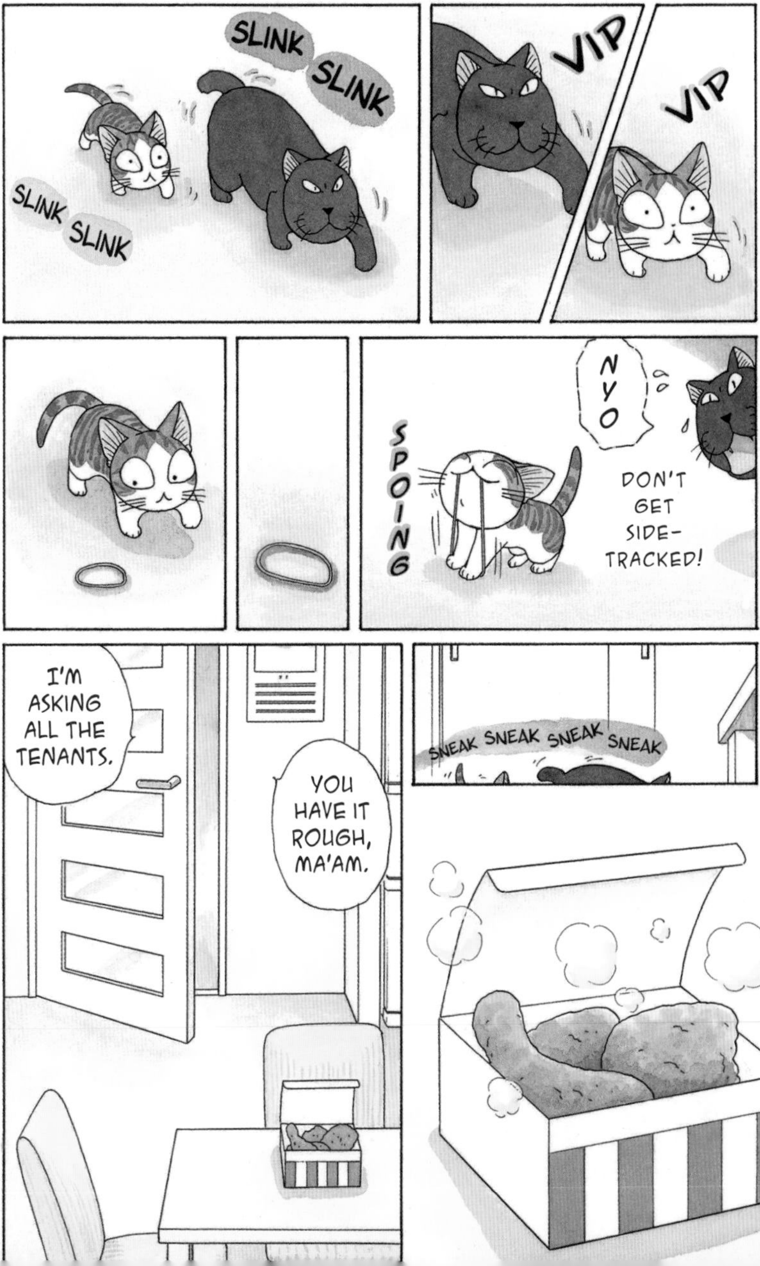
SLINK
SLINK
SLINK
SLINK
VIP
VIP
NYO
SPOING
DON'T GET SIDE-TRACKED!
I'M ASKING ALL THE TENANTS.
YOU HAVE IT ROUGH, MA'AM.
SNEAK SNEAK SNEAK SNEAK

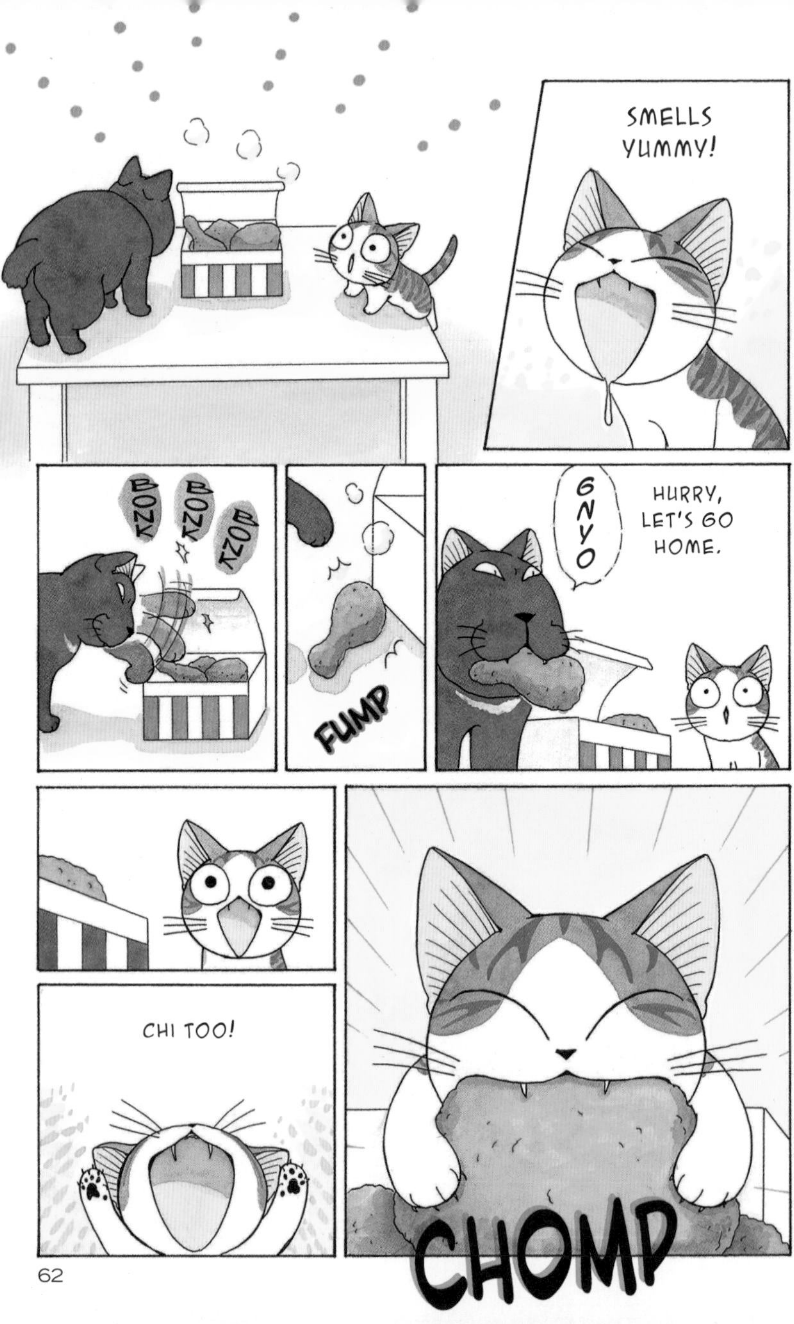
SMELLS YUMMY!
BONK BONK BONK
FUMP
GNYO
HURRY, LET'S GO HOME.
CHI TOO!
CHOMP

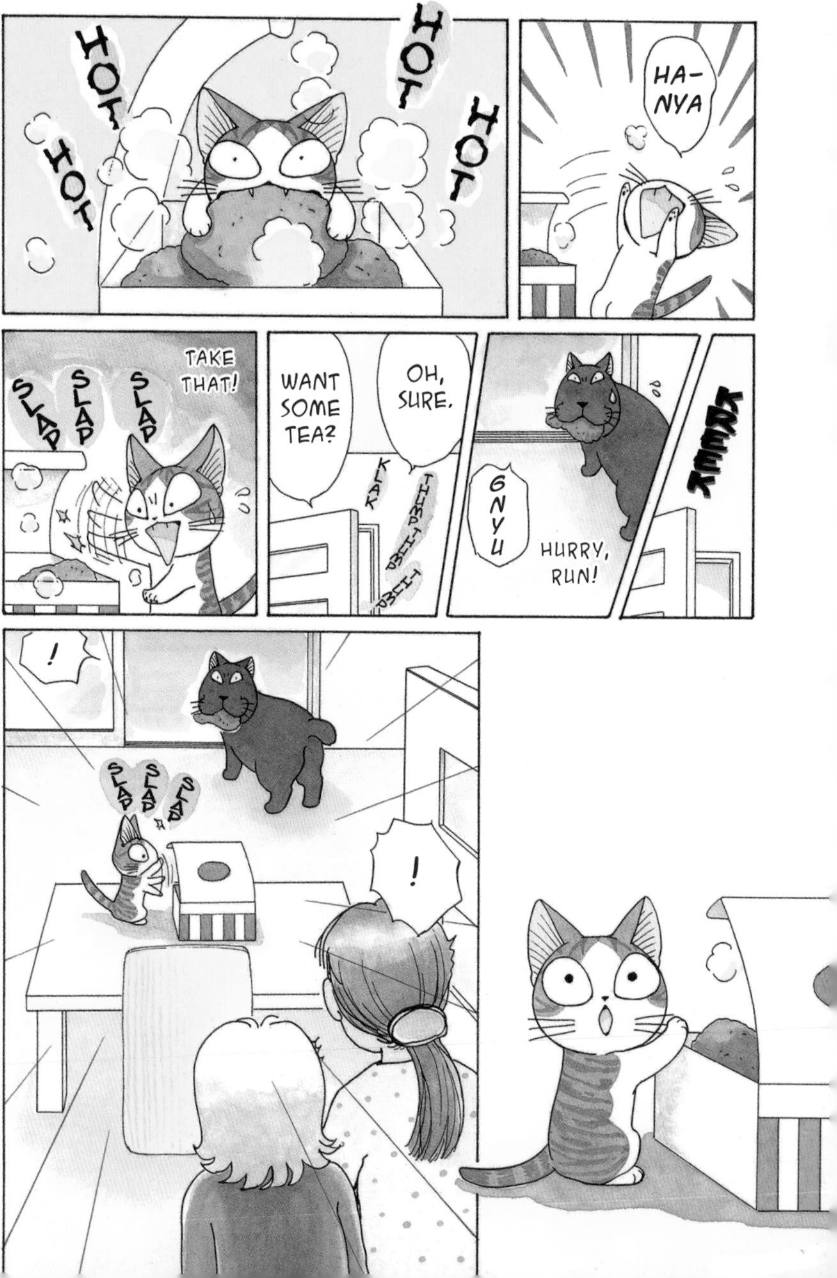
HOT
HOT
HOT
HOT
HA-NYA
TAKE THAT!
SLAP
SLAP
SLAP
WANT SOME TEA?
OH, SURE.
KLAK
THUMP THUMP
THUMP
GNYU
HURRY, RUN!
KREEK
!
SLAP
SLAP
SLAP
!

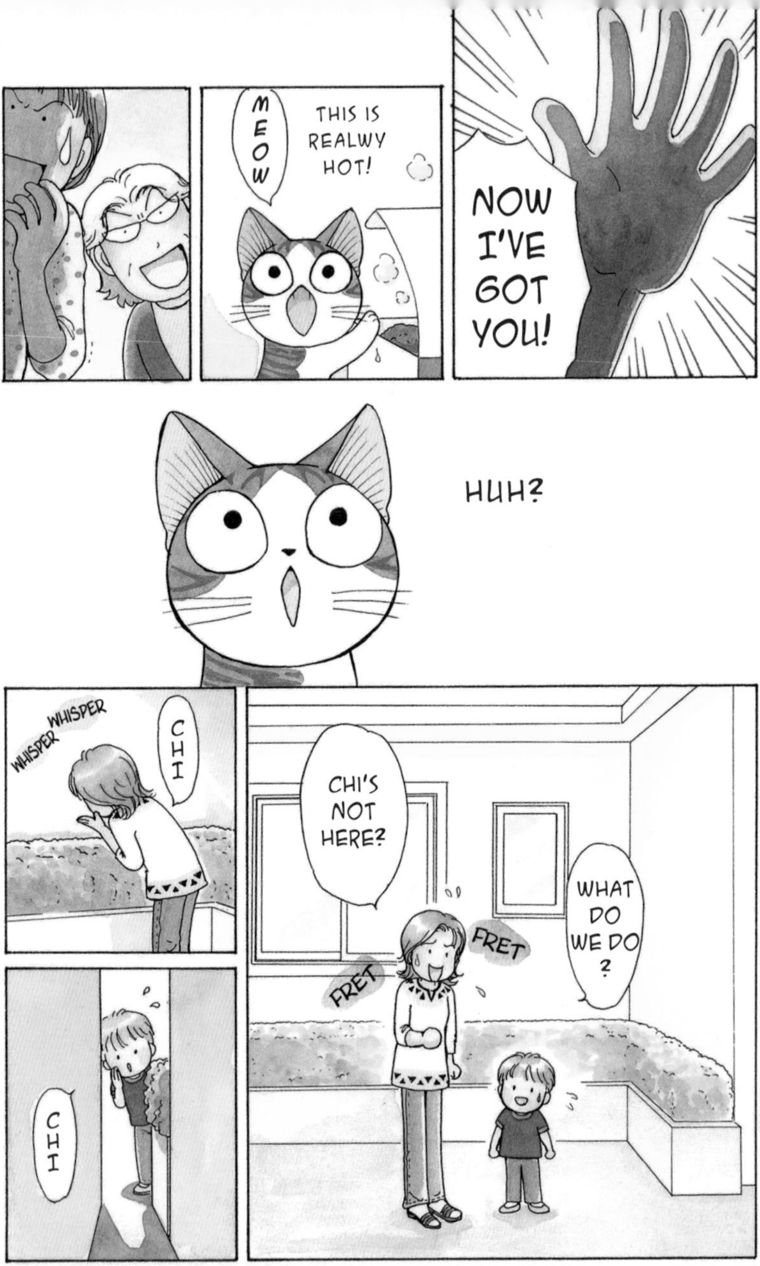
MEOW
THIS IS REALWY HOT!
NOW I'VE GOT YOU!
HUH?
WHISPER WHISPER
CHI
CHI
CHI'S NOT HERE?
FRET FRET
WHAT DO WE DO?

the end

homemade 47: a cat is cornered

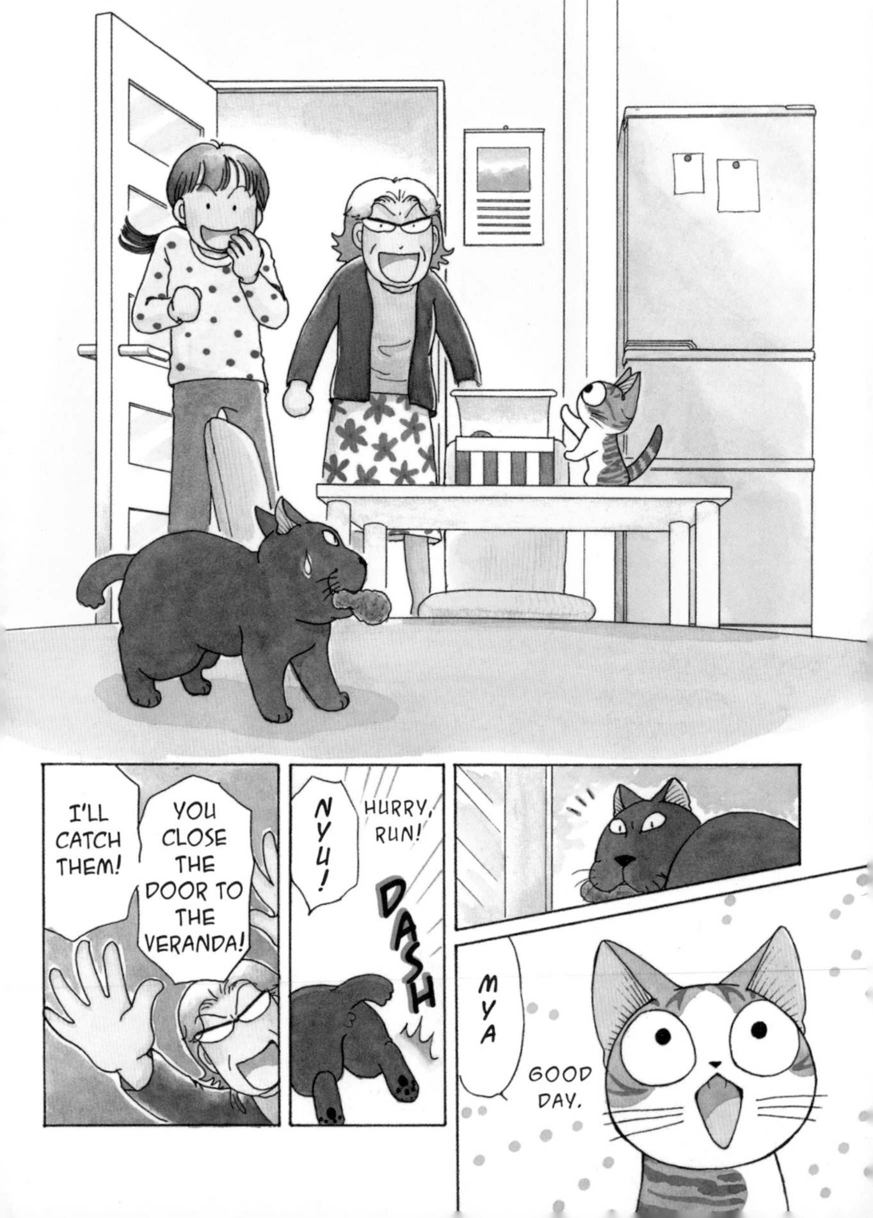
I'LL CATCH THEM!
YOU CLOSE THE DOOR TO THE VERANDA!
NYU!
HURRY, RUN!
DASH
MYA
GOOD DAY.

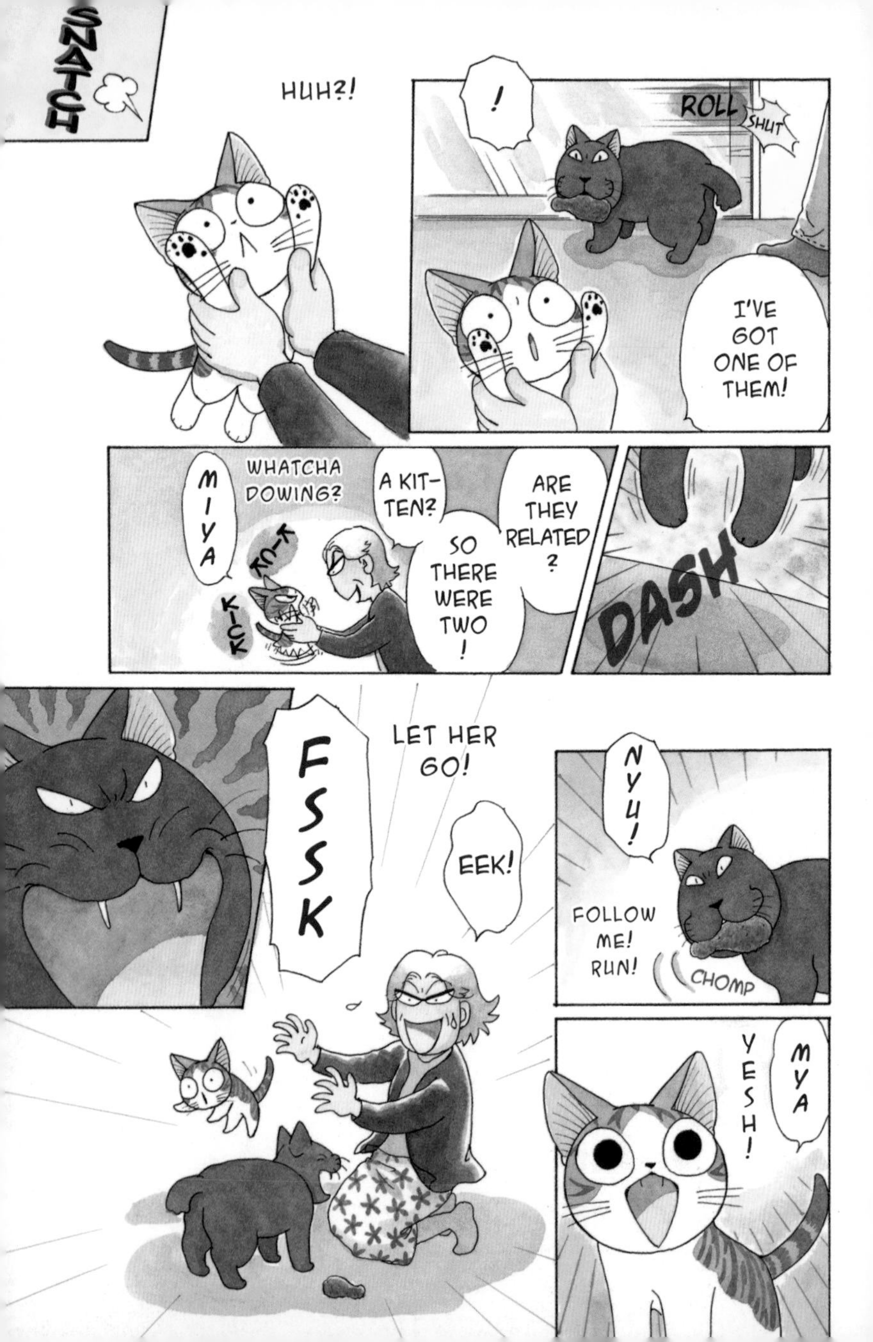
SNATCH
HUH?!
!
ROLL
SHUT
I'VE GOT ONE OF THEM!
MIYA
WHATCHA DOWING?
KICK
KICK
A KITTEN?
SO THERE WERE TWO!
ARE THEY RELATED?
DASH
FSSK
LET HER GO!
EEK!
NYU!
FOLLOW ME! RUN!
CHOMP
MYA
YESH!

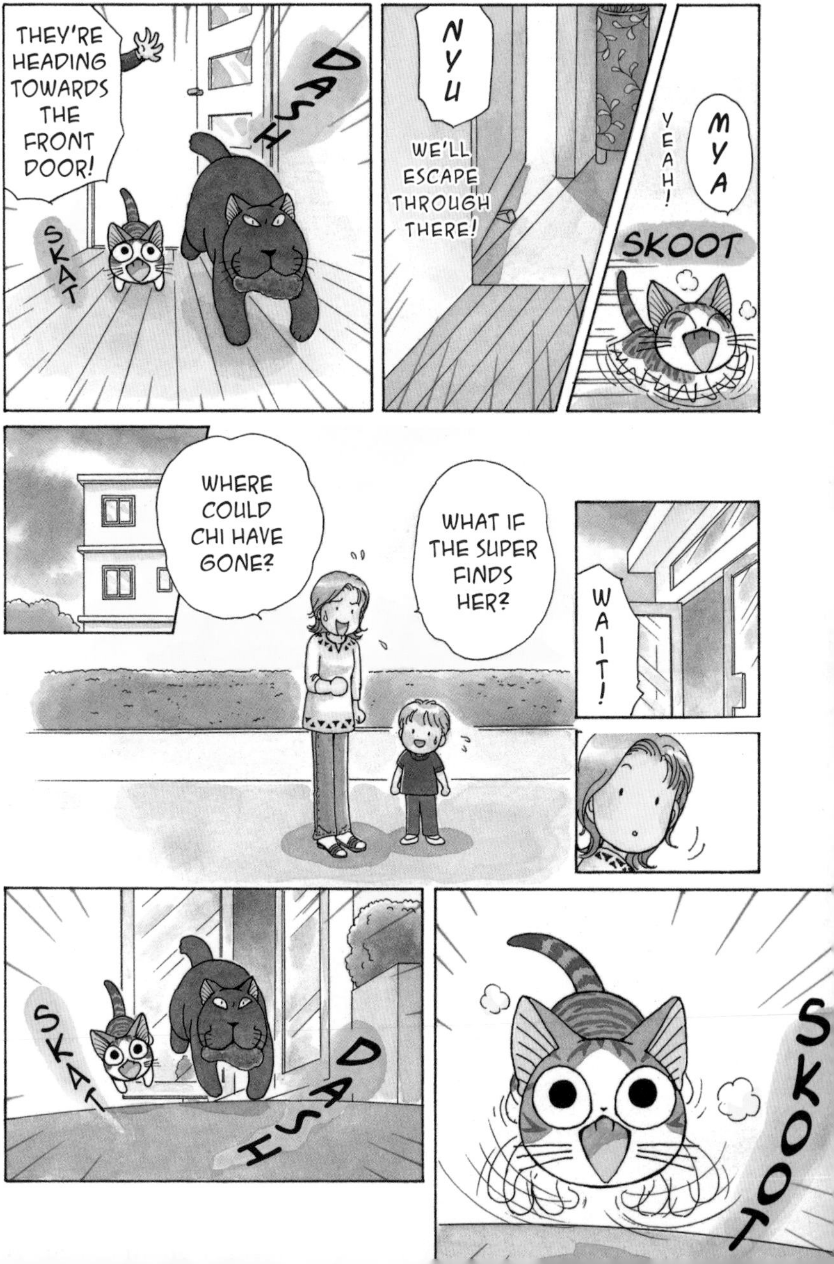
THEY'RE HEADING TOWARDS THE FRONT DOOR!
DASH
SKAT
NYU
WE'LL ESCAPE THROUGH THERE!
MYA
YEAH!
SKOOT
WHERE COULD CHI HAVE GONE?
WHAT IF THE SUPER FINDS HER?
WAIT!
SKAT
DASH
SKOOT

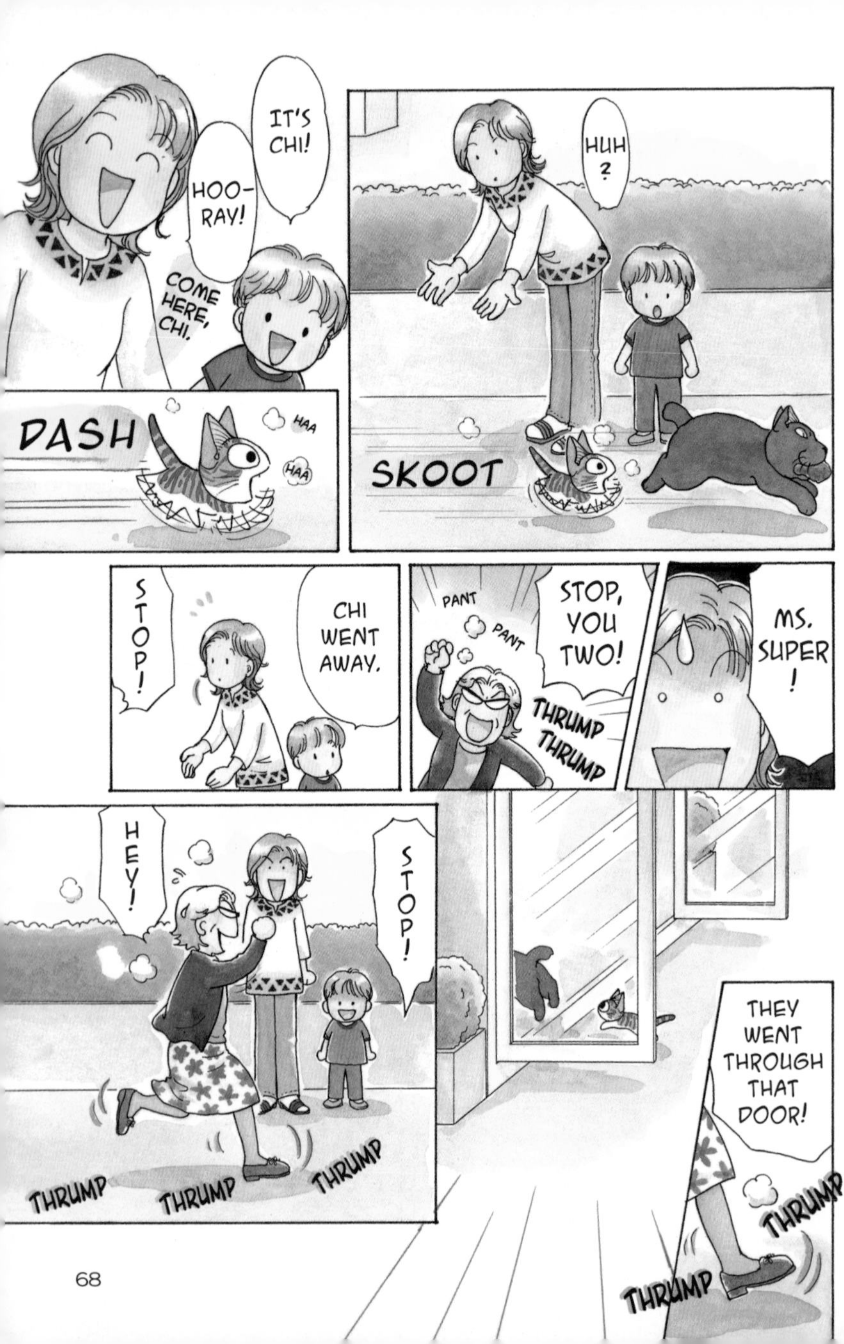
IT'S CHI!
HOO-RAY!
COME HERE, CHI.
DASH
HAA
HAA
HUH?
SKOOT
STOP!
CHI WENT AWAY.
PANT
PANT
STOP, YOU TWO!
THRUMP
THRUMP
MS. SUPER!
HEY!
STOP!
THRUMP
THRUMP
THRUMP
THEY WENT THROUGH THAT DOOR!
THRUMP
THRUMP

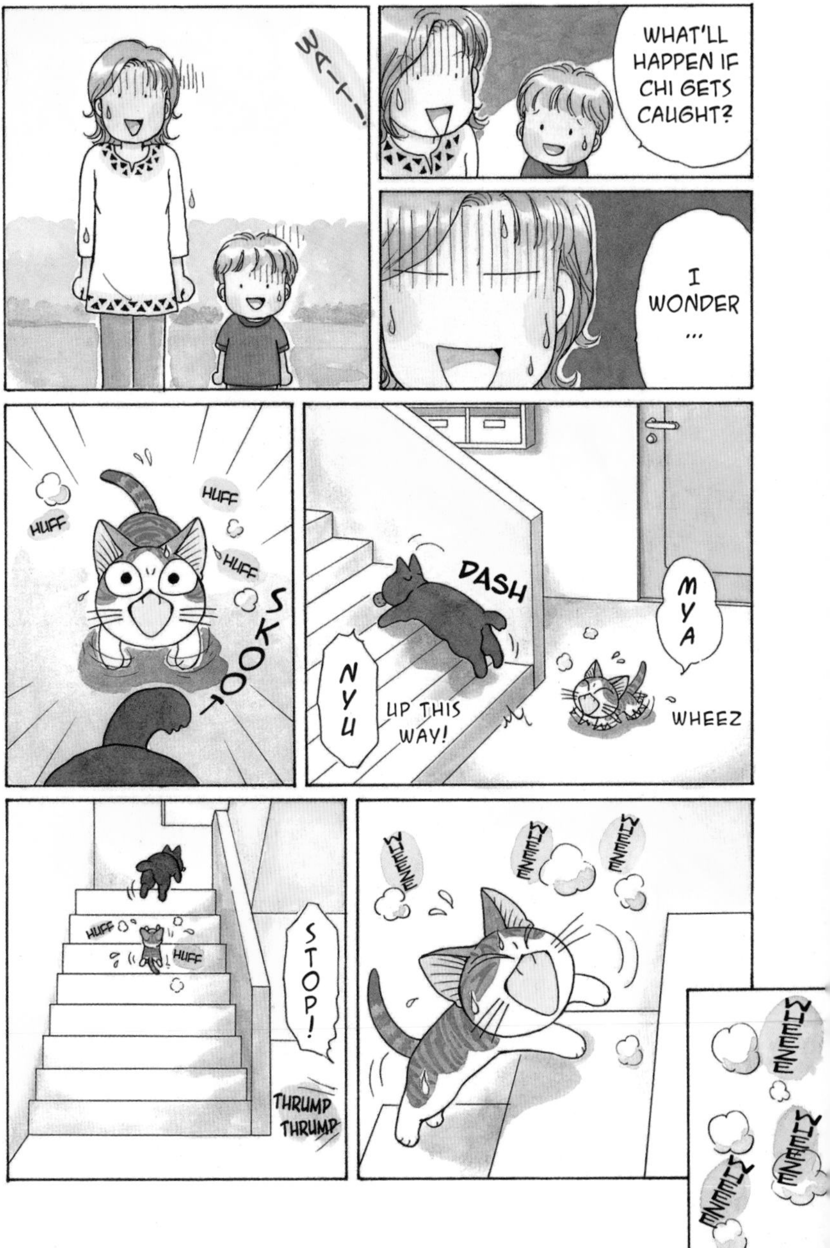
WAIT-!
WHAT'LL HAPPEN IF CHI GETS CAUGHT?
I WONDER ...
HUFF
HUFF
HUFF
SKOOOT
DASH
UP THIS WAY!
NYU
MYA
WHEEZ
HUFF
HUFF
STOP!
THRUMP THRUMP
WHEEZE
WHEEZE
WHEEZE
WHEEZE
WHEEZE
WHEEZE

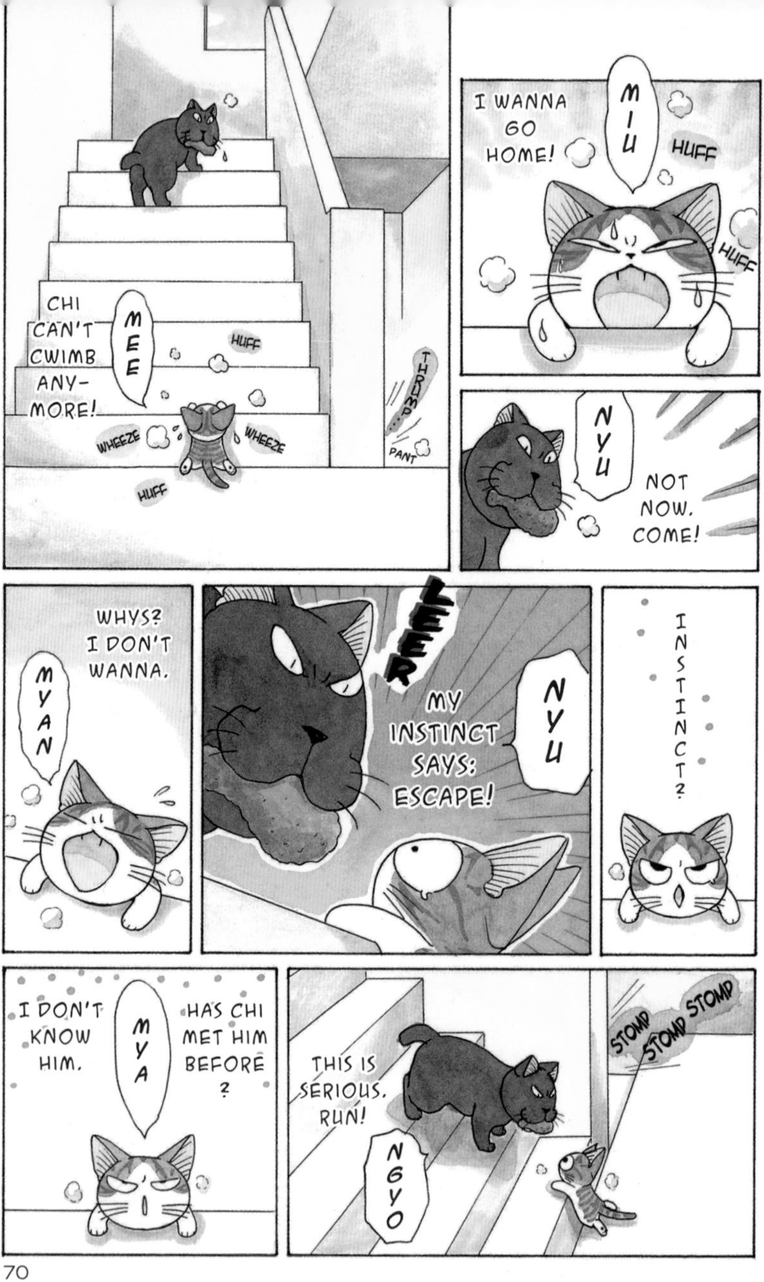
CHI CAN'T CWIMB ANY-MORE!
MEE
HUFF
WHEEZE
WHEEZE
THRUMP
PANT
HUFF
I WANNA GO HOME!
MIU
HUFF
HUFF
NYU
NOT NOW. COME!
WHYS? I DON'T WANNA.
MYAN
LEER
MY INSTINCT SAYS: ESCAPE!
NYU
INSTINCT?
I DON'T KNOW HIM.
MYA
HAS CHI MET HIM BEFORE?
THIS IS SERIOUS. RUN!
NGYO
STOMP
STOMP
STOMP

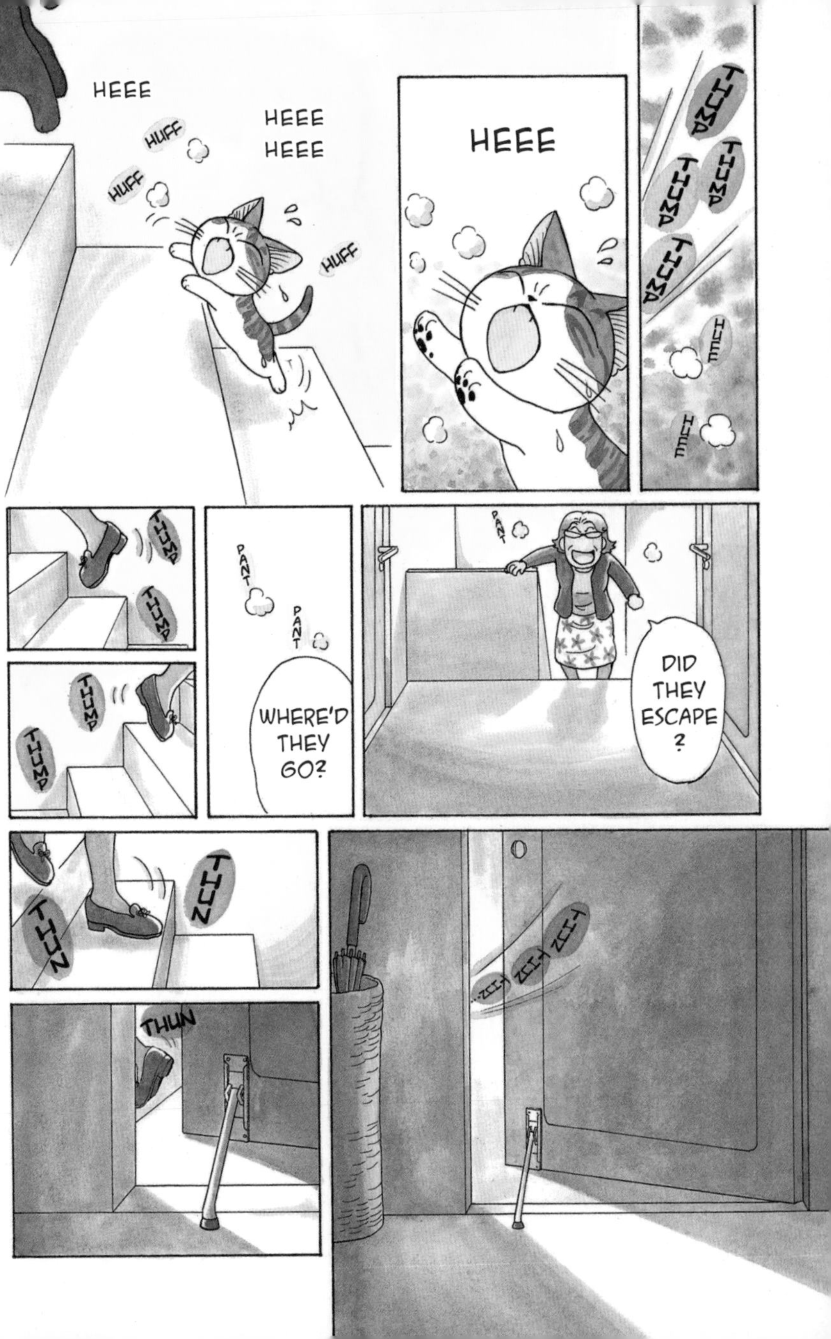
HEEE
HUFF
HEEE
HEEE
HUFF
HUFF
HEEE
THUMP
THUMP
THUMP
THUMP
HUFF
HUFF
THUMP
THUMP
THUMP
THUMP
PANT
PANT
WHERE'D THEY GO?
PANT
DID THEY ESCAPE?
THUN
THUN
THUN

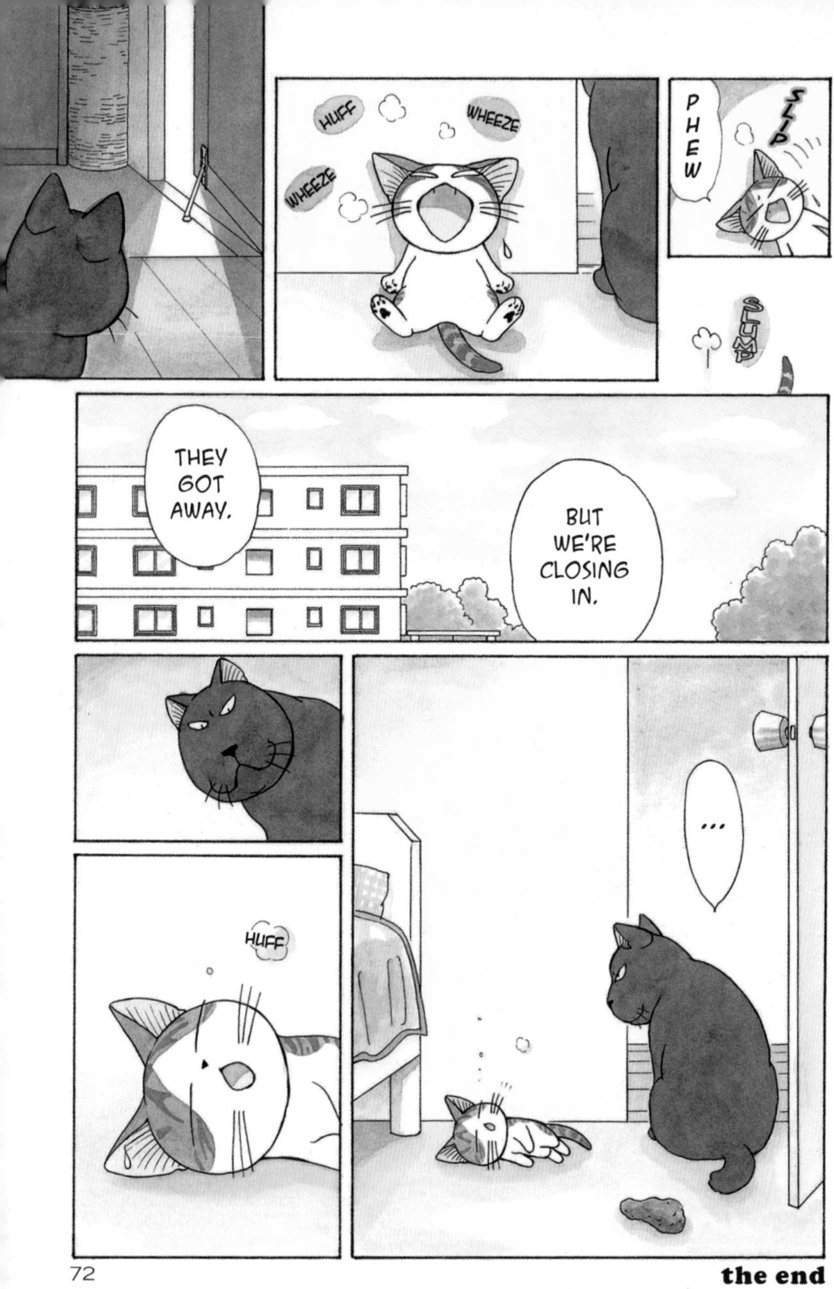
HUFF
WHEEZE
WHEEZE
SLIP
PHEW
SLUMP
THEY GOT AWAY.
BUT WE'RE CLOSING IN.
...
HUFF

the end

homemade 48: a cat studies

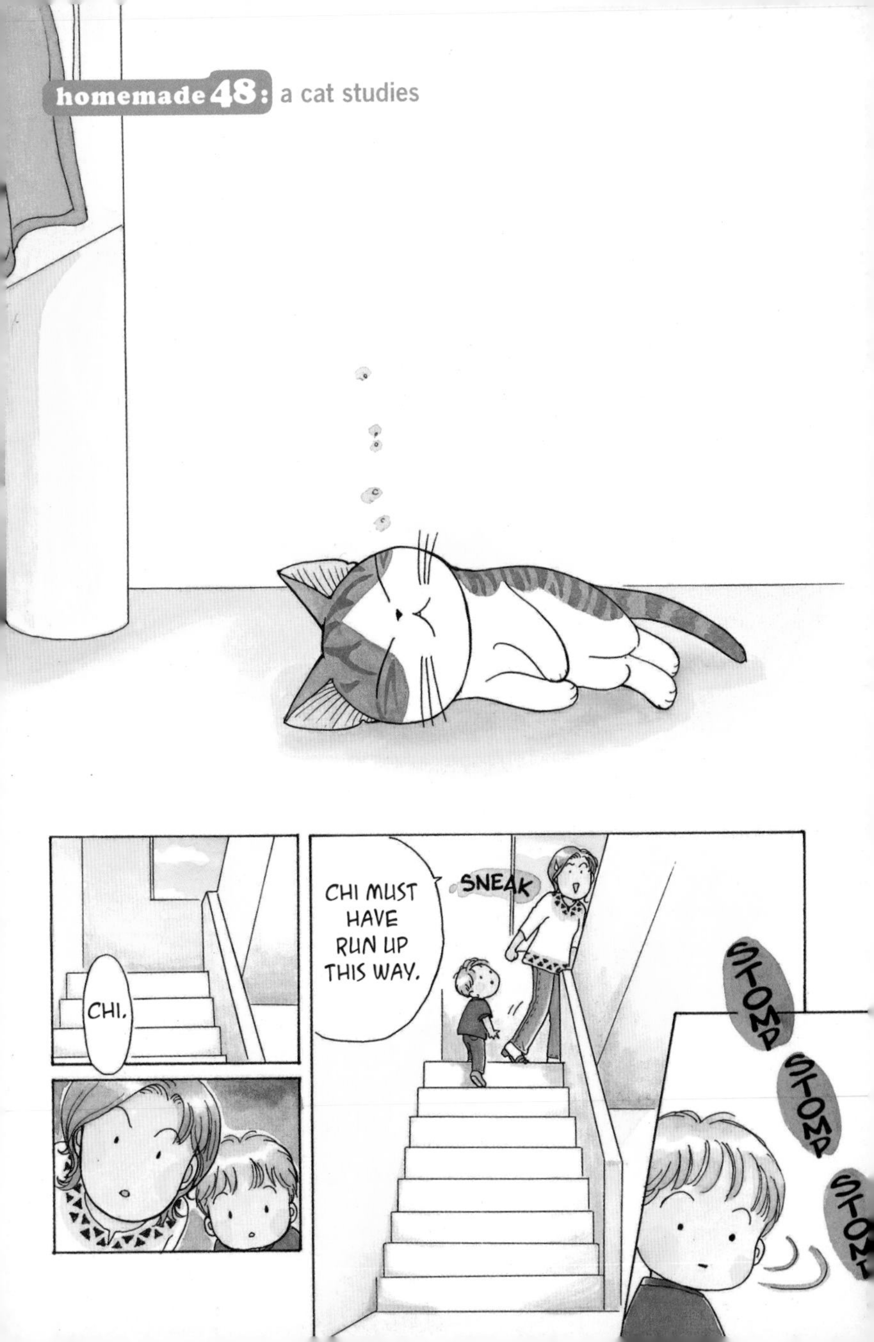
CHI.
CHI MUST HAVE RUN UP THIS WAY.
SNEAK
STOMP
STOMP
STOMP

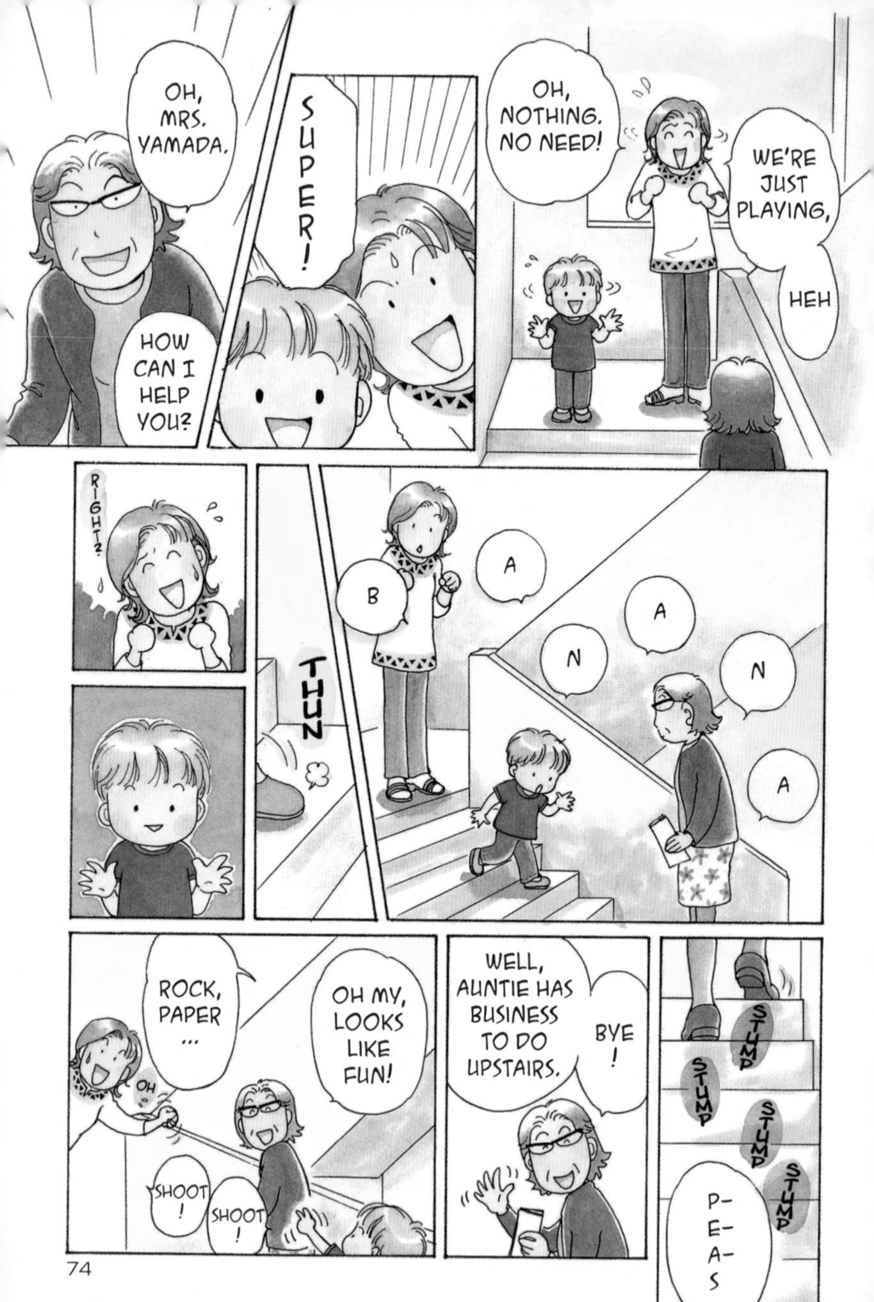
OH, MRS. YAMADA.
HOW CAN I HELP YOU?
SUPER!
OH, NOTHING. NO NEED!
WE'RE JUST PLAYING,
HEH
RIGHT?
THUN
B
A
N
A
N
A
ROCK, PAPER ...
OH
SHOOT!
SHOOT!
OH MY, LOOKS LIKE FUN!
WELL, AUNTIE HAS BUSINESS TO DO UPSTAIRS.
BYE!
STUMP
STUMP
STUMP
STUMP
P-E-A-S

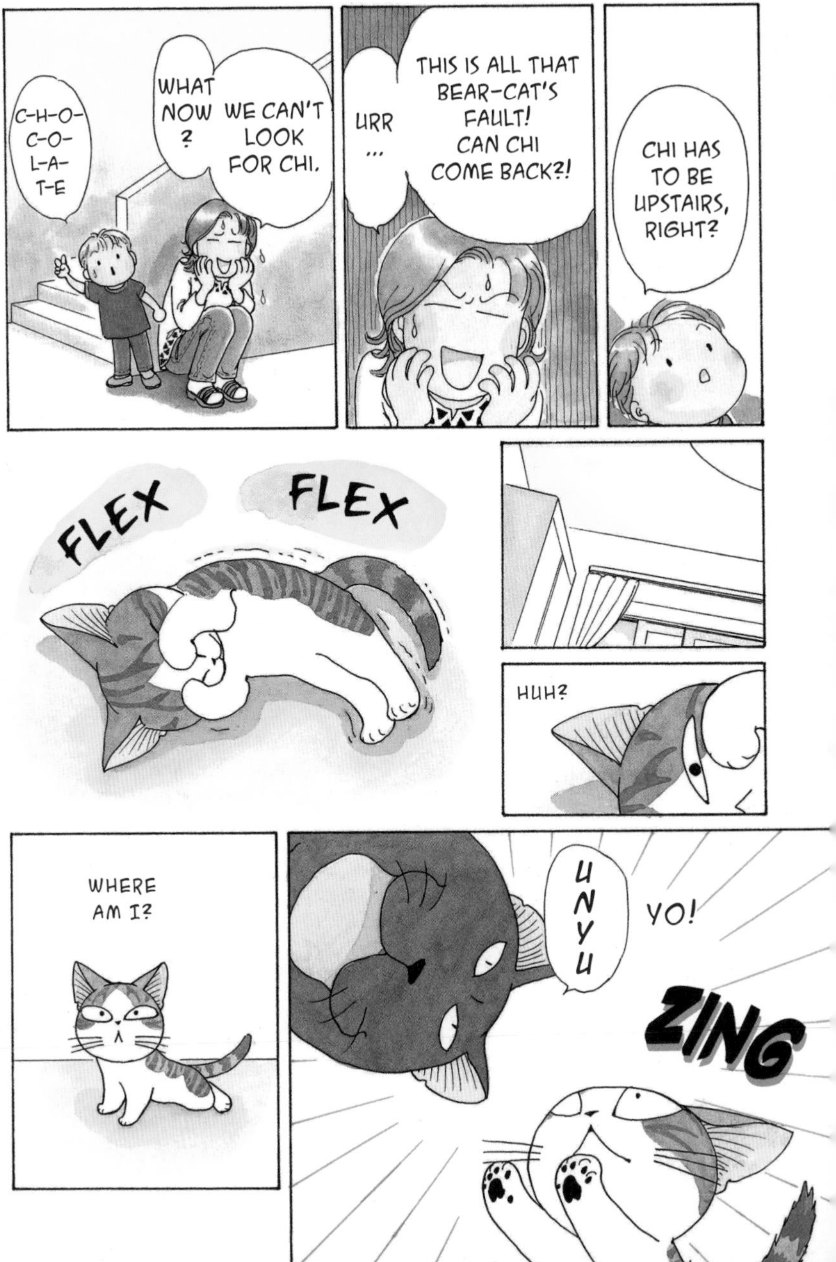
C-H-O-C-O-L-A-T-E
WHAT NOW?
WE CAN'T LOOK FOR CHI.
URR ...
THIS IS ALL THAT BEAR-CAT'S FAULT! CAN CHI COME BACK?!
CHI HAS TO BE UPSTAIRS, RIGHT?
FLEX
FLEX
HUH?
WHERE AM I?
UNYU
YO!
ZING

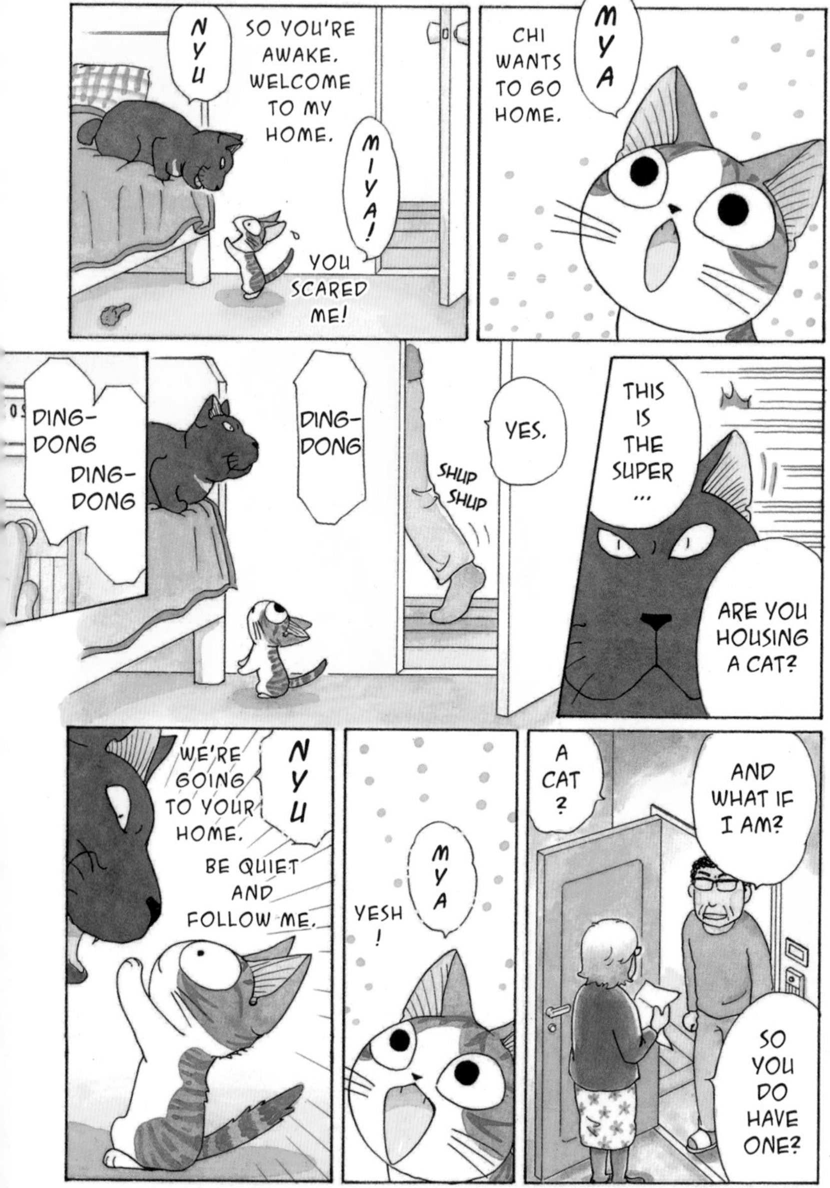

NYU
SO YOU'RE AWAKE. WELCOME TO MY HOME.
MIYA!
YOU SCARED ME!
CHI WANTS TO GO HOME.
MYA
DING-DONG DING-DONG
DING-DONG
SHUP SHUP
YES.
THIS IS THE SUPER...
ARE YOU HOUSING A CAT?
WE'RE GOING TO YOUR HOME.
NYU
BE QUIET AND FOLLOW ME.
YESH!
MYA
A CAT?
AND WHAT IF I AM?
SO YOU DO HAVE ONE?

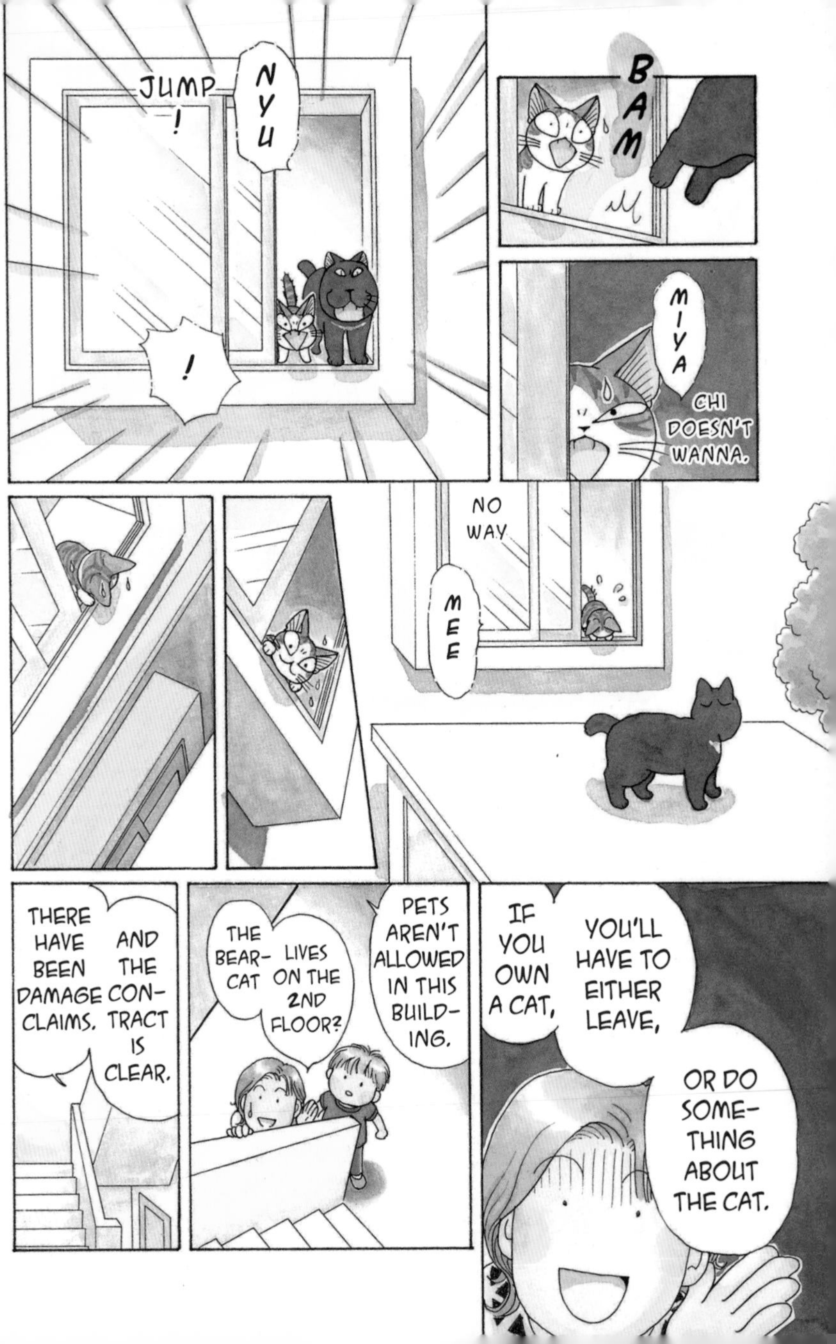
BAM
MIYA
CHI DOESN'T WANNA.
NYU
JUMP!
!
NO WAY
MEE
IF YOU OWN A CAT, YOU'LL HAVE TO EITHER LEAVE,
OR DO SOMETHING ABOUT THE CAT.
PETS AREN'T ALLOWED IN THIS BUILDING.
THE BEAR-CAT LIVES ON THE 2ND FLOOR?
THERE HAVE BEEN DAMAGE CLAIMS. AND THE CONTRACT IS CLEAR.

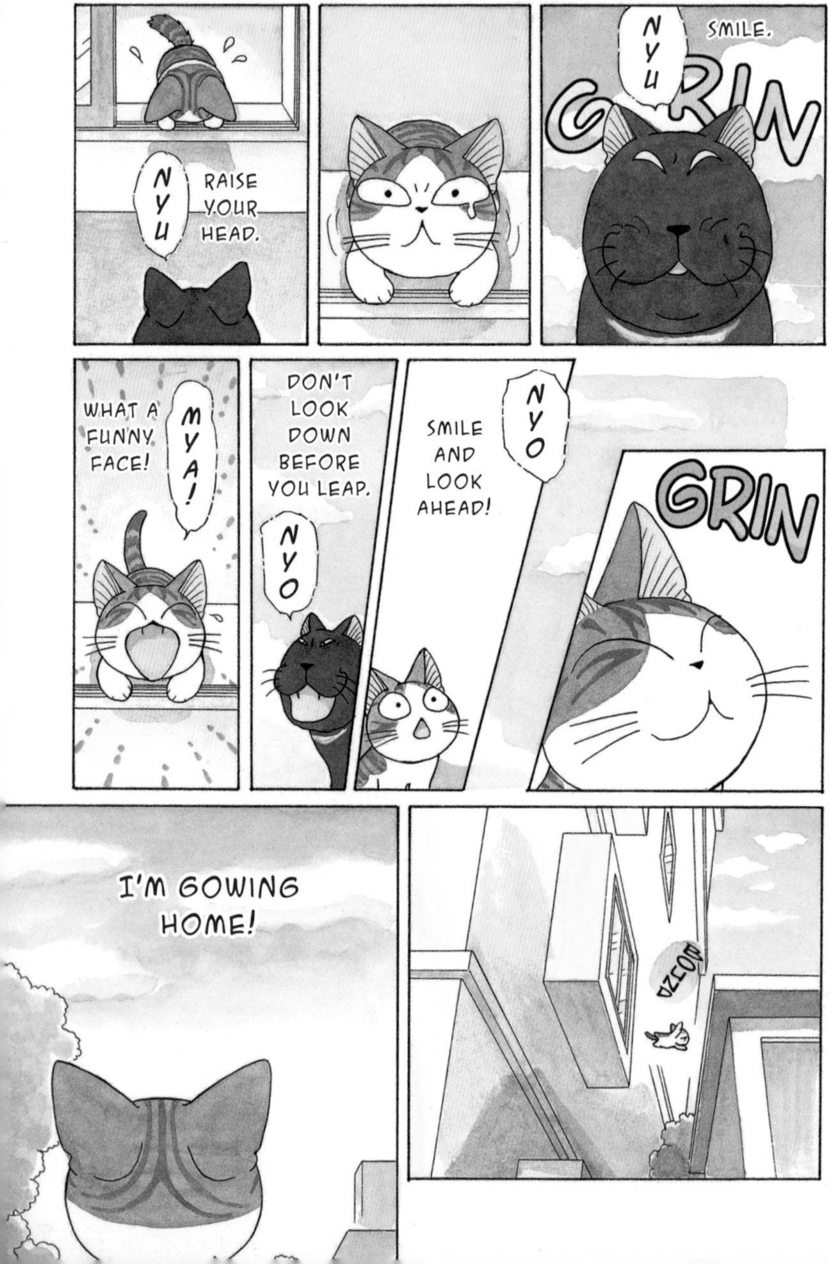
NYU
RAISE YOUR HEAD.
NYU
SMILE.
GRIN
WHAT A FUNNY FACE!
MYA!
DON'T LOOK DOWN BEFORE YOU LEAP.
NYO
SMILE AND LOOK AHEAD!
NYO
GRIN
I'M GOWING HOME!

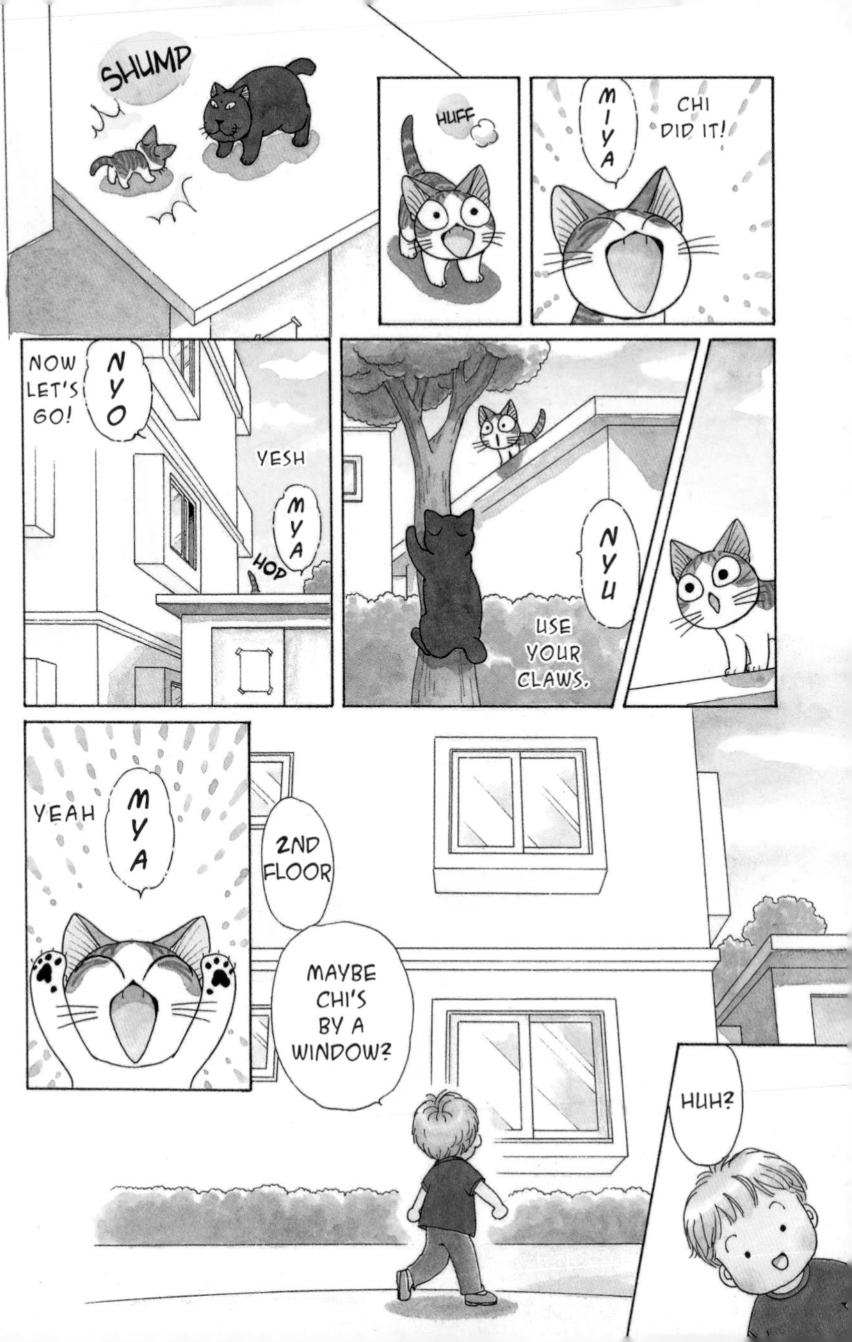
SHUMP
HUFF
MIYA
CHI DID IT!
NOW LET'S GO!
NYO
YESH
MYA
HOP
NYU
USE YOUR CLAWS.
YEAH
MYA
2ND FLOOR
MAYBE CHI'S BY A WINDOW?
HUH?

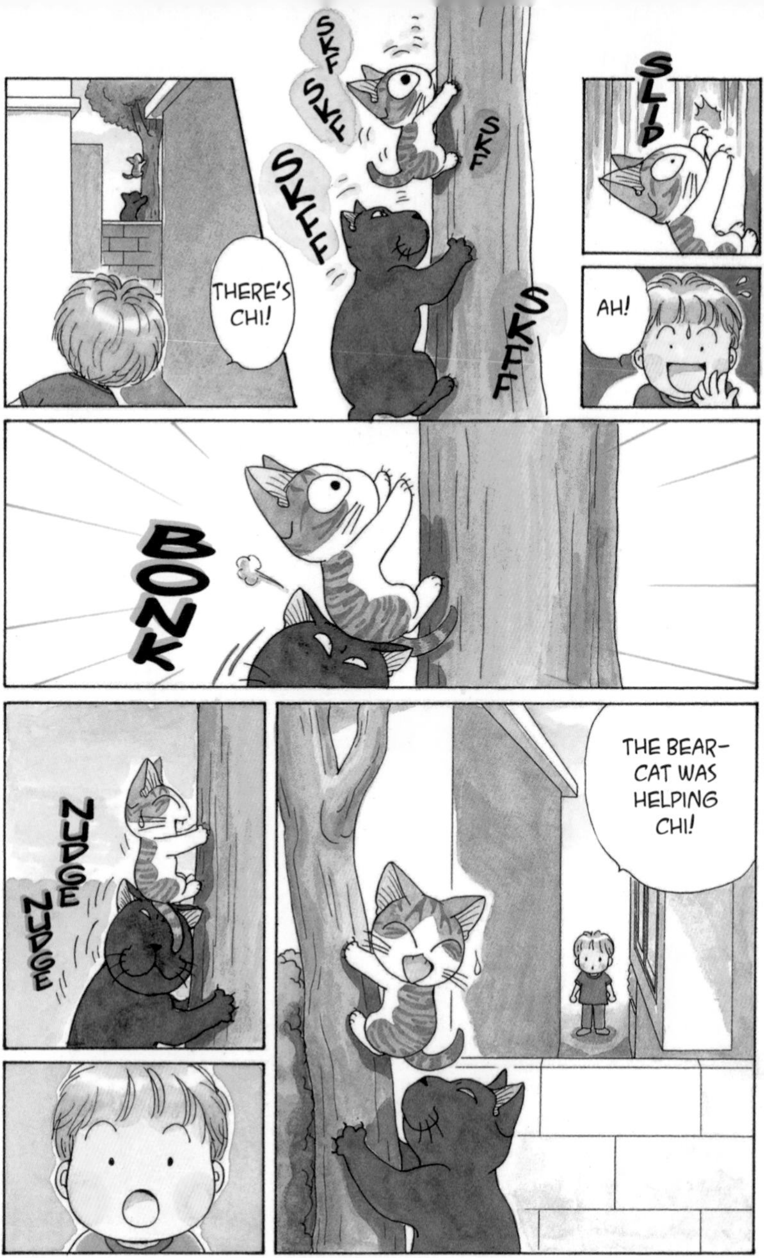
THERE'S CHI!
SKF SKF
SKFF
SKF
SKFF
SLID
AH!
BONK
NUDGE NUDGE
THE BEAR-CAT WAS HELPING CHI!

the end

homemade 49: a cat endeavoers

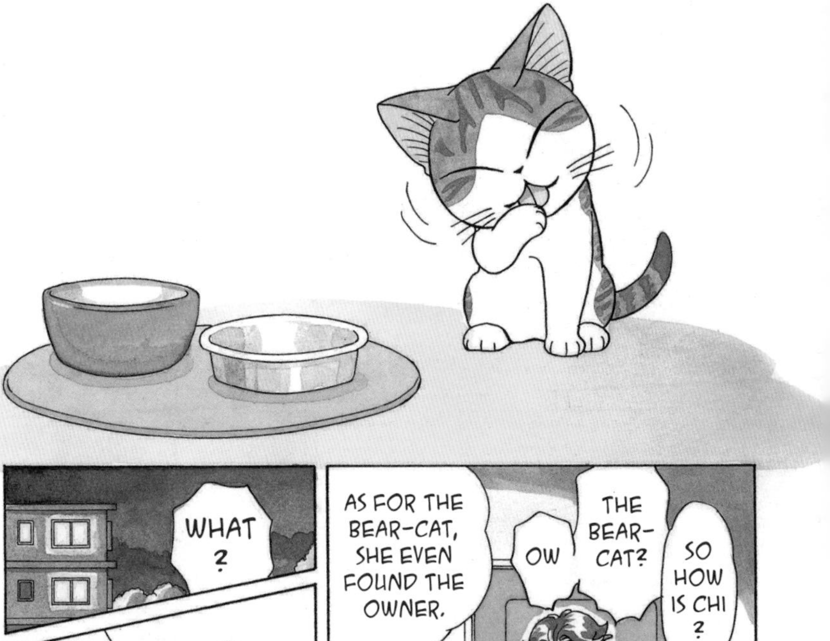

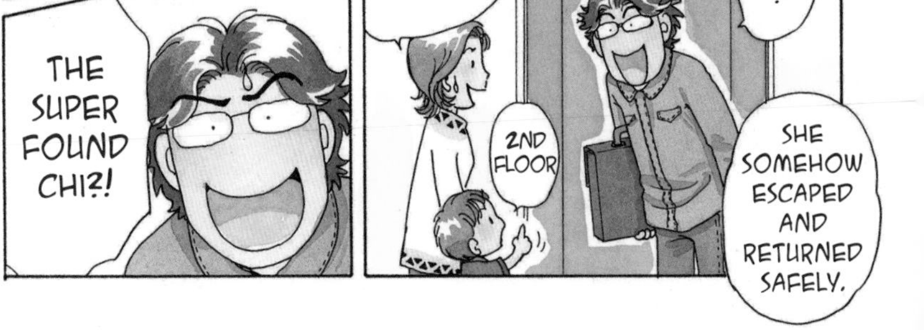
WHAT ?
THE SUPER FOUND CHI?!
AS FOR THE BEAR-CAT, SHE EVEN FOUND THE OWNER.
OW
THE BEAR-CAT?
SO HOW IS CHI ?
2ND FLOOR
SHE SOMEHOW ESCAPED AND RETURNED SAFELY.

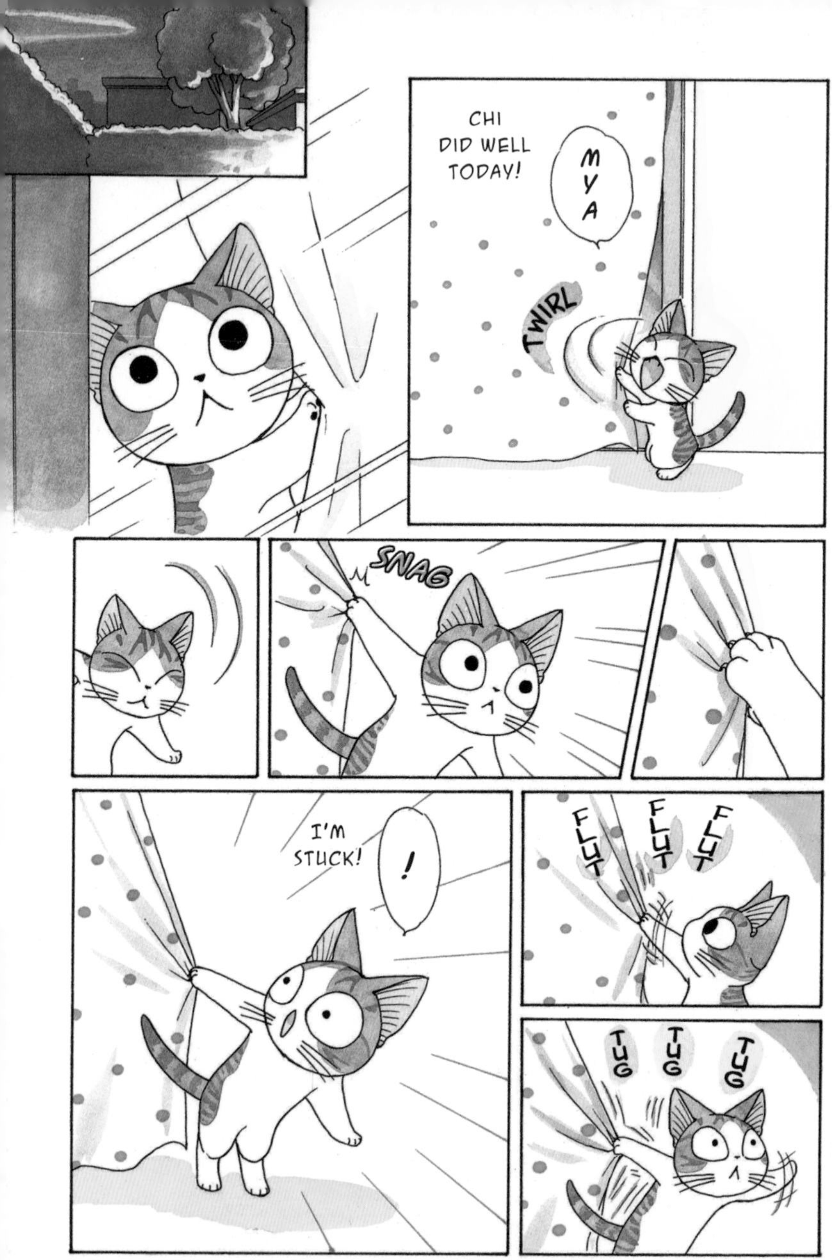
CHI DID WELL TODAY!
MYA
TWIRL
SNAG
I'M STUCK!
!
FLUT FLUT FLUT
TUG TUG TUG

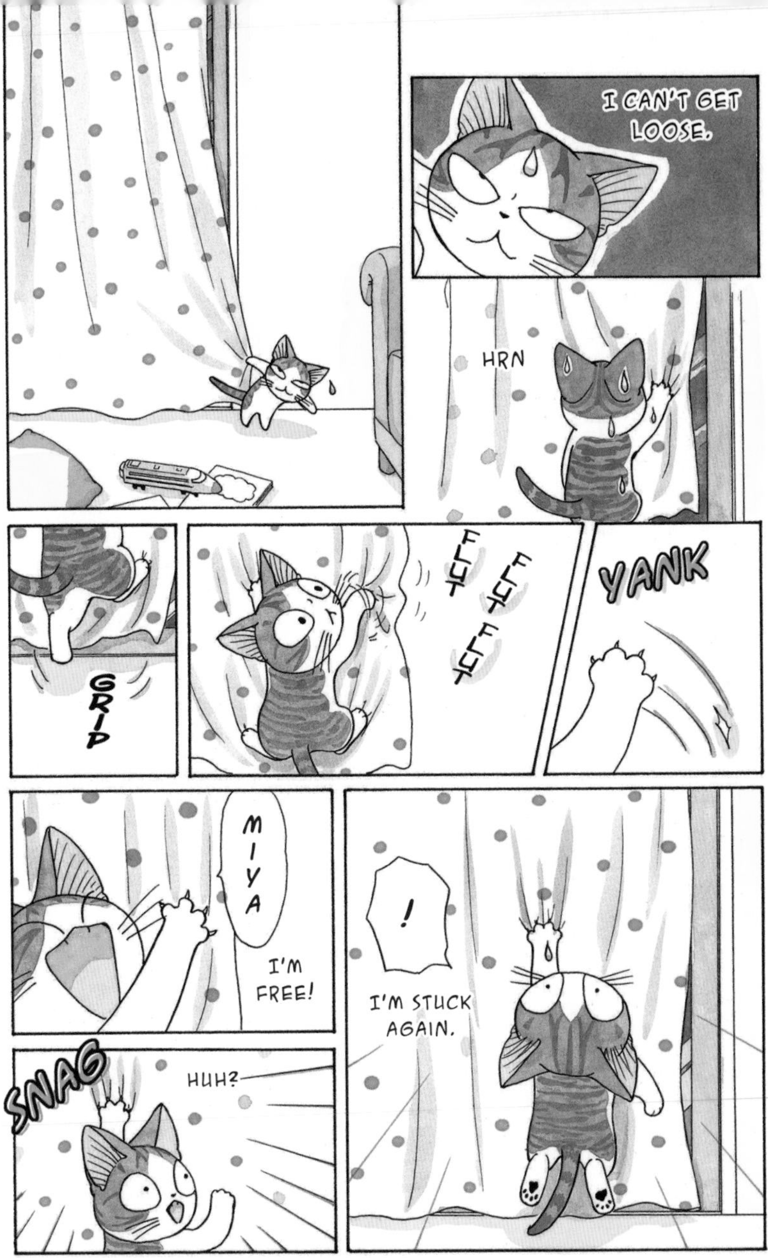
I CAN'T GET LOOSE.
HRN
GRIP
FLUT FLUT FLUT
YANK
MIYA
I'M FREE!
SNAG
HUH?
!
I'M STUCK AGAIN.

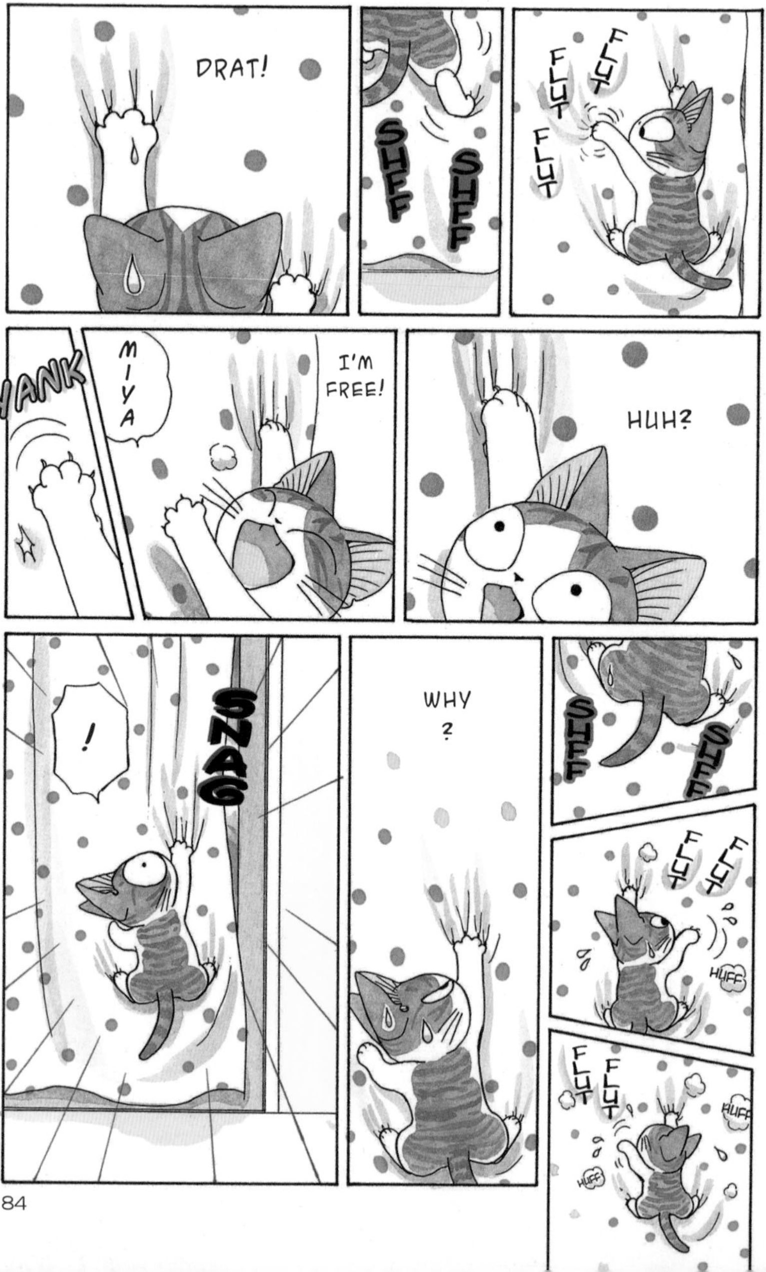

DRAT!
SHFF
SHFF
FLUT
FLUT
FLUT
YANK
MIYA
I'M FREE!
HUH?
!
SNAG
WHY ?
SHFF
SHFF
FLUT
FLUT
HUFF
FLUT
FLUT
HUFF
HUFF

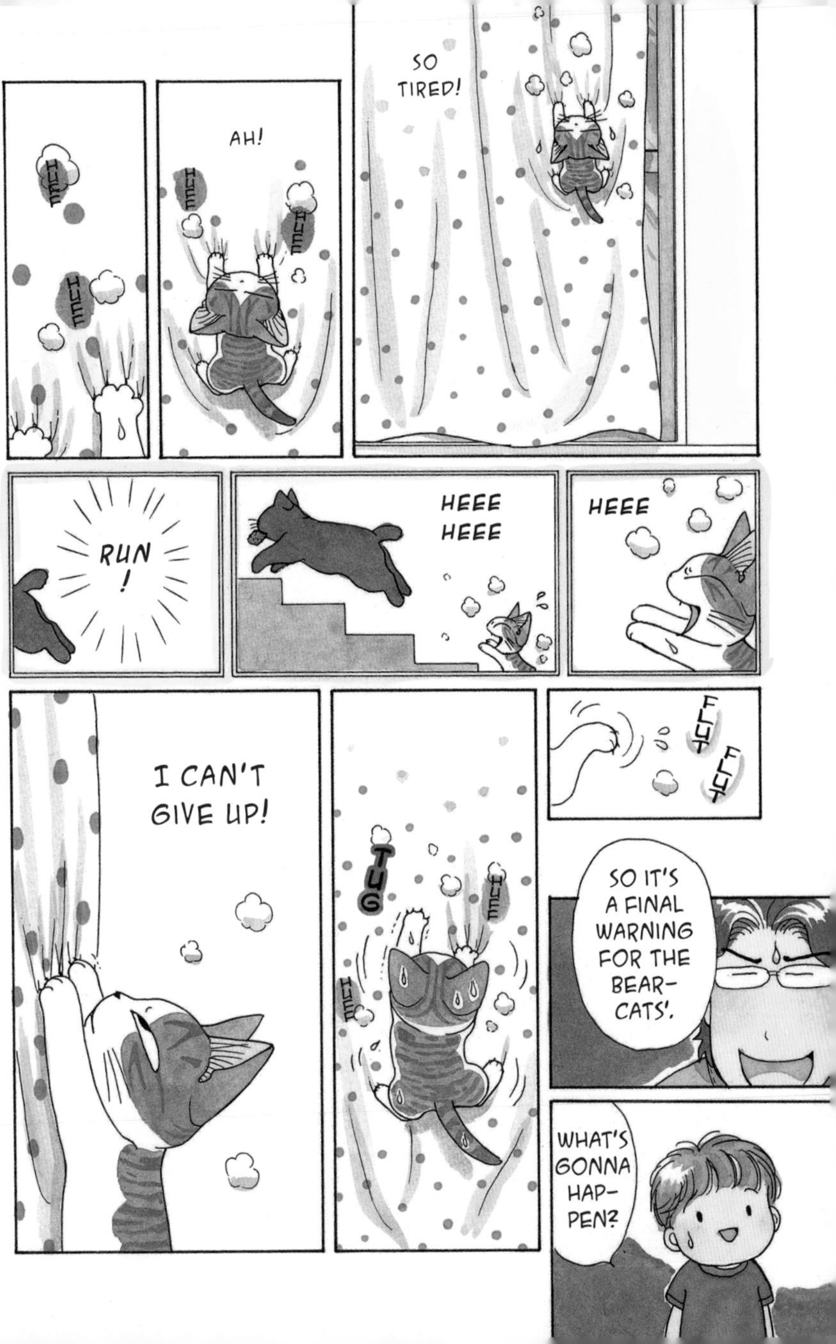
HUFF
HUFF
AH!
HUFF
HUFF
SO TIRED!
RUN!
HEEE HEEE
HEEE
I CAN'T GIVE UP!
TUG
HUFF
HUFF
FLUT FLUT
SO IT'S A FINAL WARNING FOR THE BEAR-CATS'.
WHAT'S GONNA HAP-PEN?

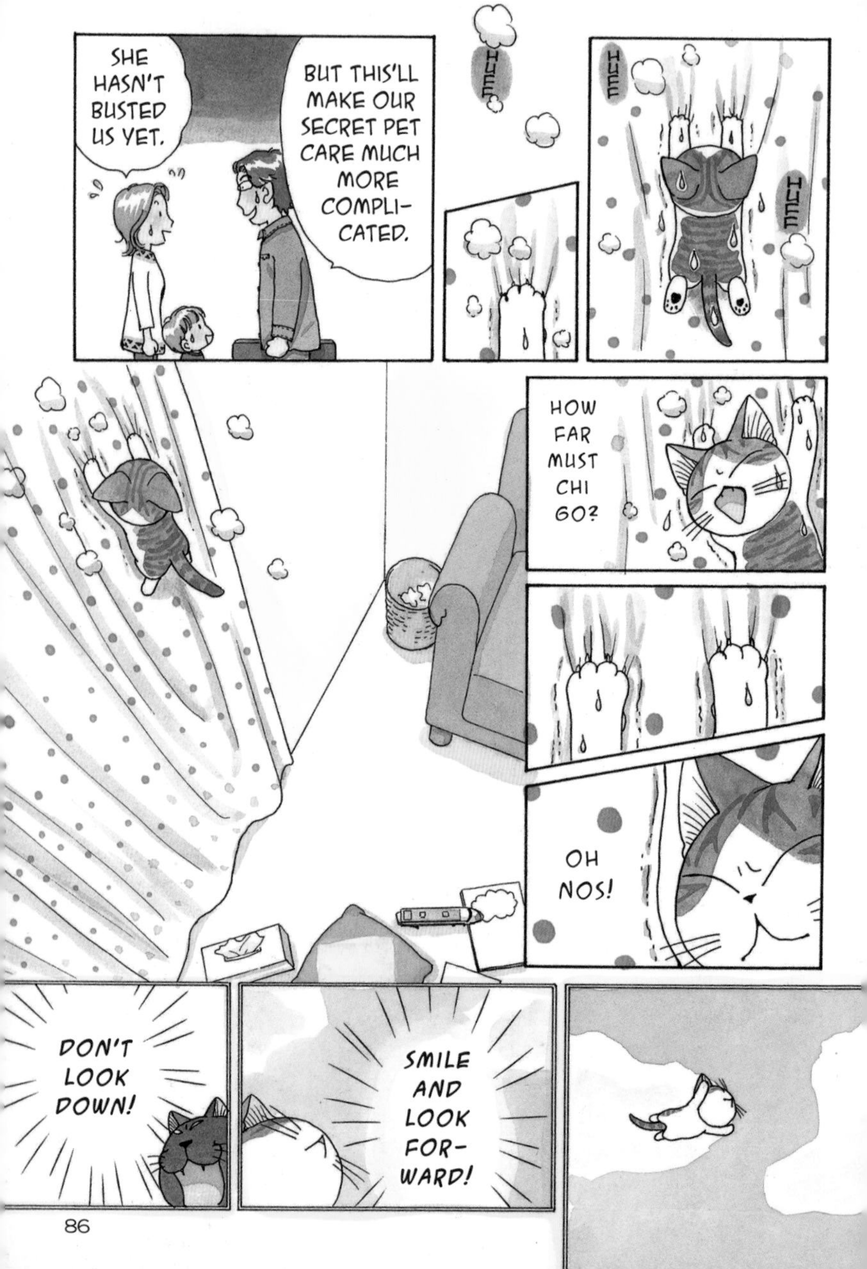
SHE HASN'T BUSTED US YET.
BUT THIS'LL MAKE OUR SECRET PET CARE MUCH MORE COMPLI-CATED.
HUFF
HUFF
HUFF
HOW FAR MUST CHI GO?
OH NOS!
DON'T LOOK DOWN!
SMILE AND LOOK FOR-WARD!

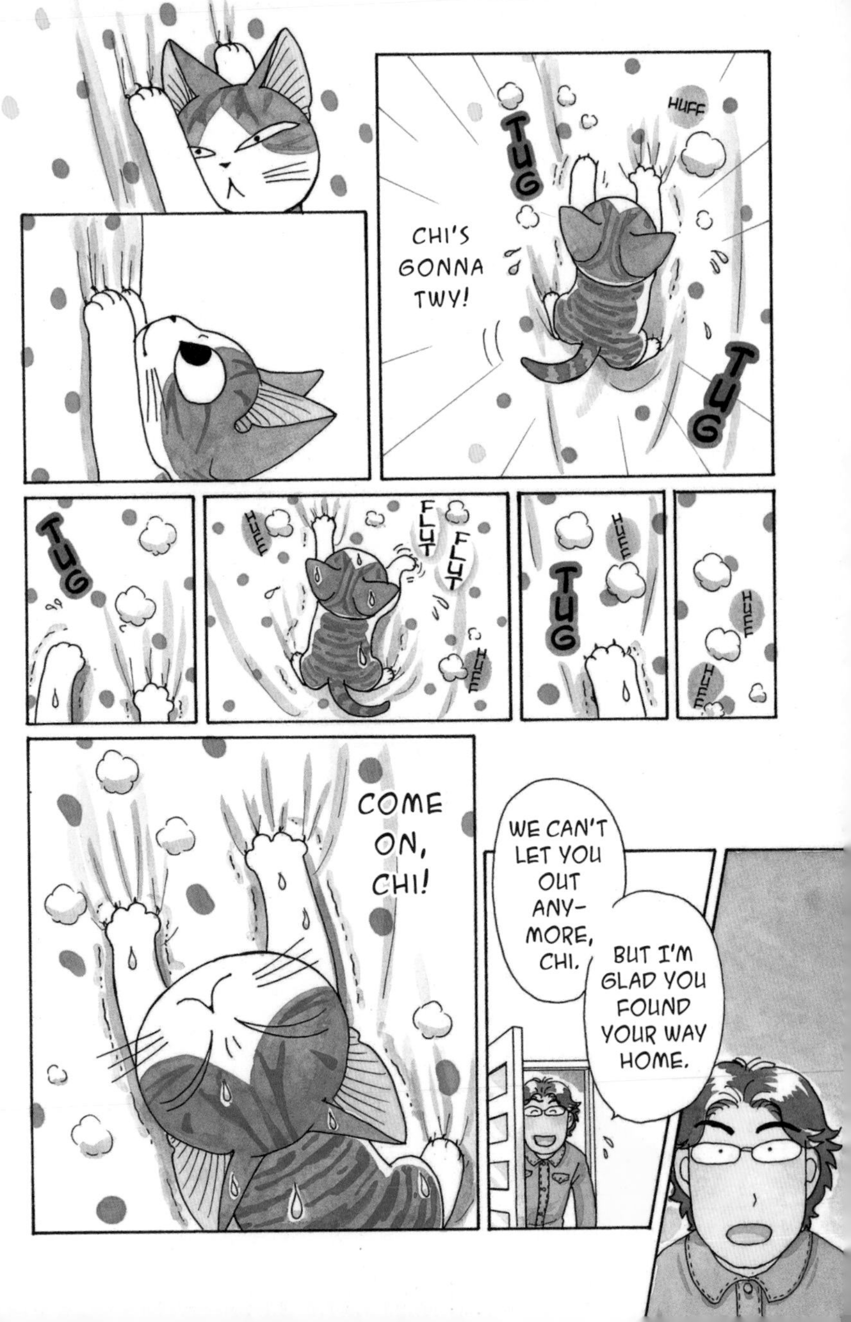
HUFF
TUG
CHI'S GONNA TWY!
TUG
TUG
HUFF
FLUT
FLUT
HUFF
TUG
HUFF
HUFF
HUFF
COME ON, CHI!
WE CAN'T LET YOU OUT ANY-MORE, CHI.
BUT I'M GLAD YOU FOUND YOUR WAY HOME.

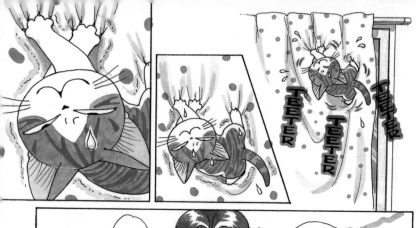

TEETER TEETER TEETER

HUH?

AND WHAT ARE YOU DOING NOW, CHI?

MEOW

DADDY, HELP ME!

SHE LOOKED LIKE A BUG CAUGHT IN A WEB.

HOW DID SHE EVER FIND HER WAY BACK?

the end

homemade 50: a cat yearns

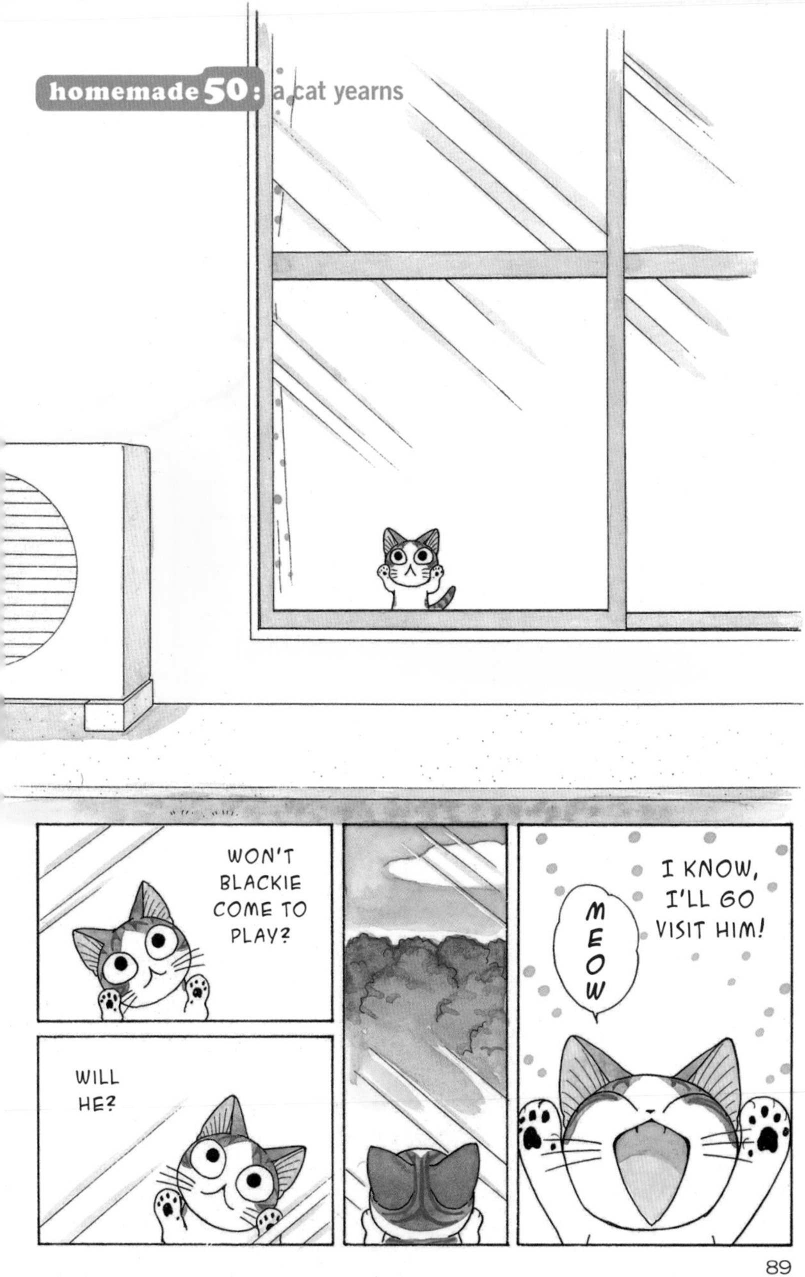
WON'T BLACKIE COME TO PLAY?
WILL HE?
MEOW
I KNOW, I'LL GO VISIT HIM!

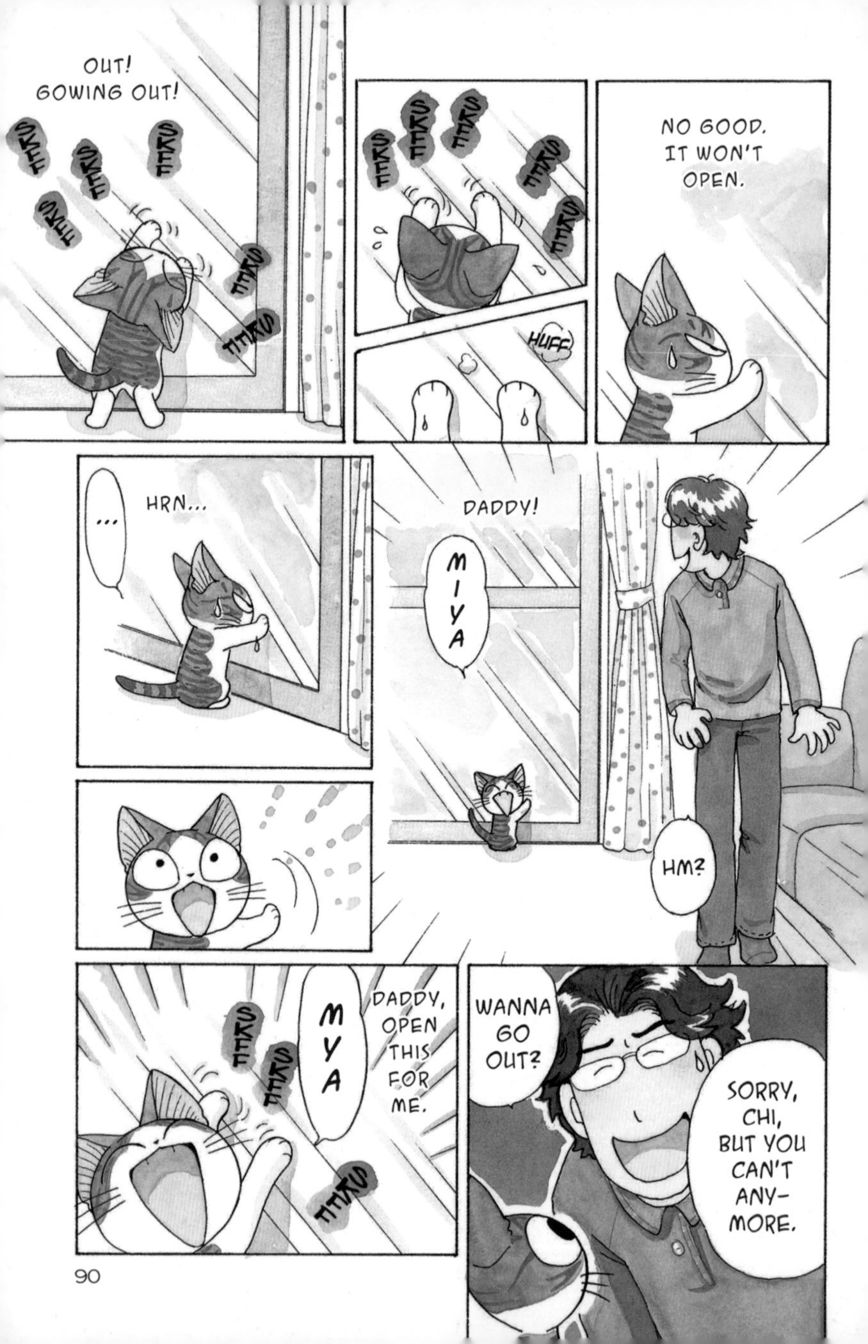
OUT!
GOWING OUT!
SKFF
SKFF
SKFF
SKFF
SKFF
SKFF
SKFF
SKFF
SKFF
HUFF
NO GOOD. IT WON'T OPEN.
...
HRN...
DADDY!
MIYA
HM?
SKFF
SKFF
MYA
DADDY, OPEN THIS FOR ME.
WANNA GO OUT?
SORRY, CHI, BUT YOU CAN'T ANY-MORE.

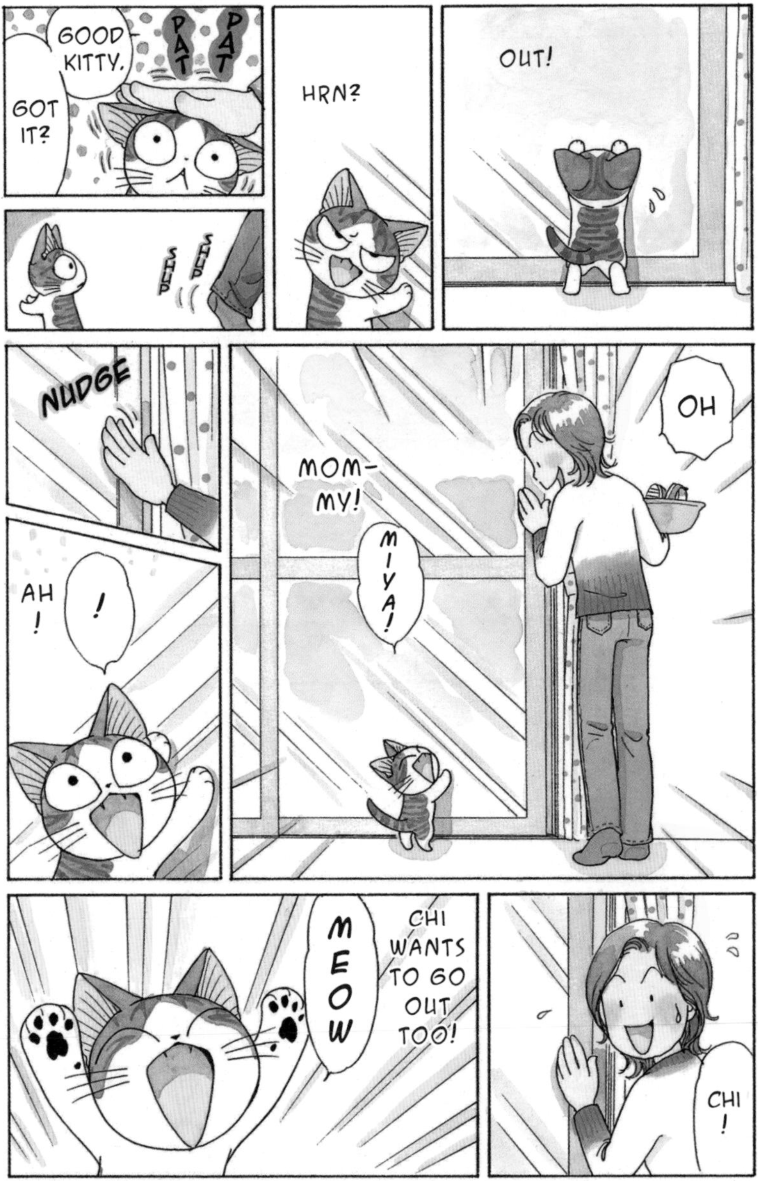
GOOD KITTY.
GOT IT?
PAT PAT
SHUP SHUP
HRN?
OUT!
NUDGE
AH!
!
MOM-MY!
MIYA!
OH
MEOW
CHI WANTS TO GO OUT TOO!
CHI!

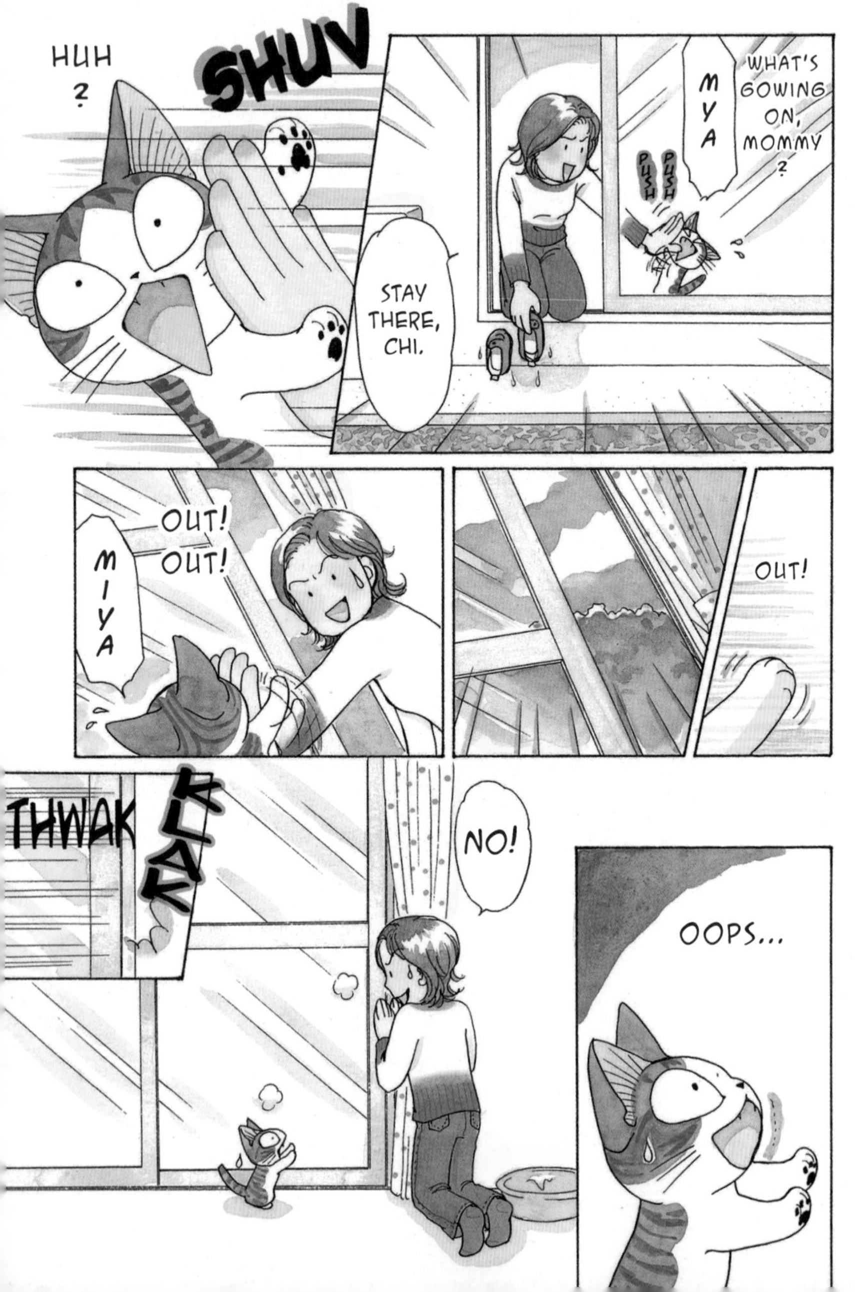
HUH ?
SHUV
STAY THERE, CHI.
MYA
PUSH PUSH
WHAT'S GOWING ON, MOMMY ?
OUT! OUT!
MIYA
OUT!
THWAK
KLAK
NO!
OOPS...

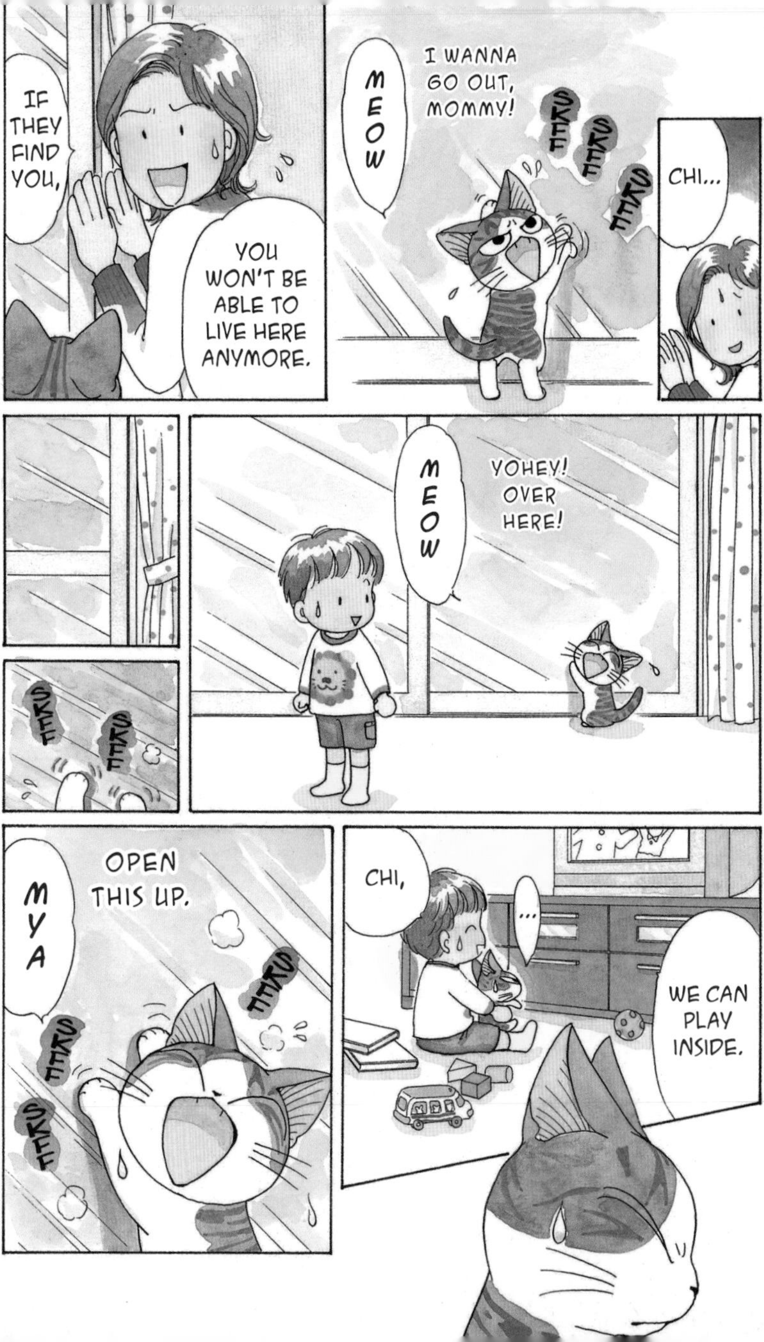
IF THEY FIND YOU,
YOU WON'T BE ABLE TO LIVE HERE ANYMORE.
MEOW
I WANNA GO OUT, MOMMY!
SKFF SKFF SKFF
CHI...
MEOW
YOHEY! OVER HERE!
SKFF SKFF
MYA
OPEN THIS UP.
SKFF SKFF SKFF
CHI,
...
WE CAN PLAY INSIDE.

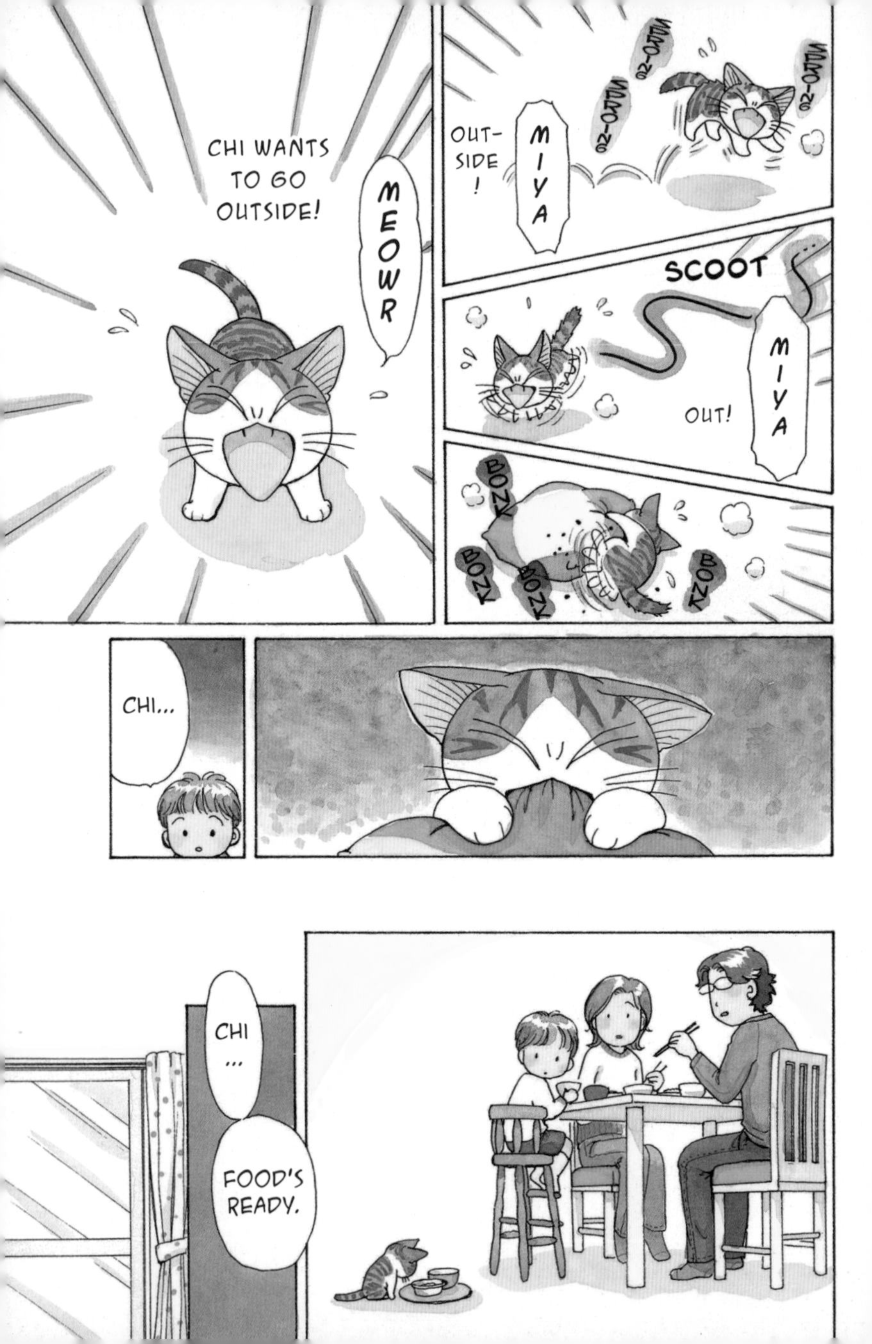

CHI WANTS TO GO OUTSIDE!
MEOWR
SPROING
SPROING
SPROING
OUT-SIDE!
MIYA
SCOOT
OUT!
MIYA
BONK
BONK
BONK
BONK
CHI...
CHI ...
FOOD'S READY.

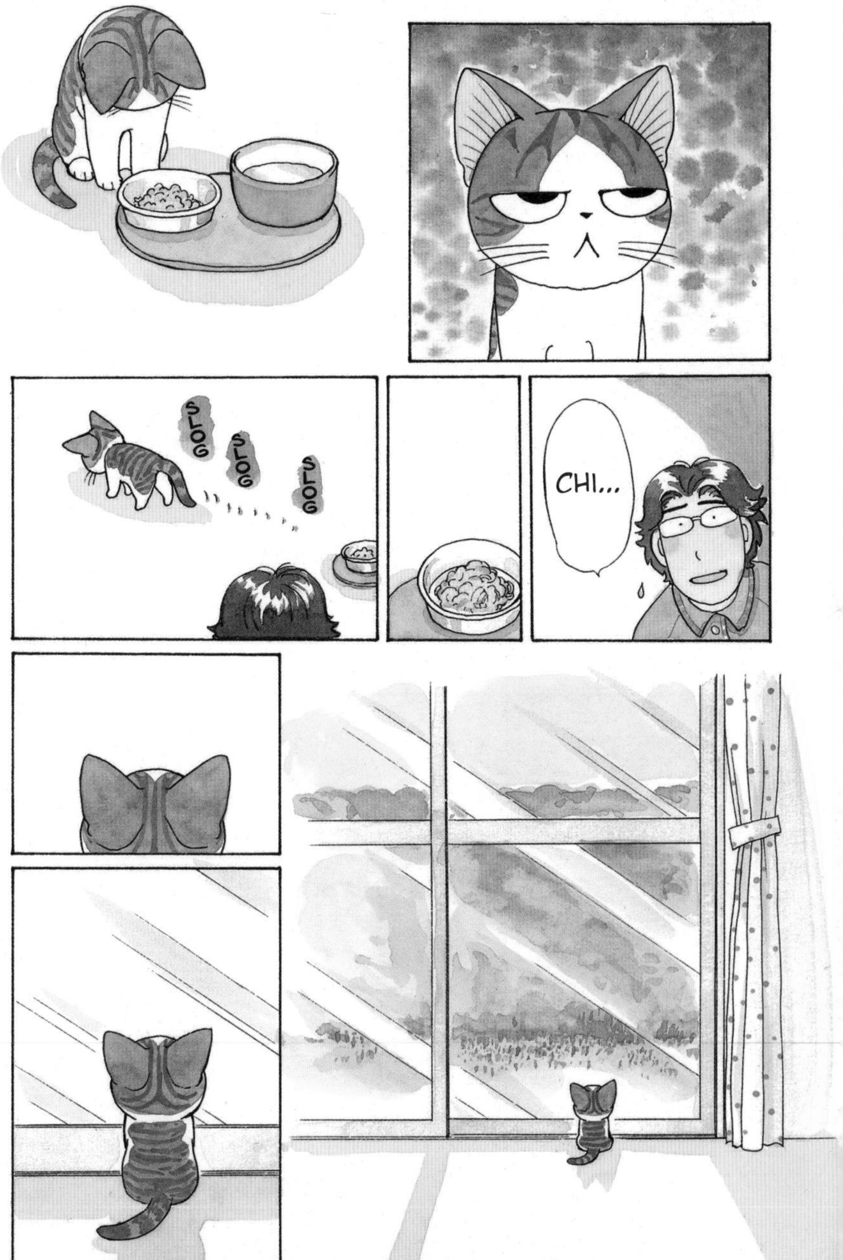
SLOG
SLOG
SLOG
CHI...

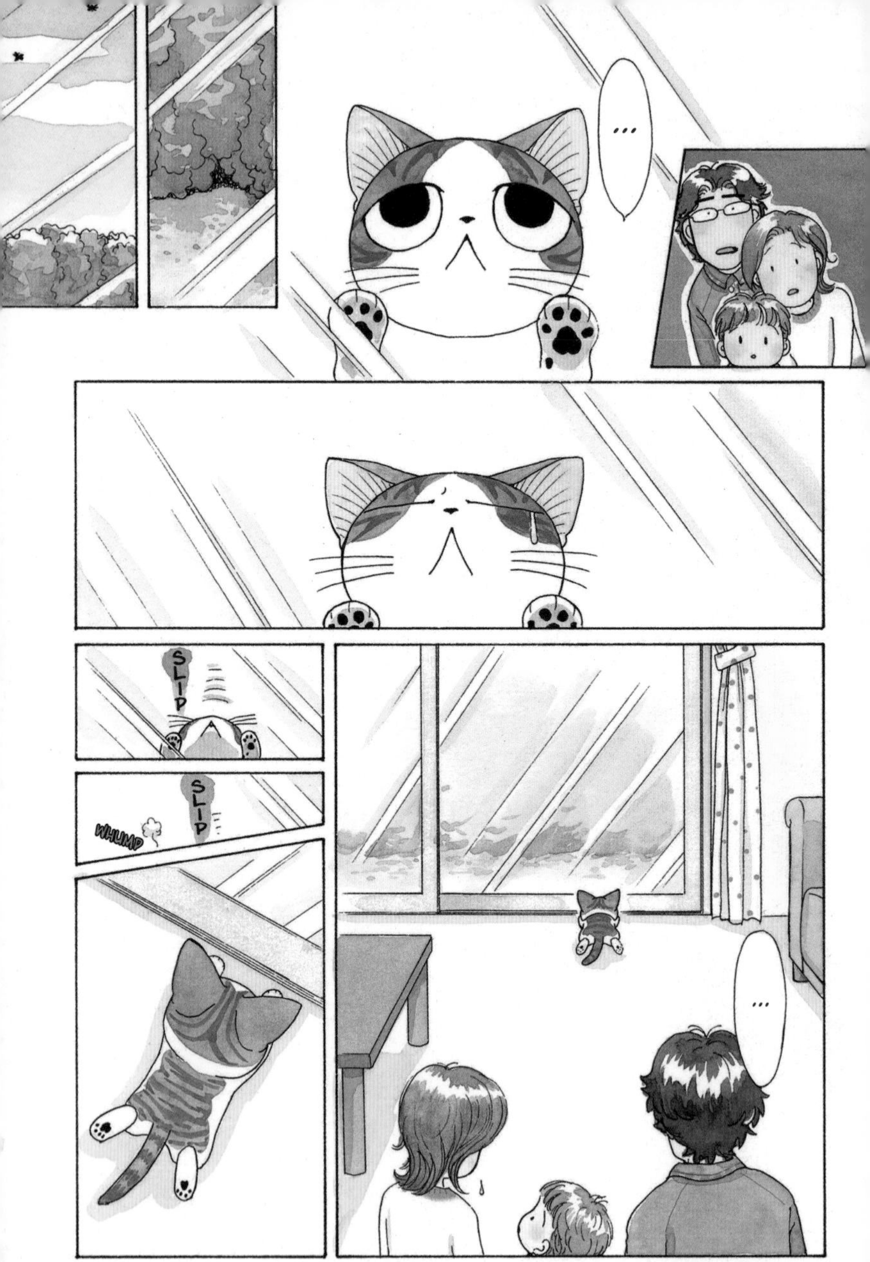
...
SLIP
SLIP
WHUMP
...

the end

homemade 51: a cat appeals

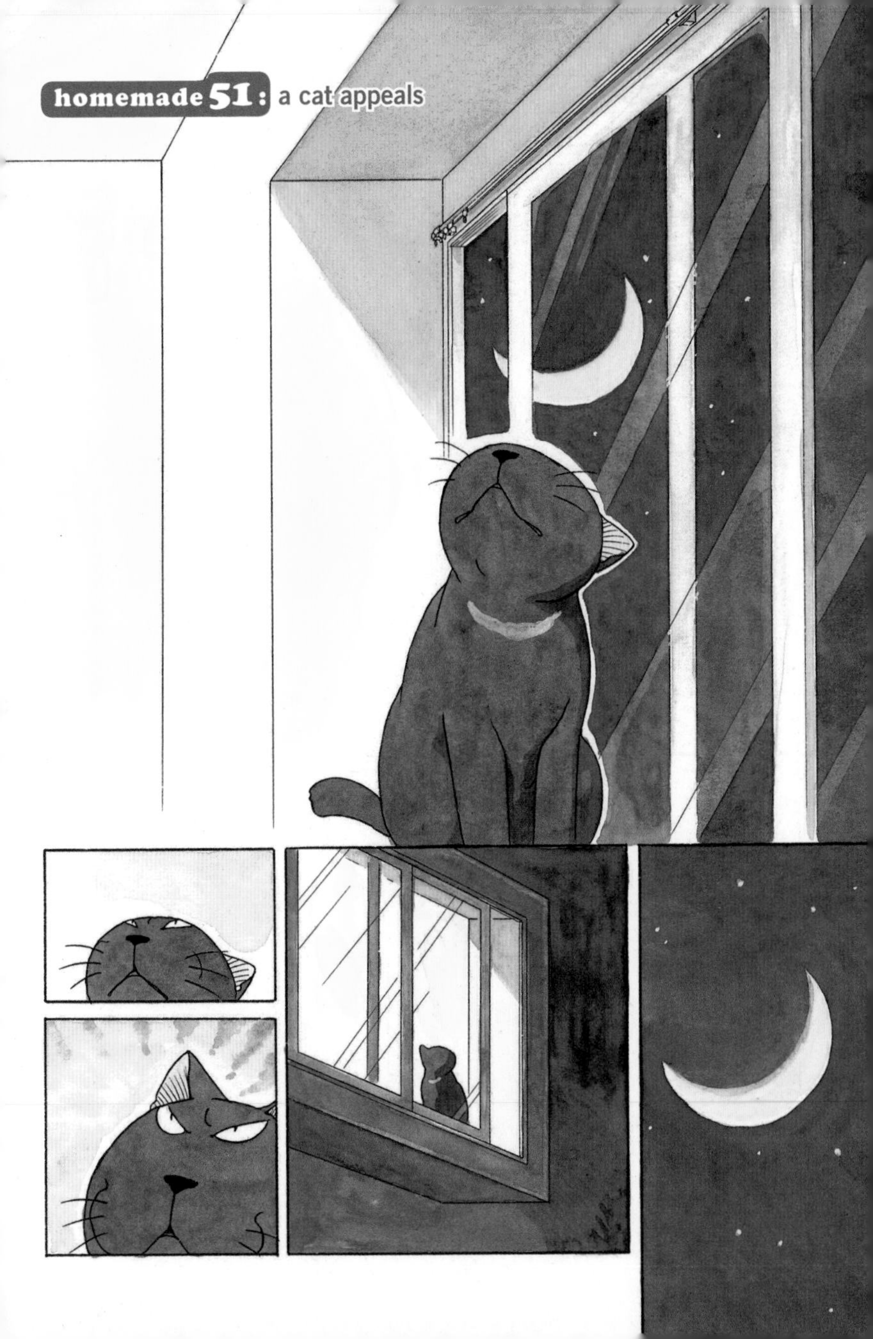

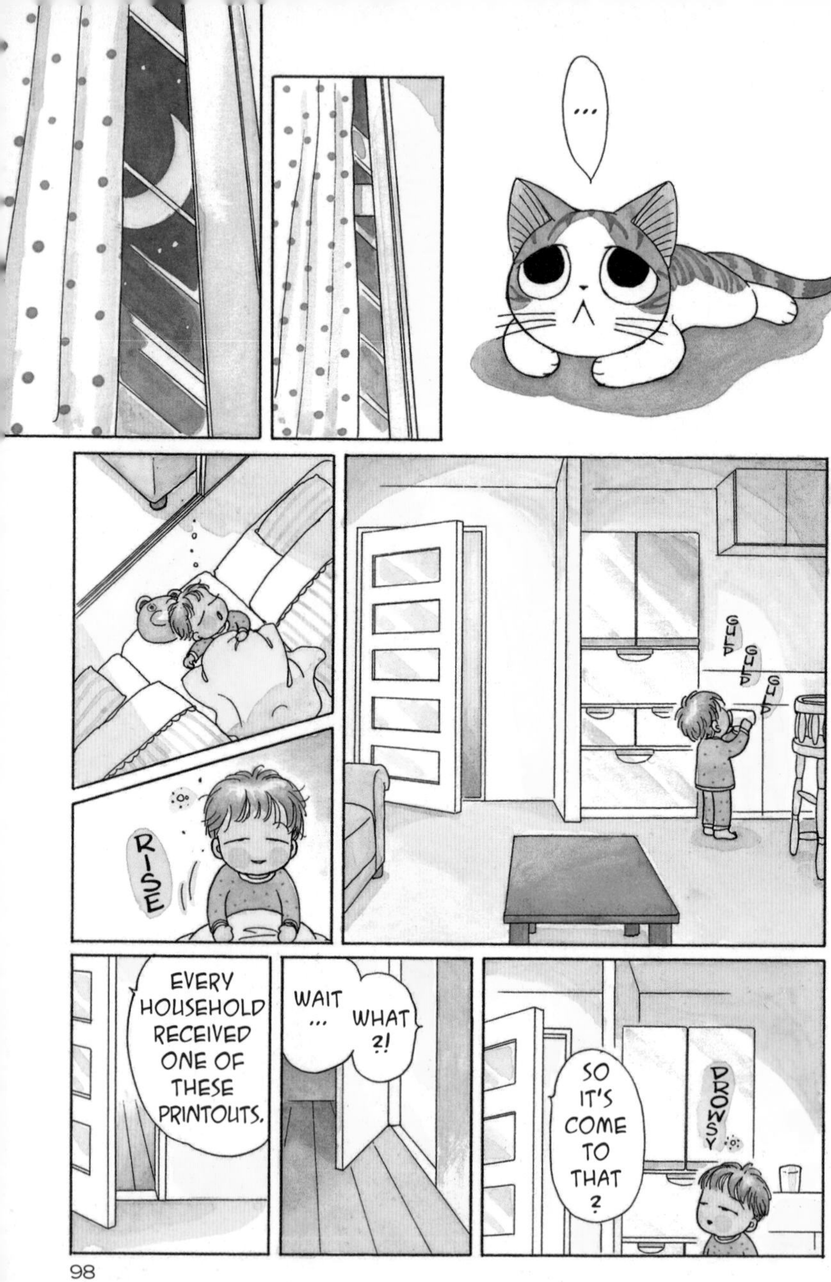
...
RISE
GULP
GULP
GULP
EVERY HOUSEHOLD RECEIVED ONE OF THESE PRINTOUTS.
WAIT ...
WHAT ?!
SO IT'S COME TO THAT ?
DROWSY

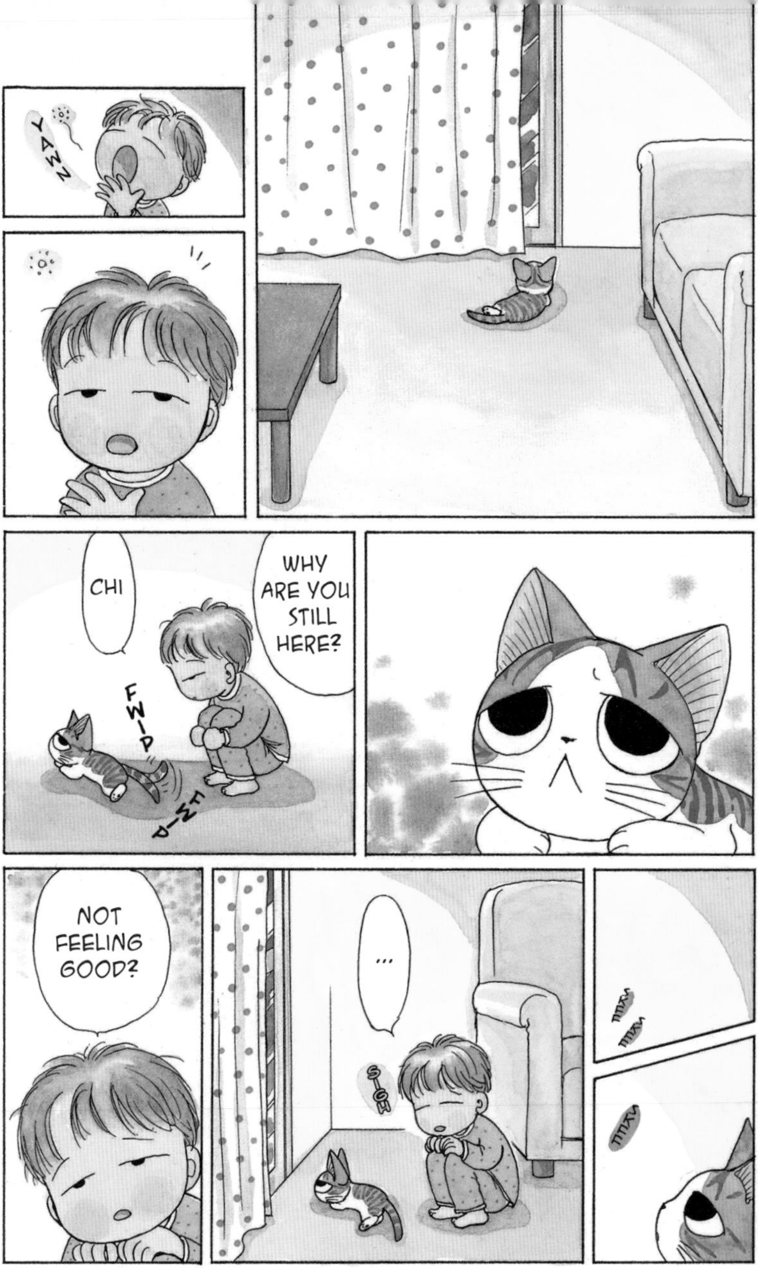
YAWN
CHI
WHY ARE YOU STILL HERE?
FWIP
TWIP
NOT FEELING GOOD?
...
SIGH

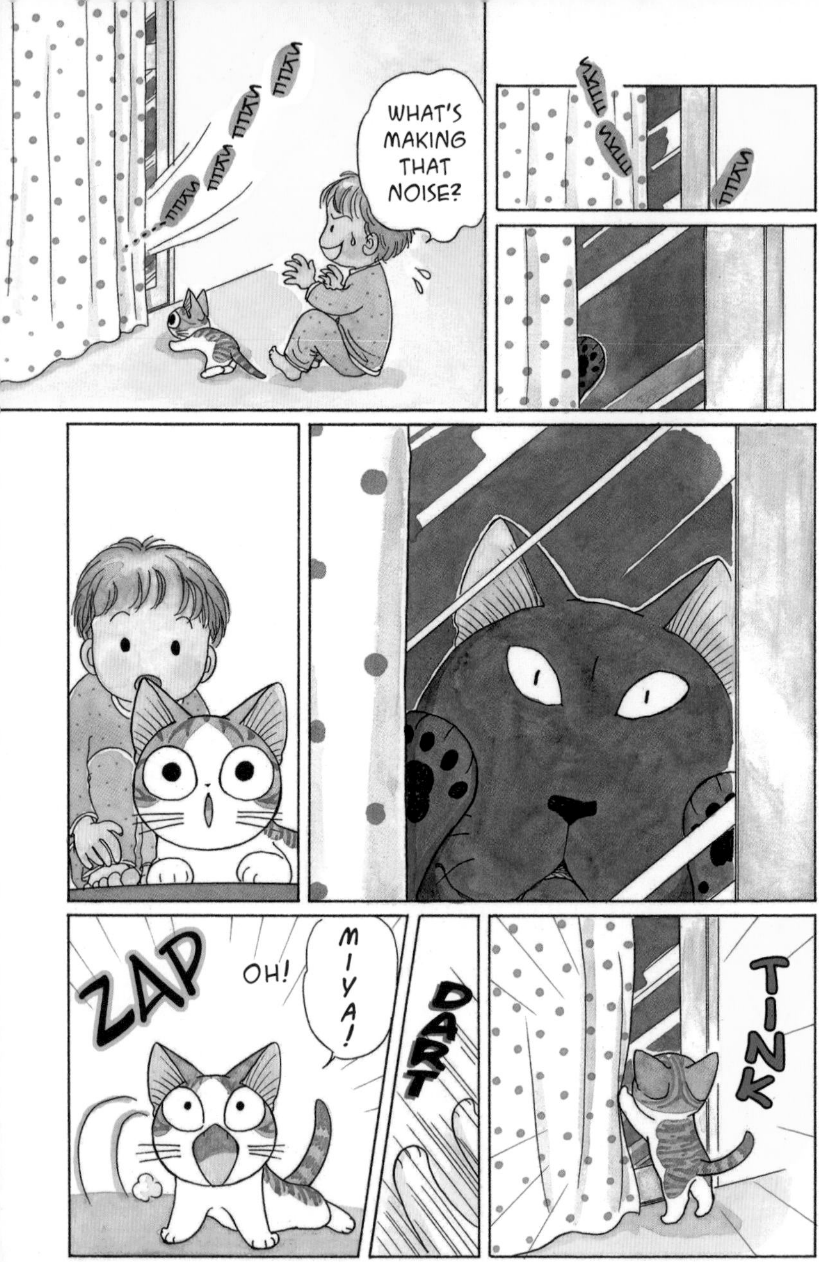
WHAT'S MAKING THAT NOISE?
ZAP
OH!
MIYA!
DART
TINK

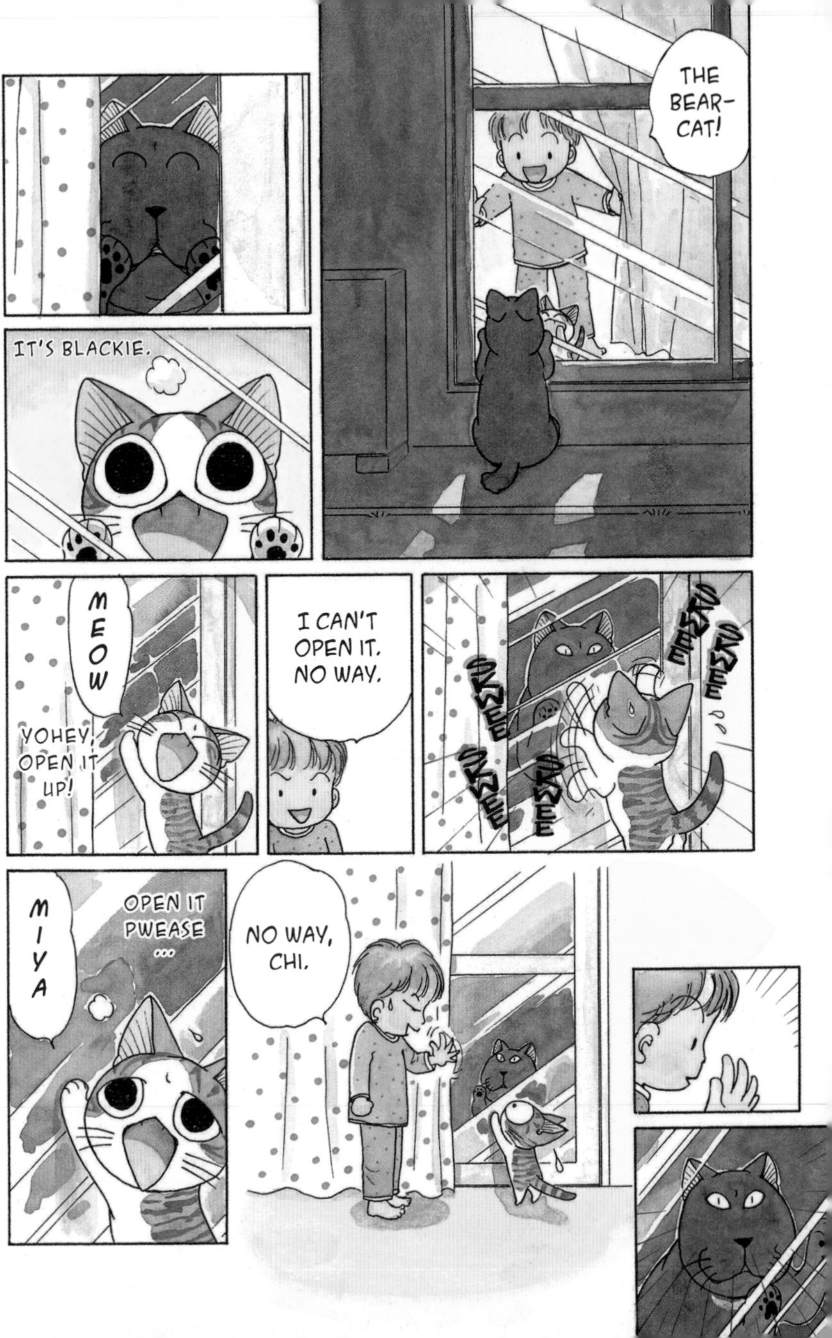
IT'S BLACKIE.
THE BEAR-CAT!
MEOW
YOHEY, OPEN IT UP!
I CAN'T OPEN IT. NO WAY.
SKWEE
SKWEE
SKWEE
SKWEE
SKWEE
MIYA
OPEN IT PWEASE...
NO WAY, CHI.

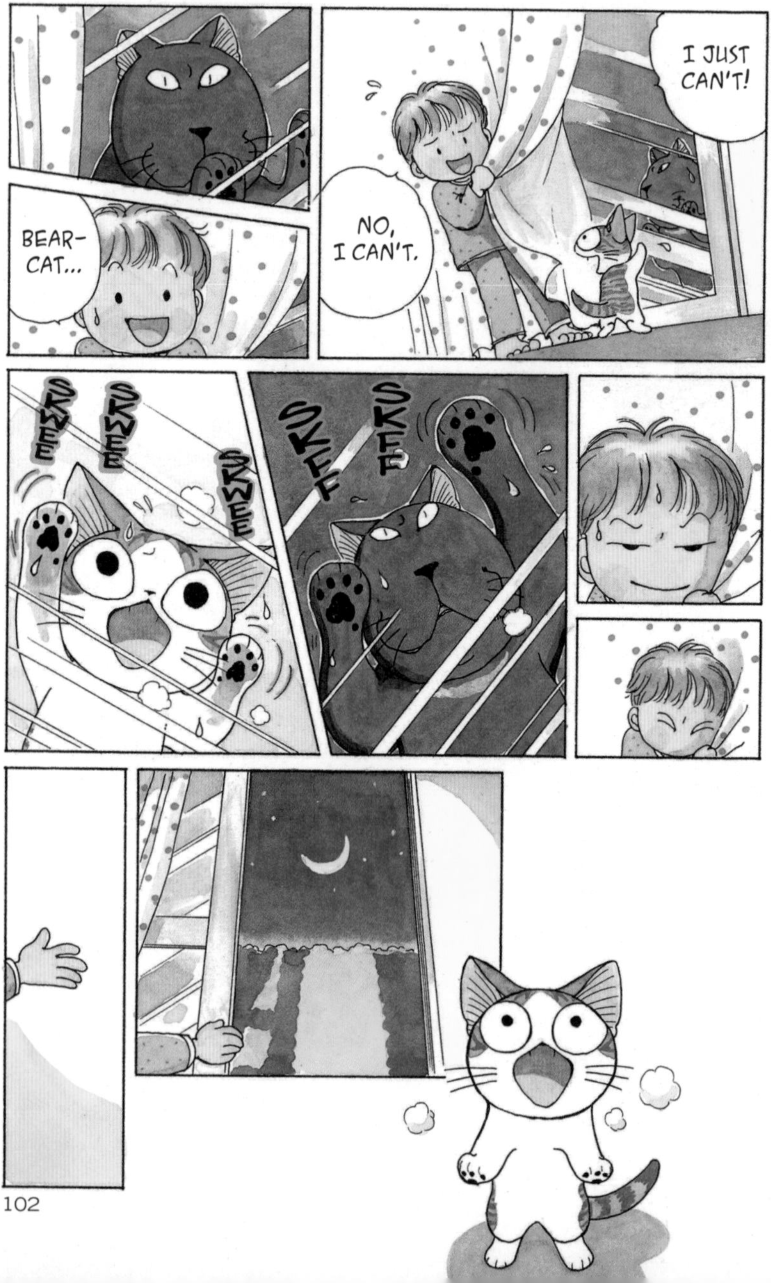
BEAR-CAT...
NO, I CAN'T.
I JUST CAN'T!
SKWEE
SKWEE
SKWEE
SKEFF
SKEFF

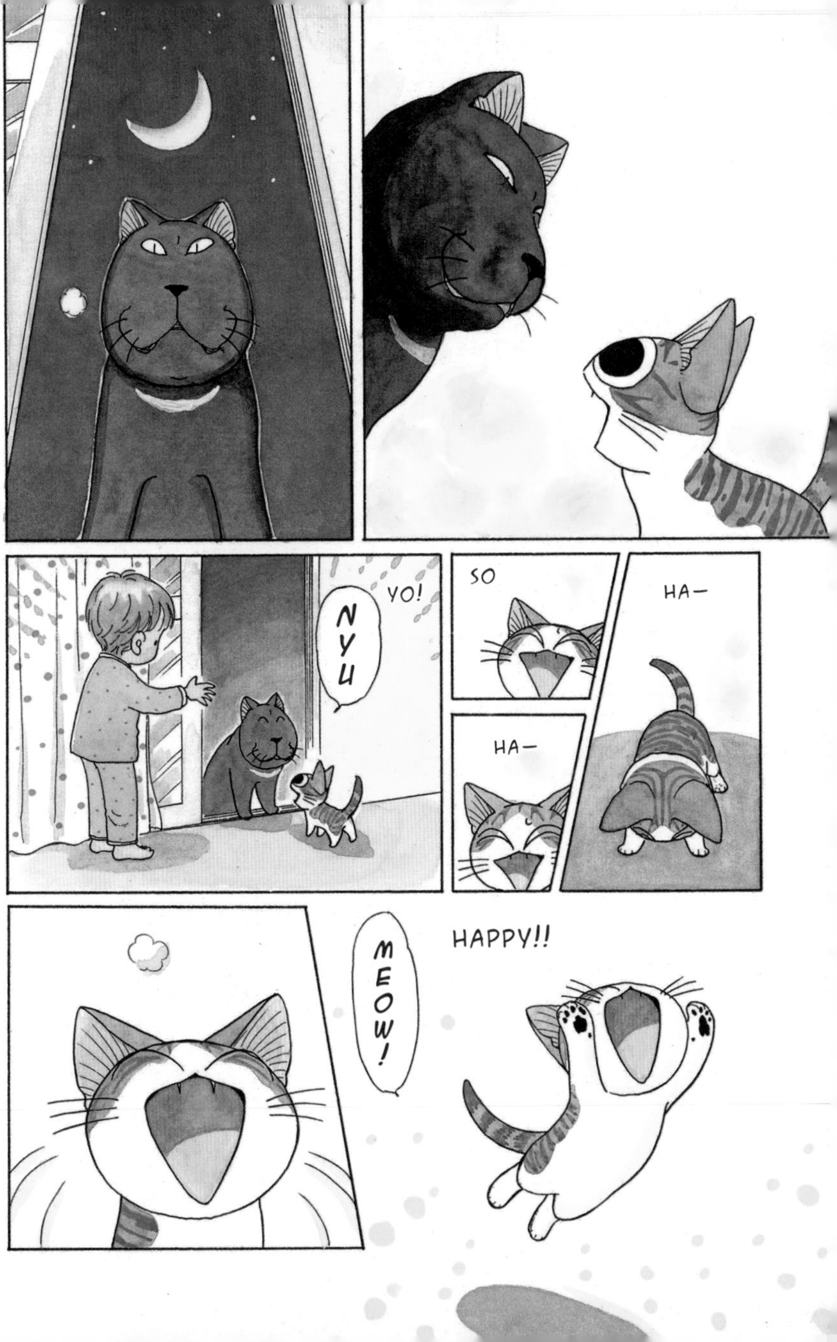
NYU
YO!
SO
HA–
HA–
MEOW!
HAPPY!!

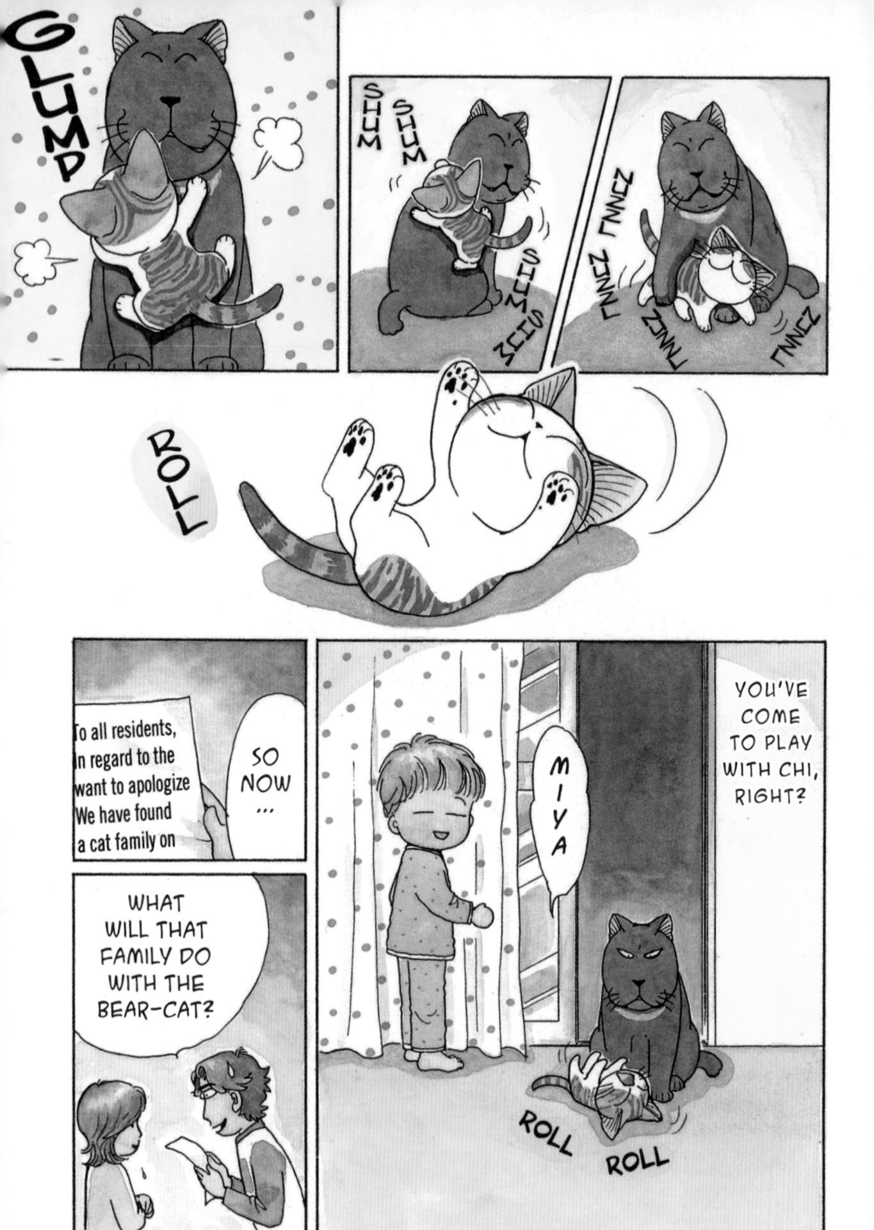
GLUMP
SHUM SHUM
SHUM SHUM
ROLL
To all residents,
In regard to the
want to apologize
We have found
a cat family on
SO NOW ...
WHAT WILL THAT FAMILY DO WITH THE BEAR-CAT?
MIYA
YOU'VE COME TO PLAY WITH CHI, RIGHT?
ROLL
ROLL

the end

homemade 52: a cat promises

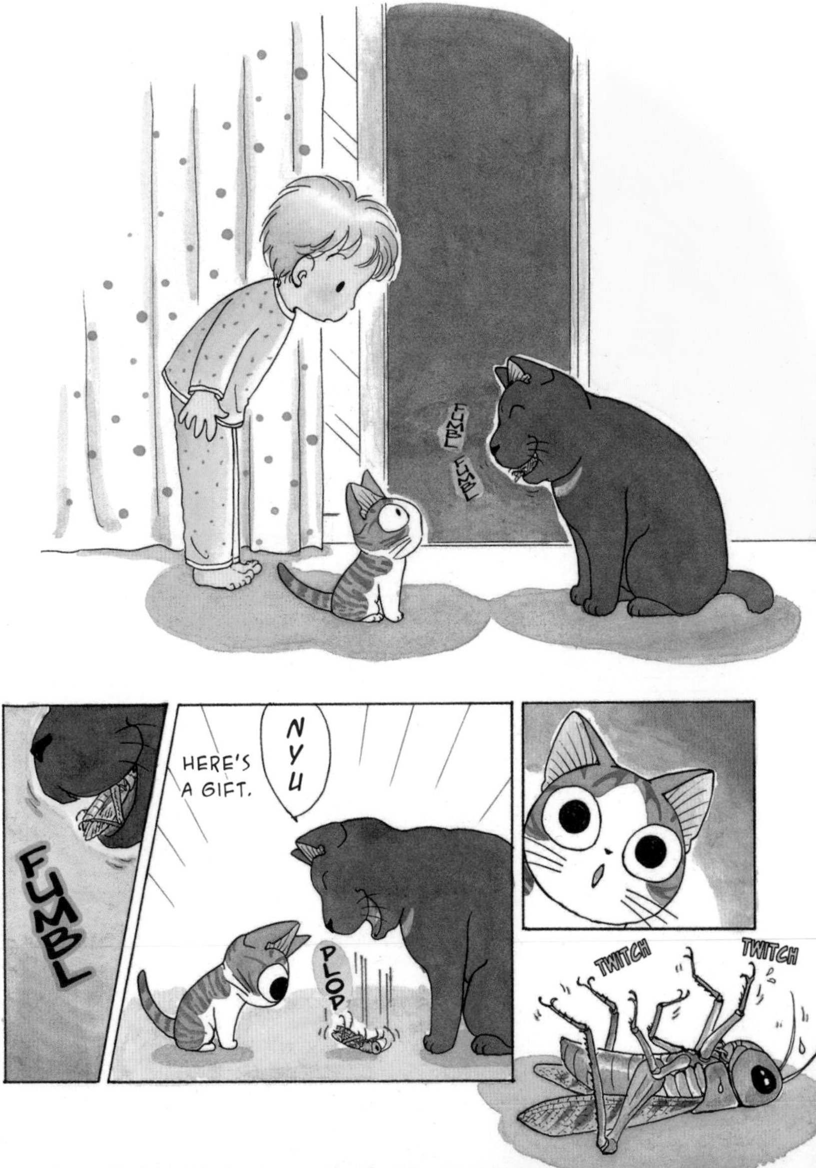
FUMBL FUMBL
FUMBL
HERE'S A GIFT.
NYU
PLOP
TWITCH
TWITCH

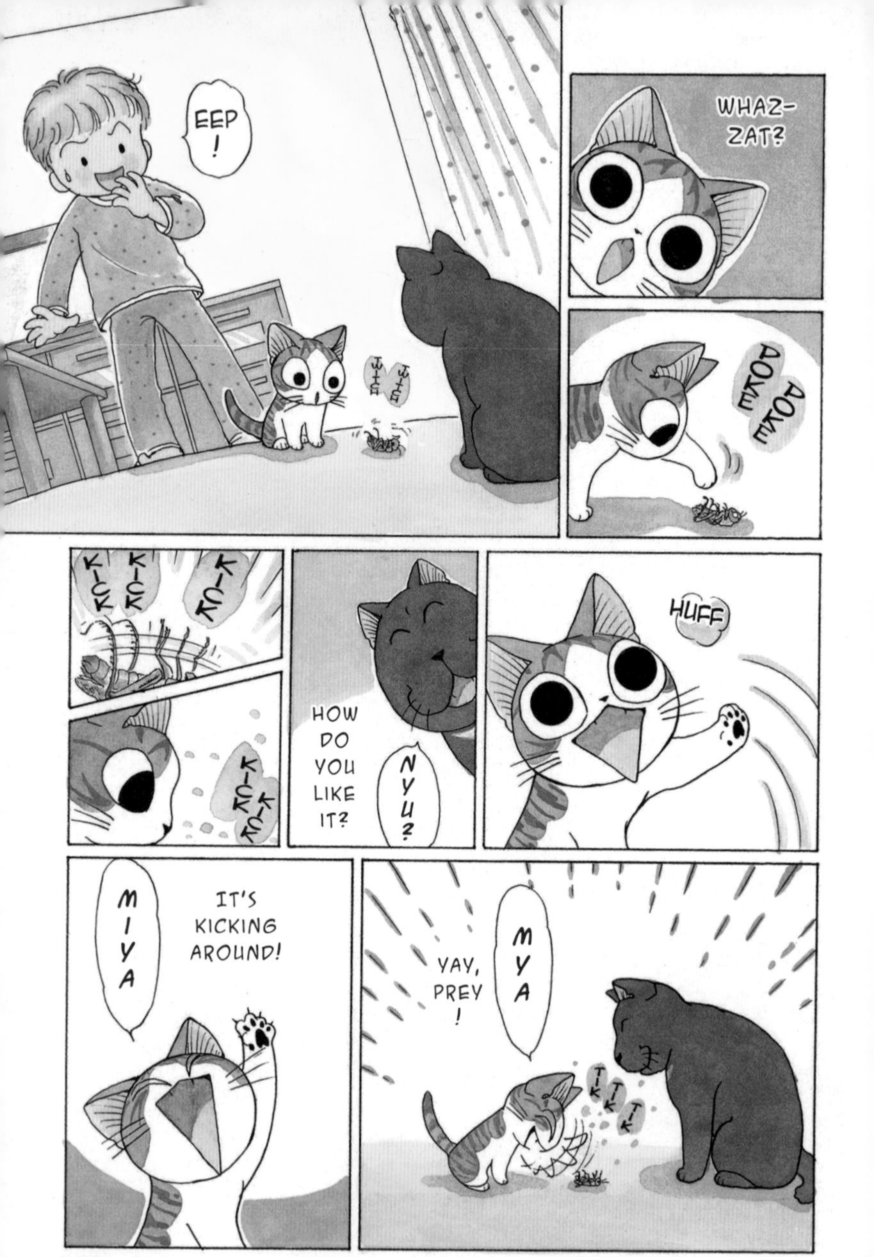
EEP!
TWITCH
TWITCH
WHAZ-ZAT?
POKE POKE
KICK KICK KICK
KICK KICK
HOW DO YOU LIKE IT?
NYU?
HUFF
MIYA
IT'S KICKING AROUND!
MYA
YAY, PREY!
TIK TIK TIK

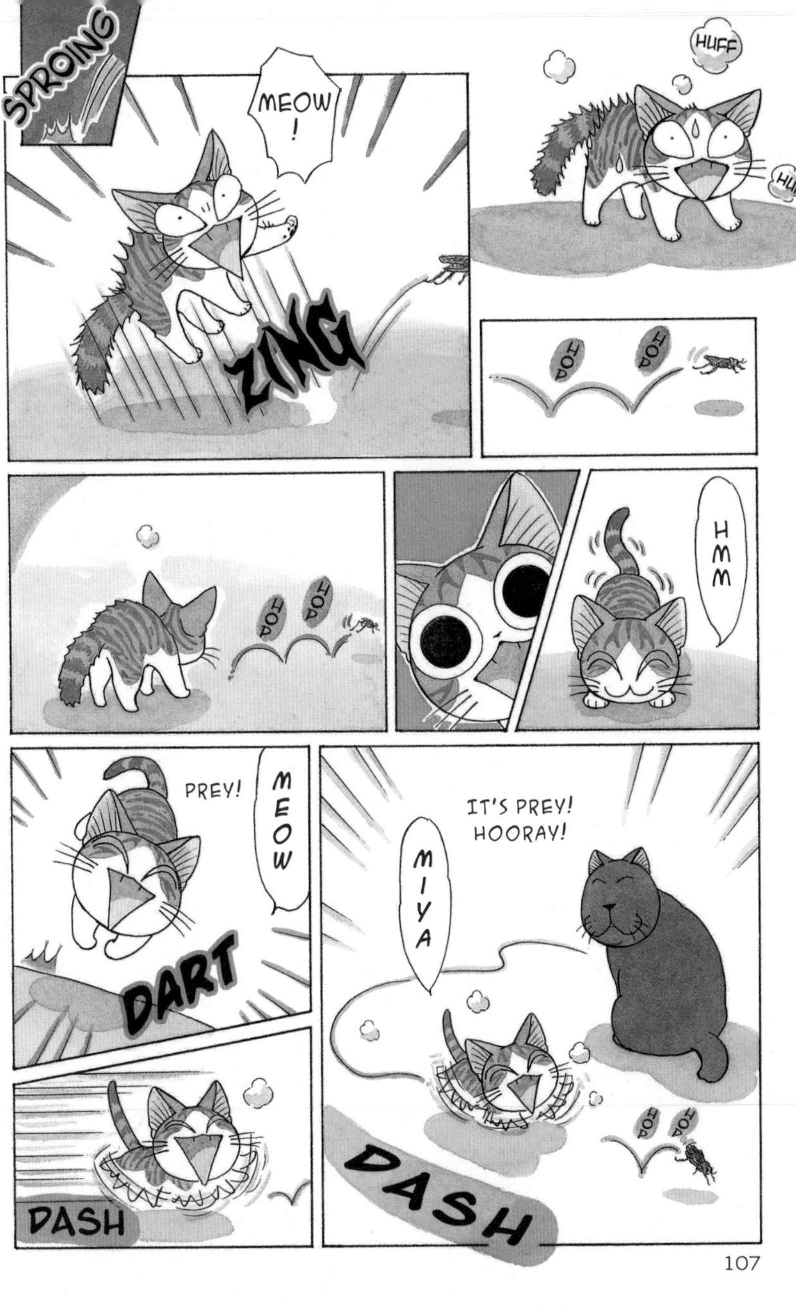
SPROING
MEOW!
ZING
HUFF
HUFF
HOP
HOP
HOP
HOP
HMM
PREY!
MEOW
DART
DASH
IT'S PREY! HOORAY!
MIYA
HOP
HOP
DASH

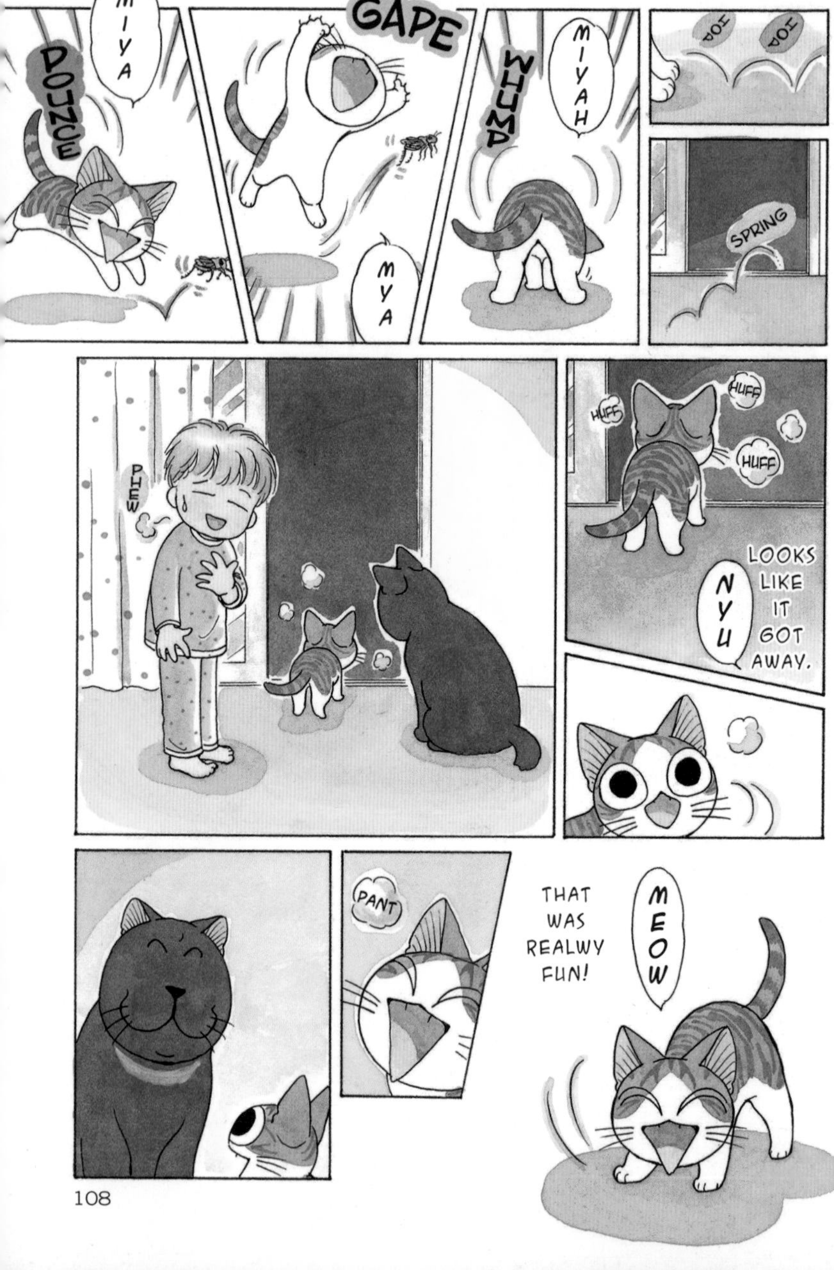
POUNCE
MIYA
GAPE
MYA
WHUMP
MIYAH
HOP HOP
SPRING
PHEW
HUFF HUFF HUFF
LOOKS LIKE IT GOT AWAY.
NYU
PANT
THAT WAS REALWY FUN!
MEOW

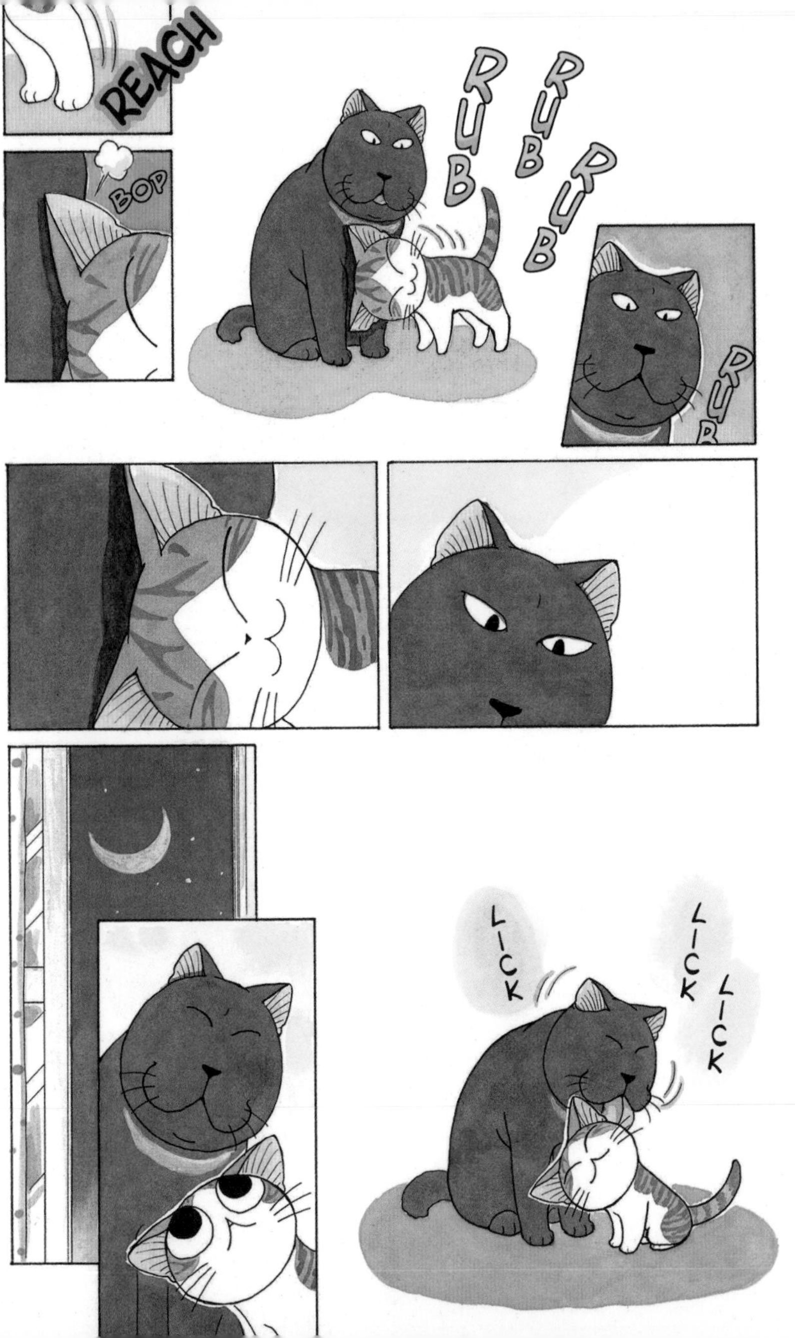
REACH
BOP
RUB RUB
RUB RUB
RUB RUB
RUB
LICK
LICK
LICK

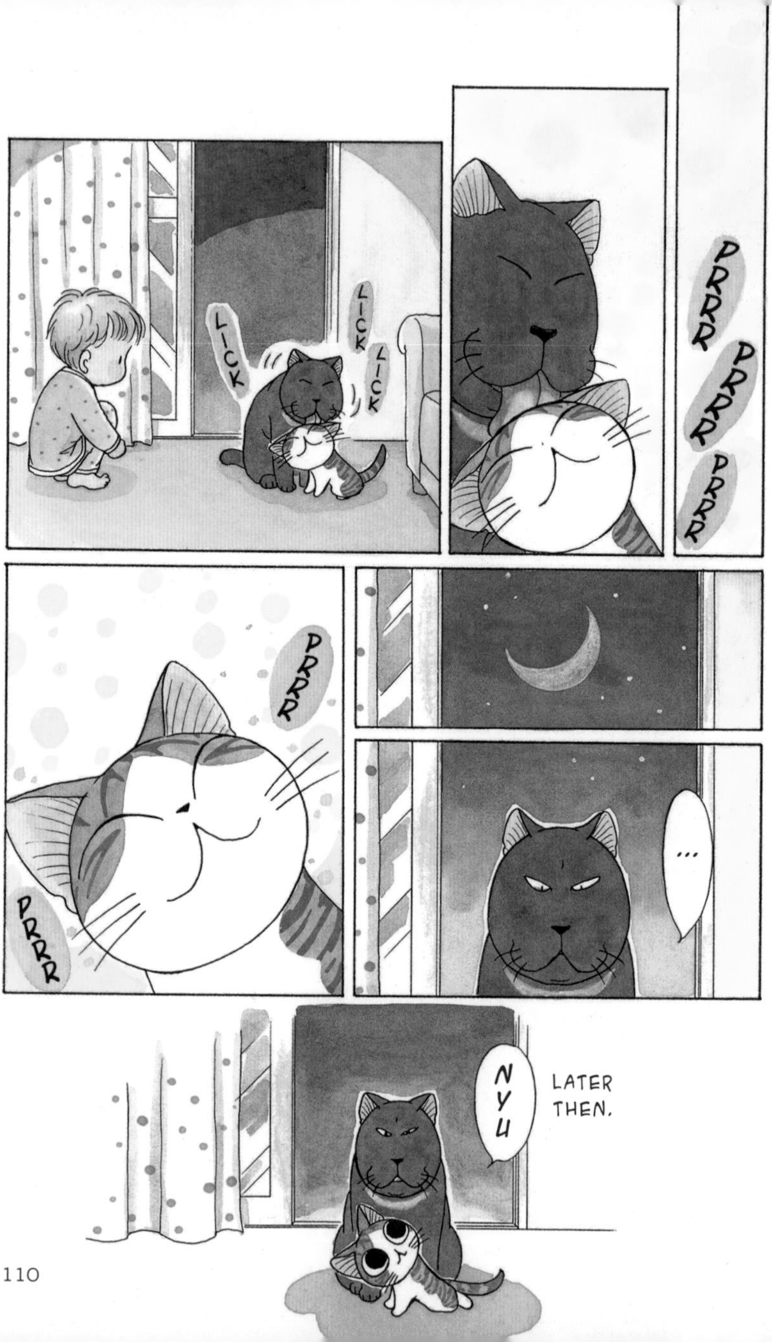
LICK
LICK
LICK
PRRR
PRRR
PRRR
PRRR
PRRR
...
NYU
LATER THEN.

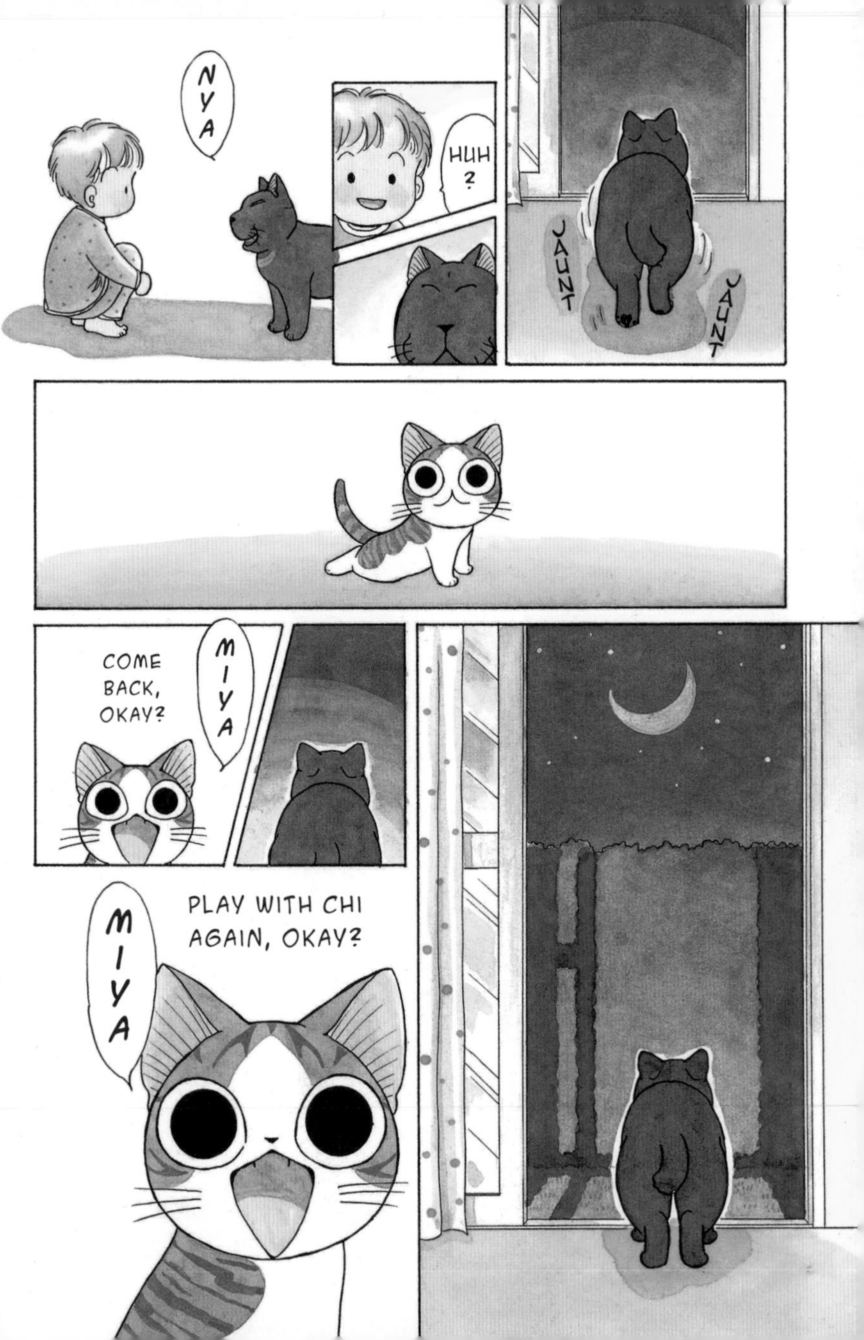
NYA
HUH?
JAUNT
JAUNT
COME BACK, OKAY?
MIYA
MIYA
PLAY WITH CHI AGAIN, OKAY?

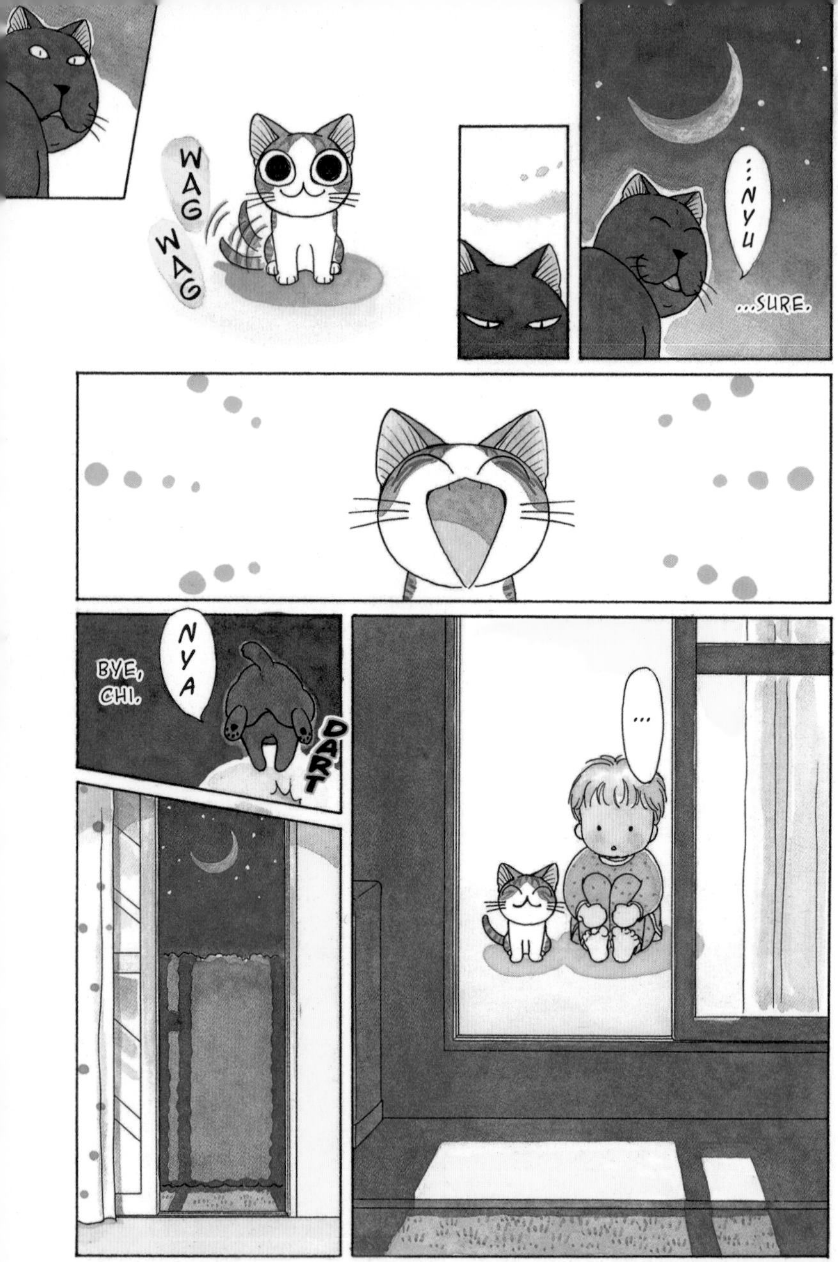
WAG WAG
...NYU
...SURE.
BYE, CHI.
NYA
DART
...

the end

homemade 53: a cat sends off

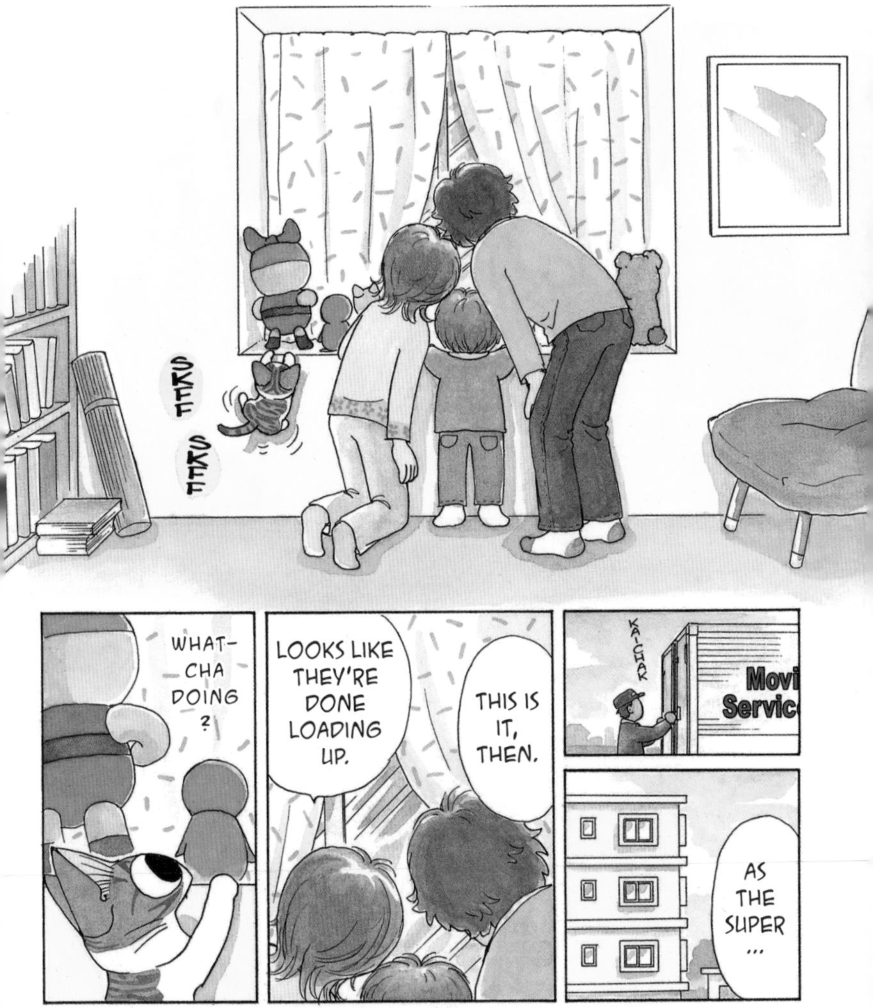
SKFF
SKFF
WHAT-CHA DOING?
LOOKS LIKE THEY'RE DONE LOADING UP.
THIS IS IT, THEN.
KAICHAK
AS THE SUPER ...

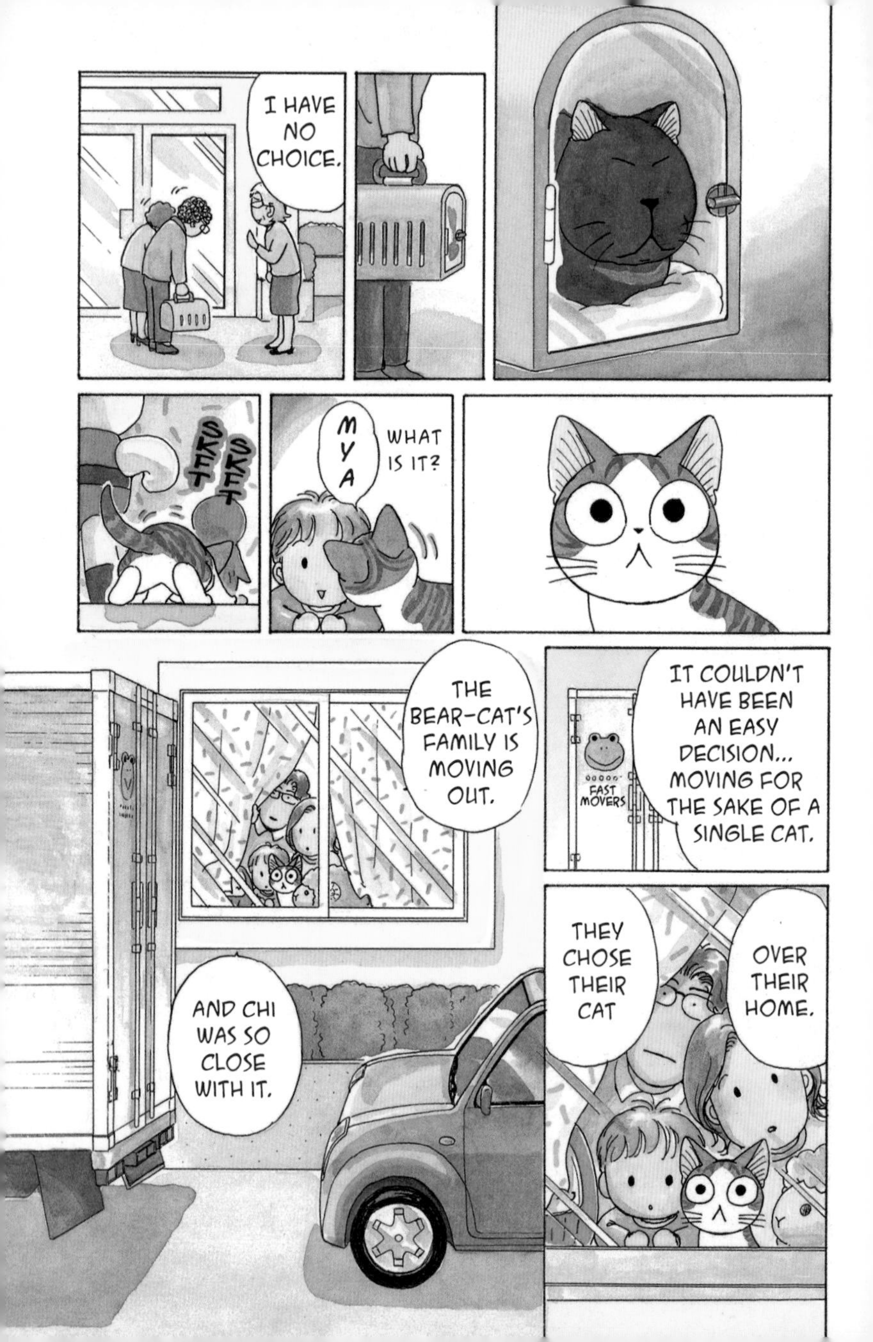
I HAVE NO CHOICE.
SKET SKET
MYA
WHAT IS IT?
THE BEAR-CAT'S FAMILY IS MOVING OUT.
AND CHI WAS SO CLOSE WITH IT.
FAST MOVERS
IT COULDN'T HAVE BEEN AN EASY DECISION... MOVING FOR THE SAKE OF A SINGLE CAT.
THEY CHOSE THEIR CAT
OVER THEIR HOME.

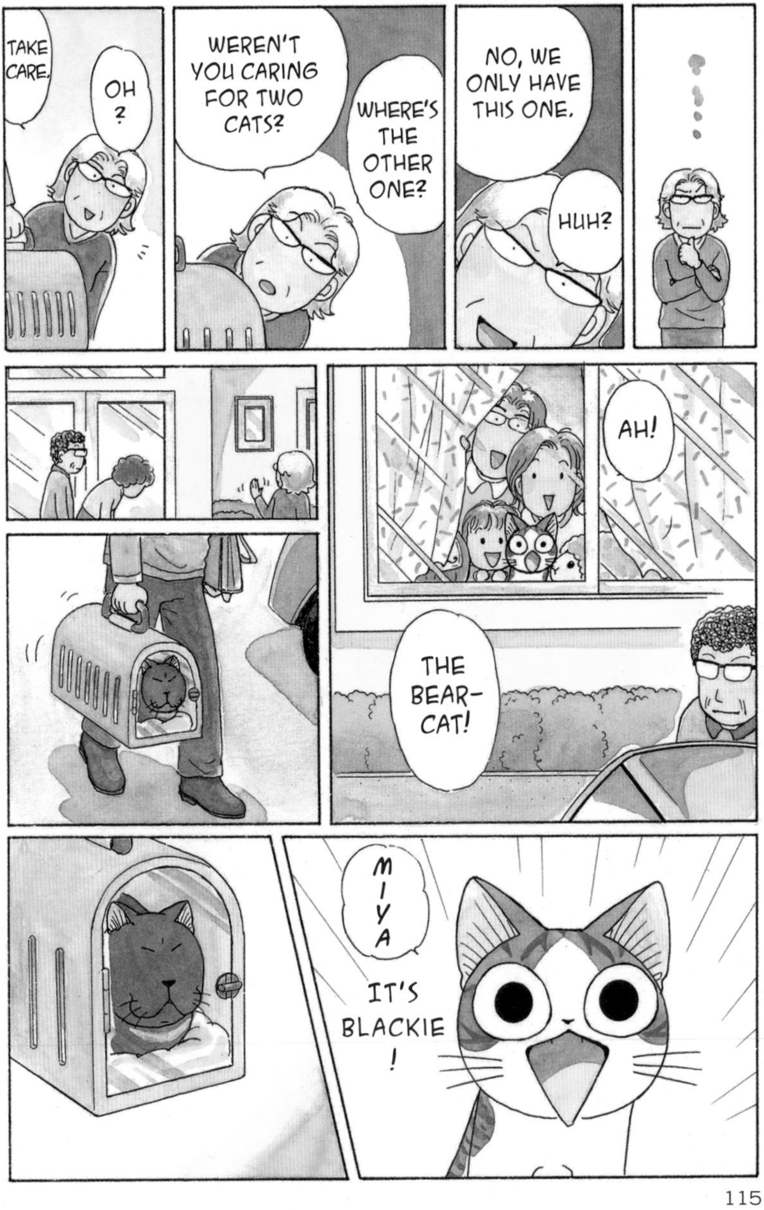
TAKE CARE.
OH?
WEREN'T YOU CARING FOR TWO CATS?
WHERE'S THE OTHER ONE?
NO, WE ONLY HAVE THIS ONE.
HUH?
AH!
THE BEAR-CAT!
MIYA
IT'S BLACKIE!

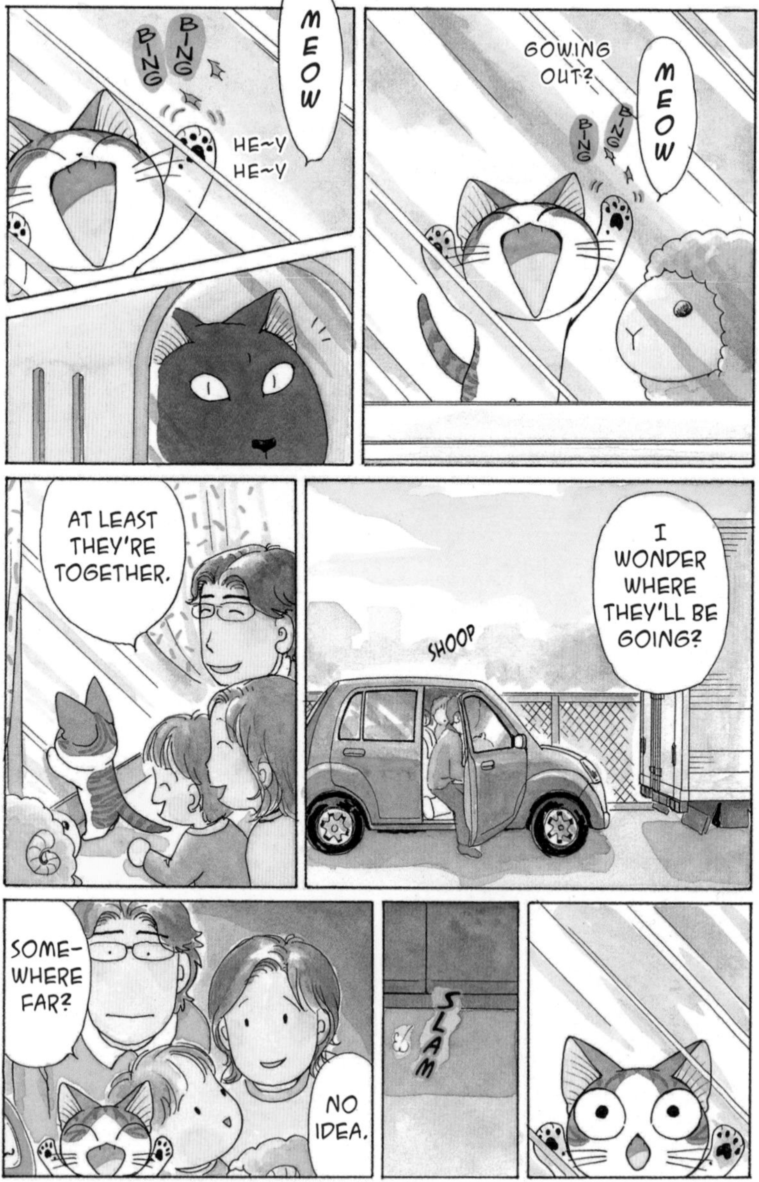
BING BING
MEOW
HE~Y HE~Y
GOWING OUT?
MEOW
BING BING
AT LEAST THEY'RE TOGETHER.
SHOOP
I WONDER WHERE THEY'LL BE GOING?
SOME-WHERE FAR?
NO IDEA.
SLAM

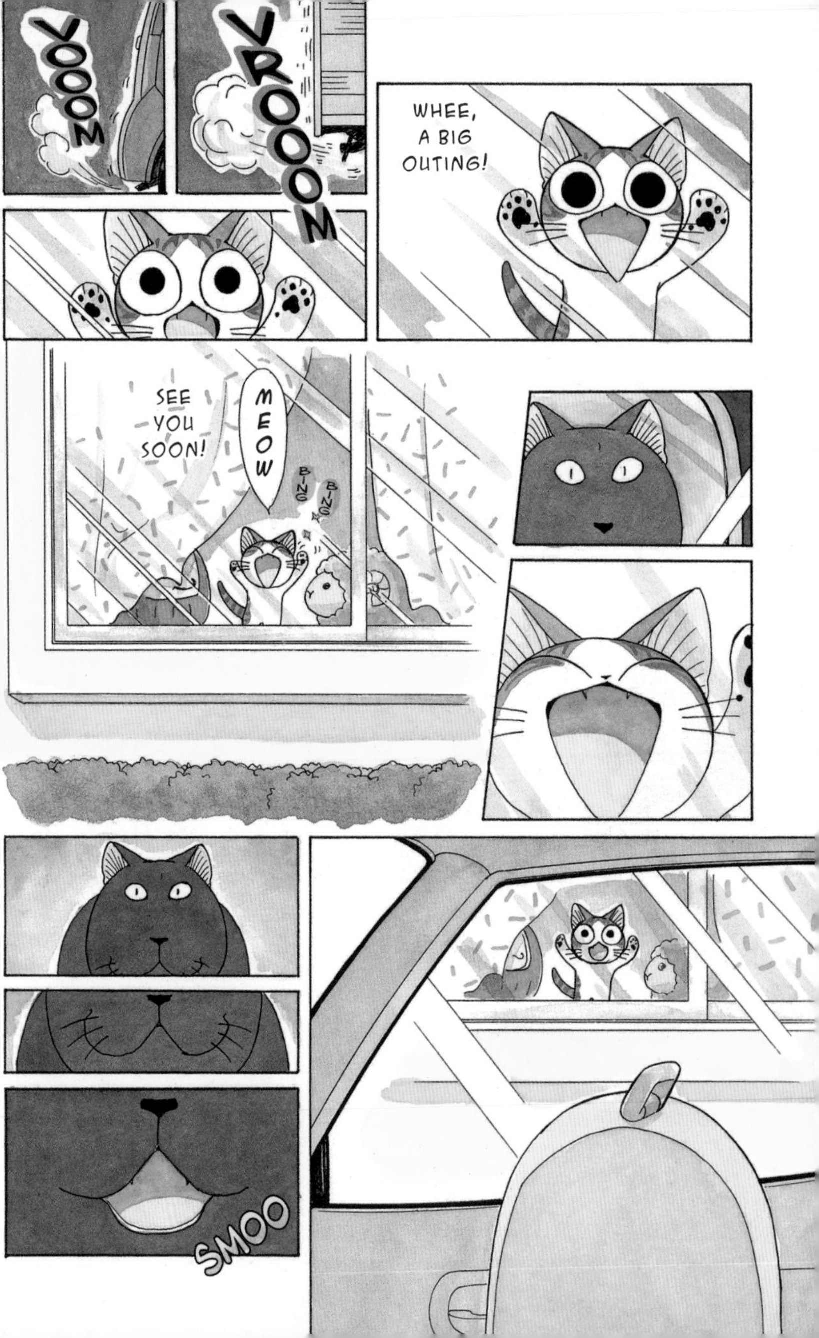
VOOOM
VROOOM
WHEE, A BIG OUTING!
SEE YOU SOON!
MEOW
BING BING
SMOO

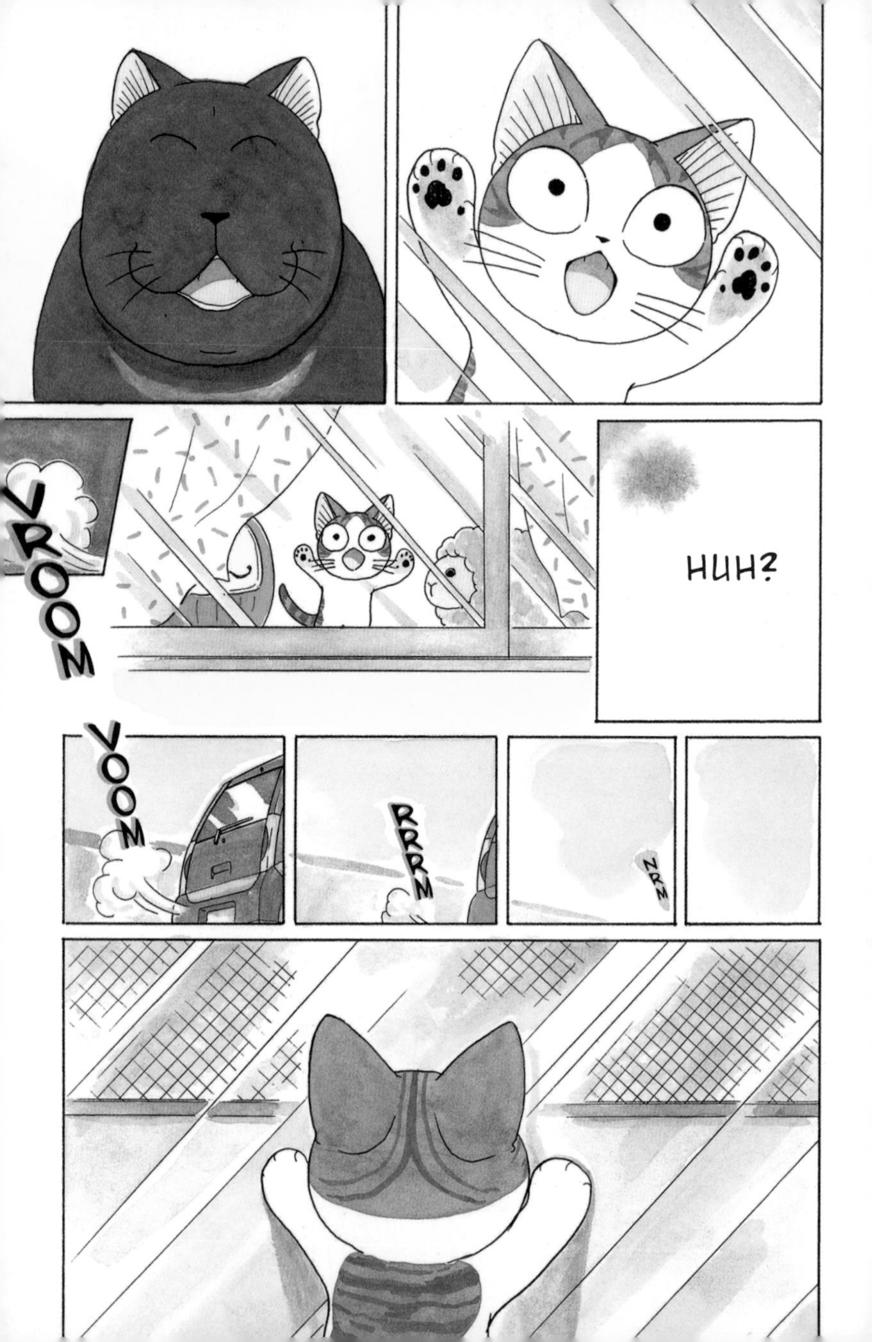
HUH?
VROOM
NRM
RRRM
VOOM

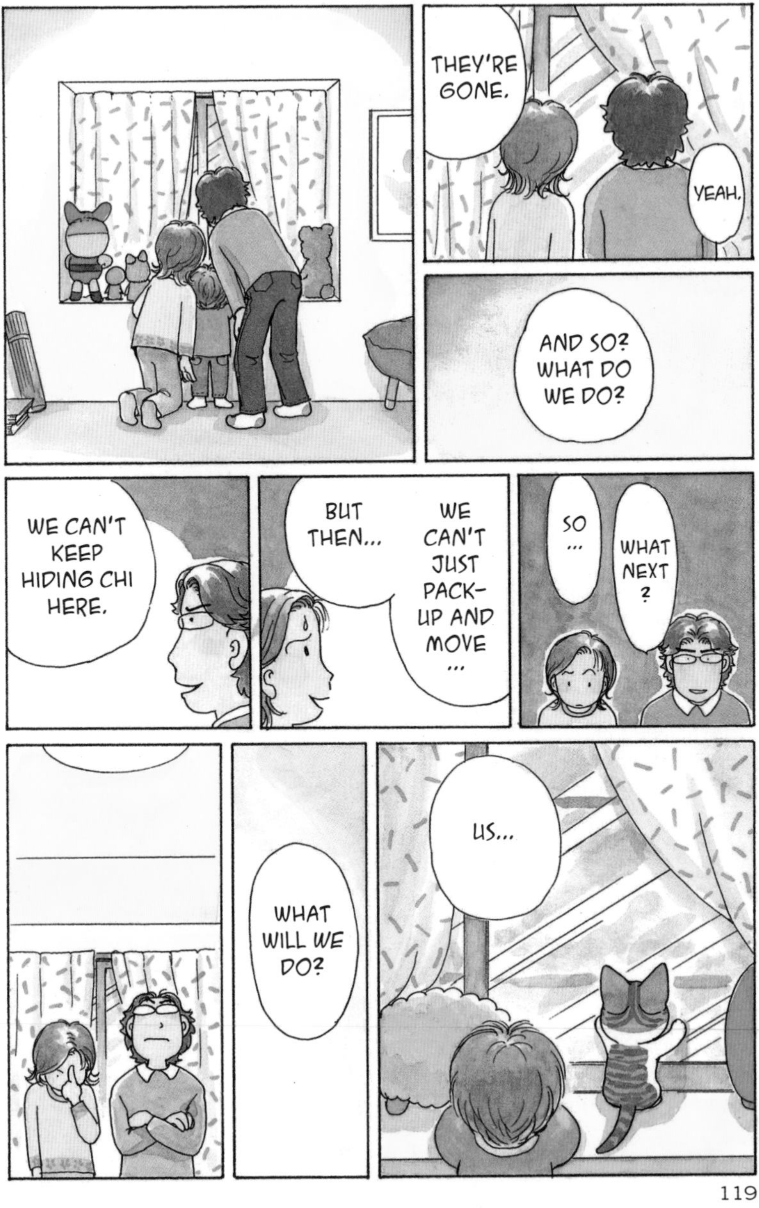
THEY'RE GONE.
YEAH.
AND SO? WHAT DO WE DO?
WE CAN'T KEEP HIDING CHI HERE.
BUT THEN...
WE CAN'T JUST PACK-UP AND MOVE ...
SO ...
WHAT NEXT ?
WHAT WILL WE DO?
US...

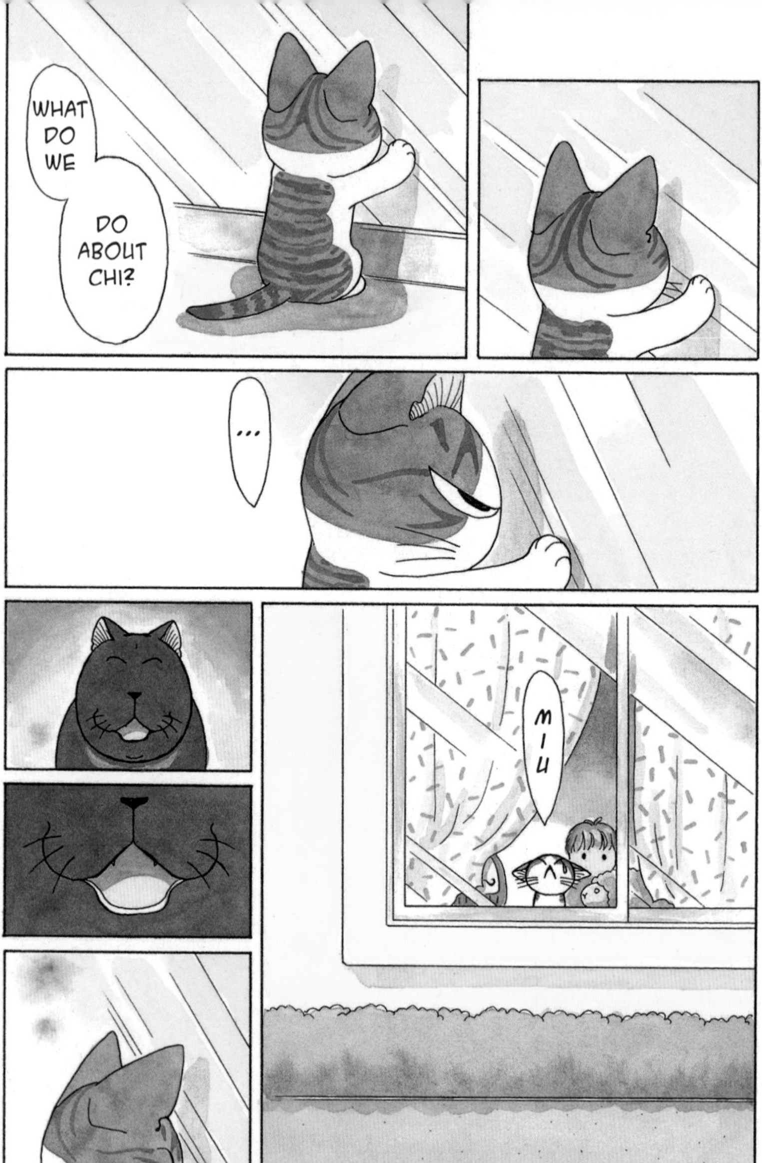
WHAT DO WE DO ABOUT CHI?
...
MIU

the end

homemade 54: a cat finds out

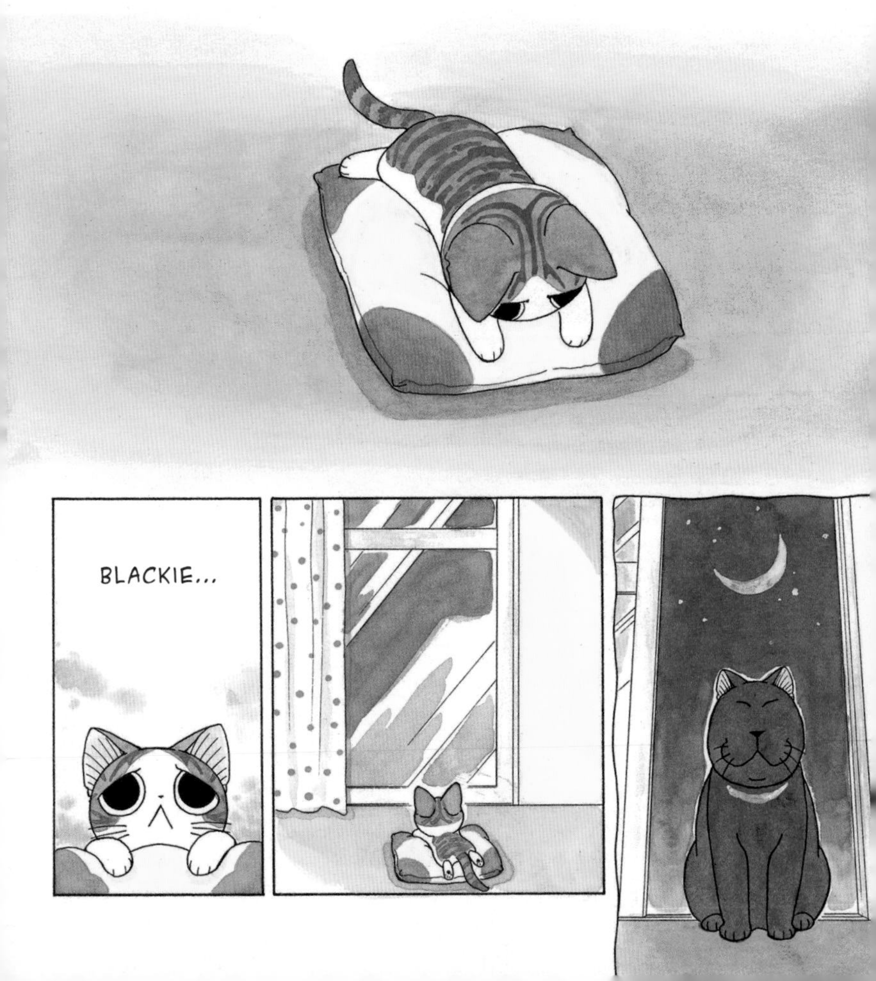
BLACKIE...

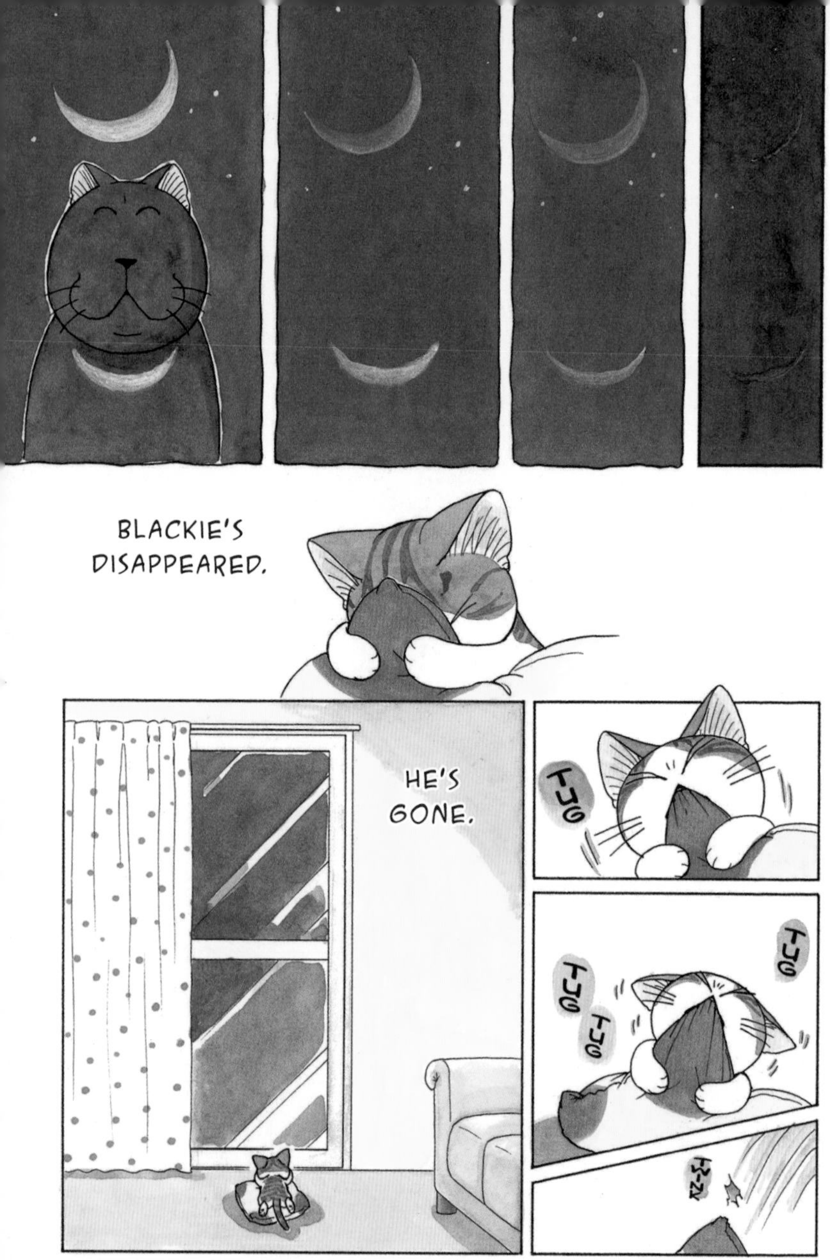
BLACKIE'S DISAPPEARED.
HE'S GONE.
TUG
TUG
TUG
TUG
TW-NK

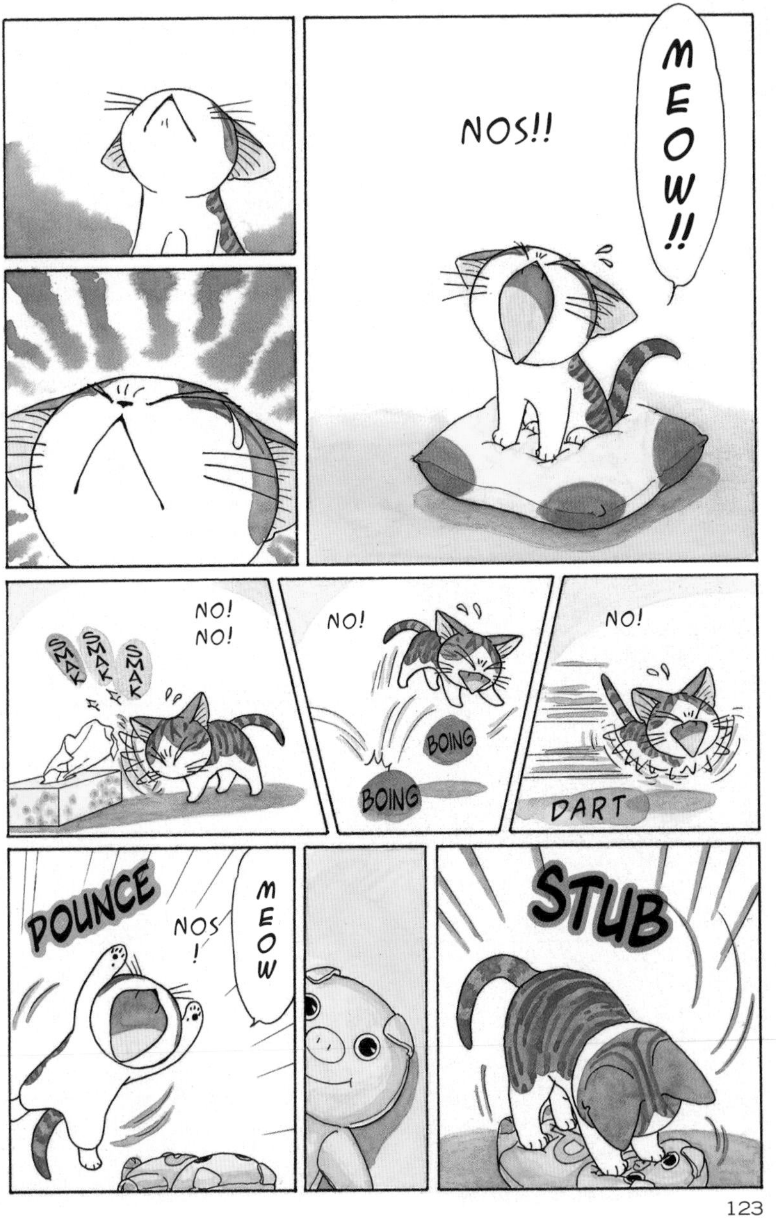
NOS!!
MEOW!!
NO!
NO!
SMAK
SMAK
SMAK
NO!
BOING
BOING
NO!
DART
POUNCE
NOS!
MEOW
STUB

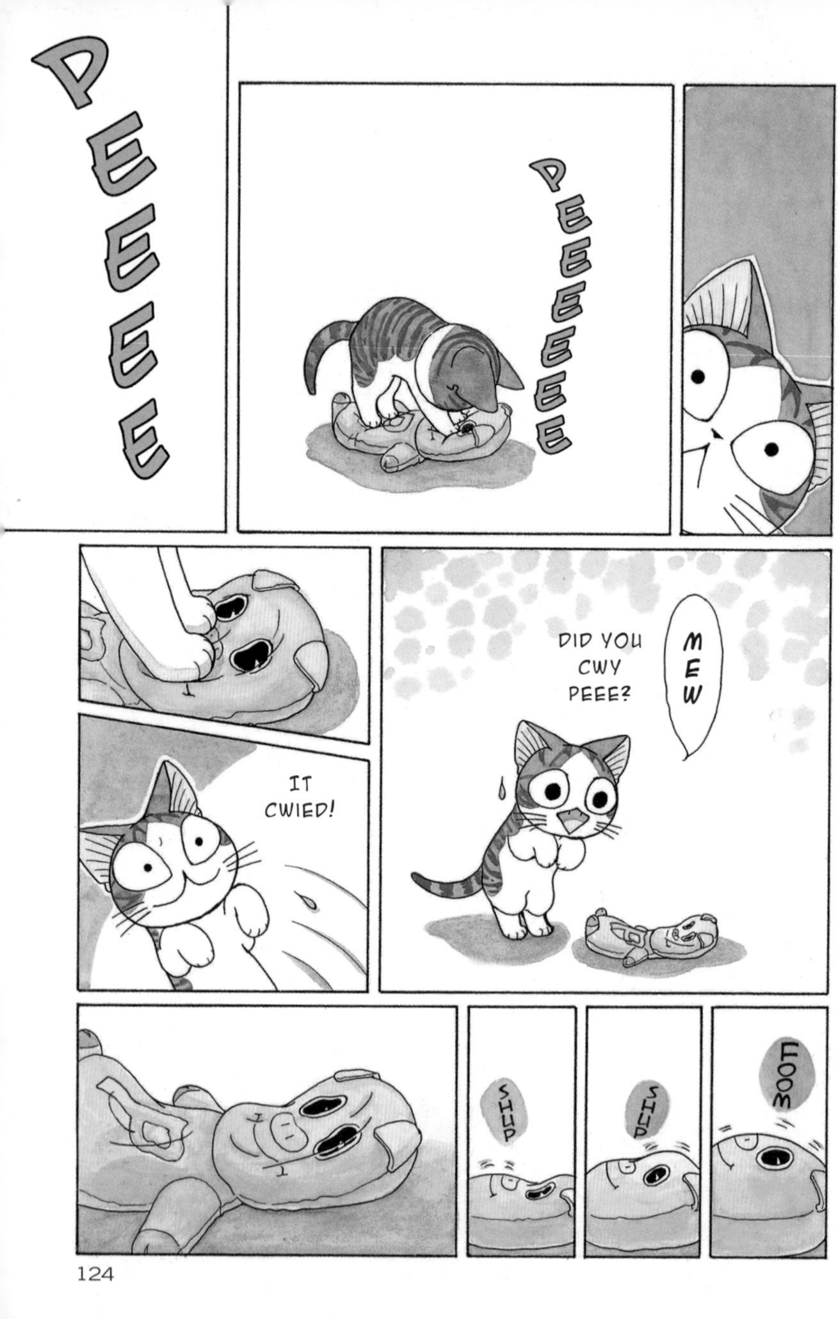
PEEEEE
PEEEEEE
IT CWIED!
DID YOU CWY PEEE?
MEW
SHUP
SHUP
FOOM

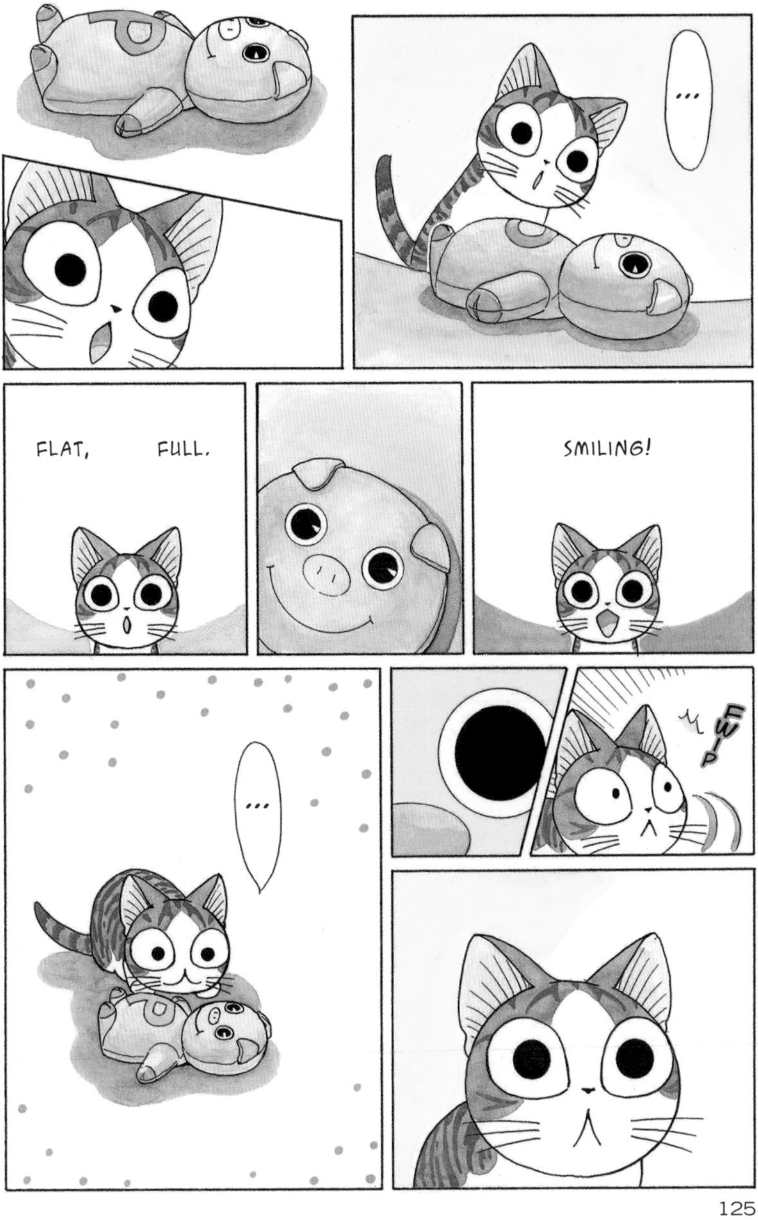
...
FLAT,
FULL.
SMILING!
...
EWIP

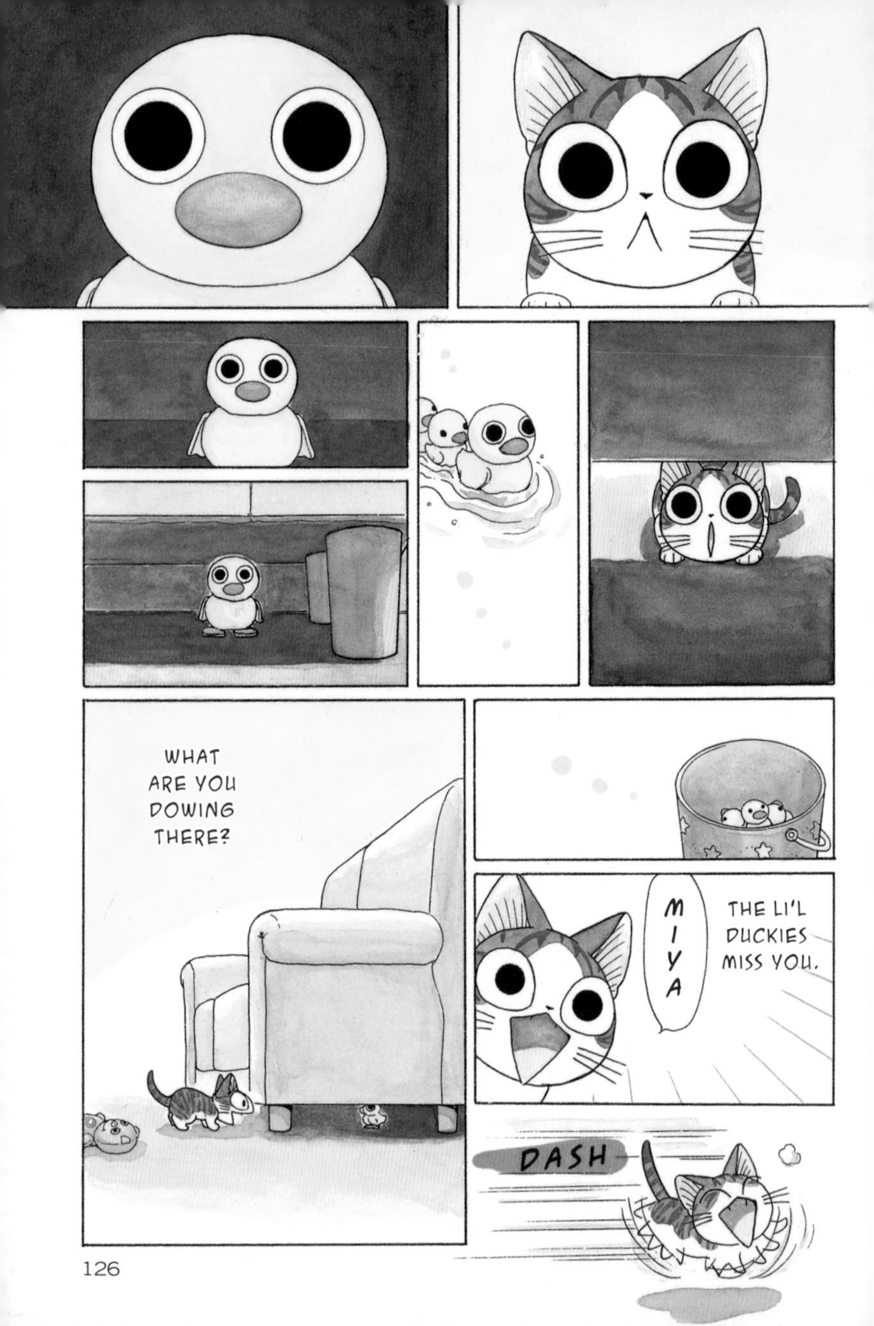
WHAT ARE YOU DOWING THERE?
MIYA
THE LI'L DUCKIES MISS YOU.
DASH

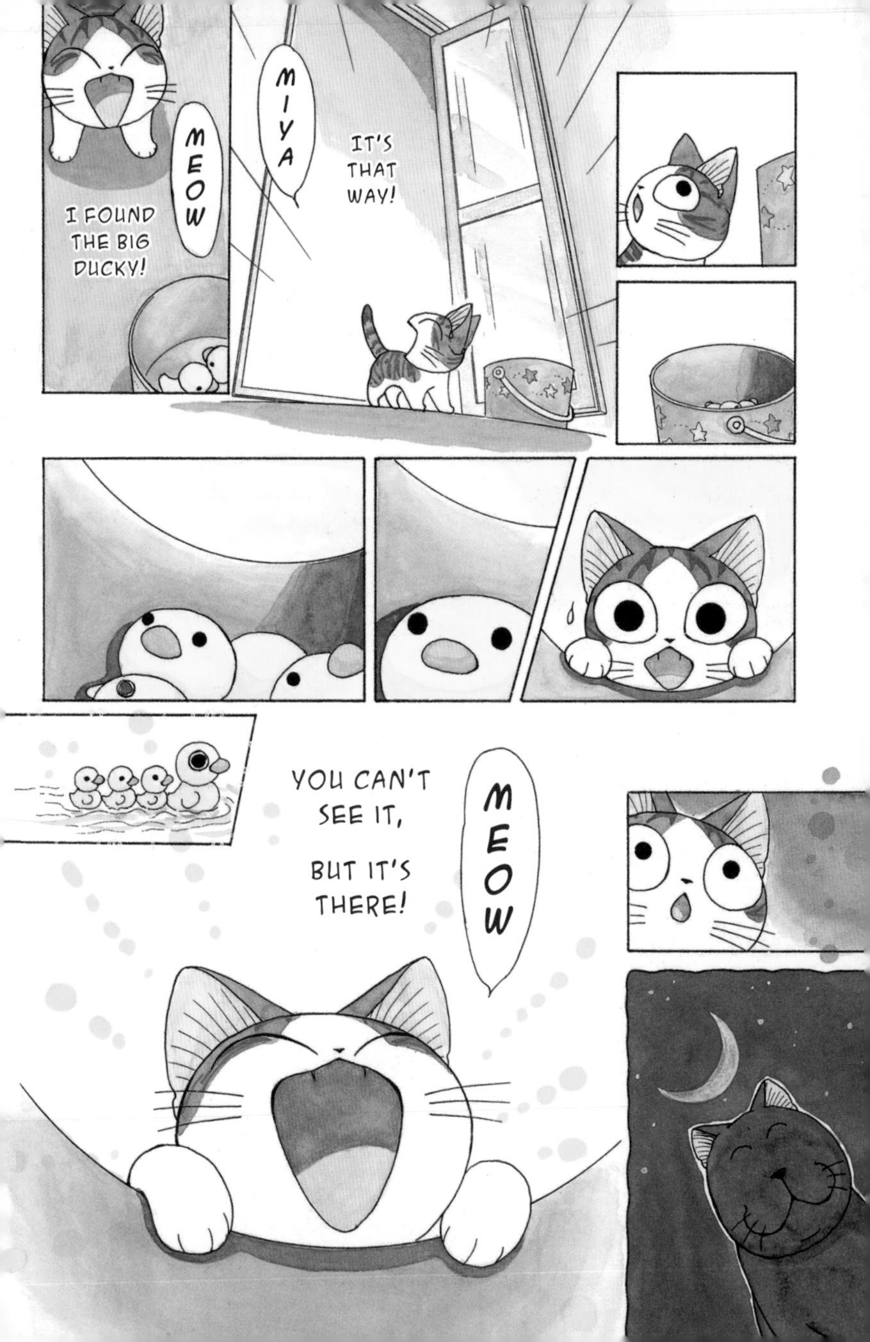

MEOW
I FOUND THE BIG DUCKY!
MIYA
IT'S THAT WAY!
YOU CAN'T SEE IT,
BUT IT'S THERE!
MEOW

I CAN'T SEE YA, BUT...

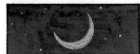

I KNOW YOU'RE THERE!

MEOW

the end

homemade 55: a cat is taken

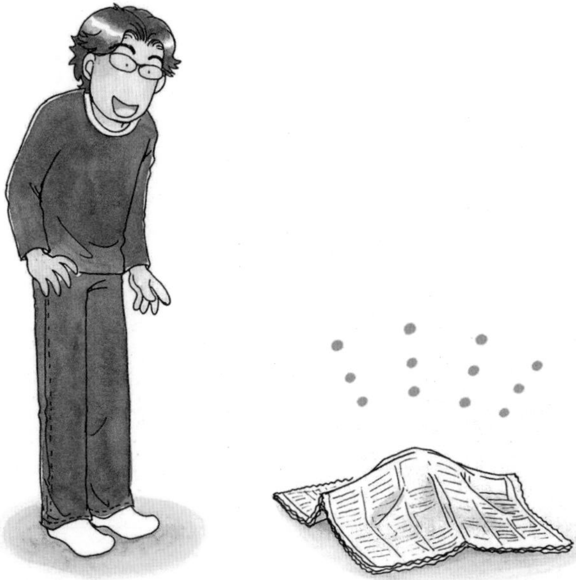

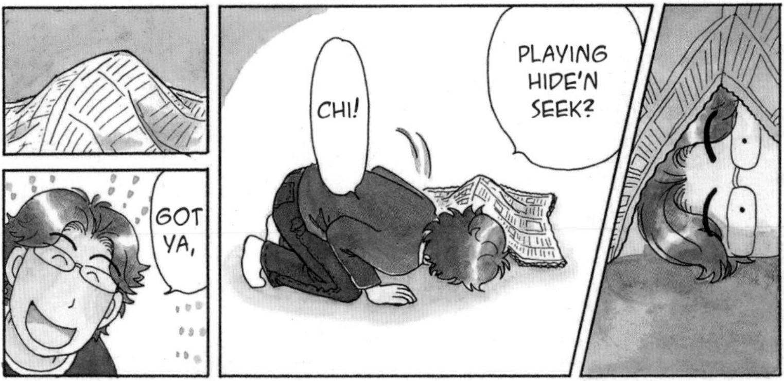
GOT YA,
CHI!
PLAYING HIDE'N SEEK?

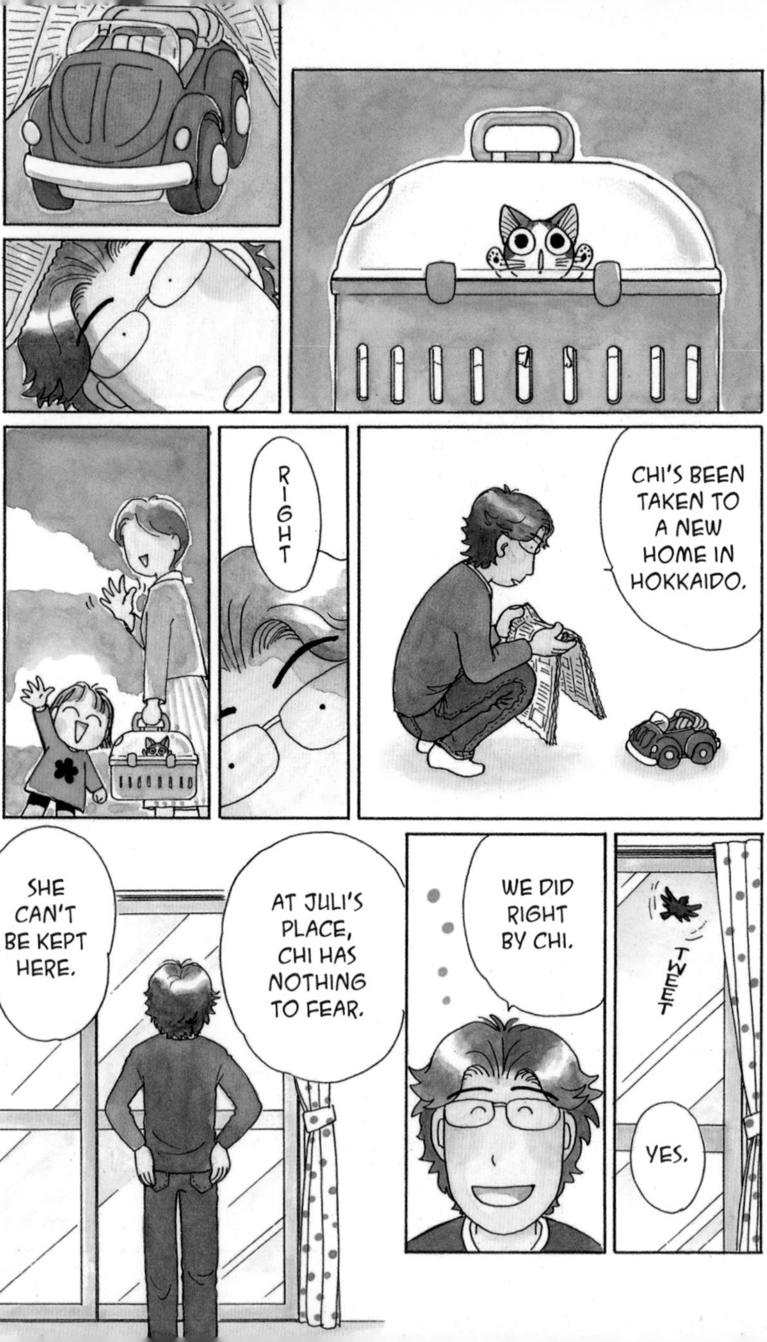
RIGHT
CHI'S BEEN TAKEN TO A NEW HOME IN HOKKAIDO.
SHE CAN'T BE KEPT HERE.
AT JULI'S PLACE, CHI HAS NOTHING TO FEAR.
WE DID RIGHT BY CHI.
TWEET
YES.

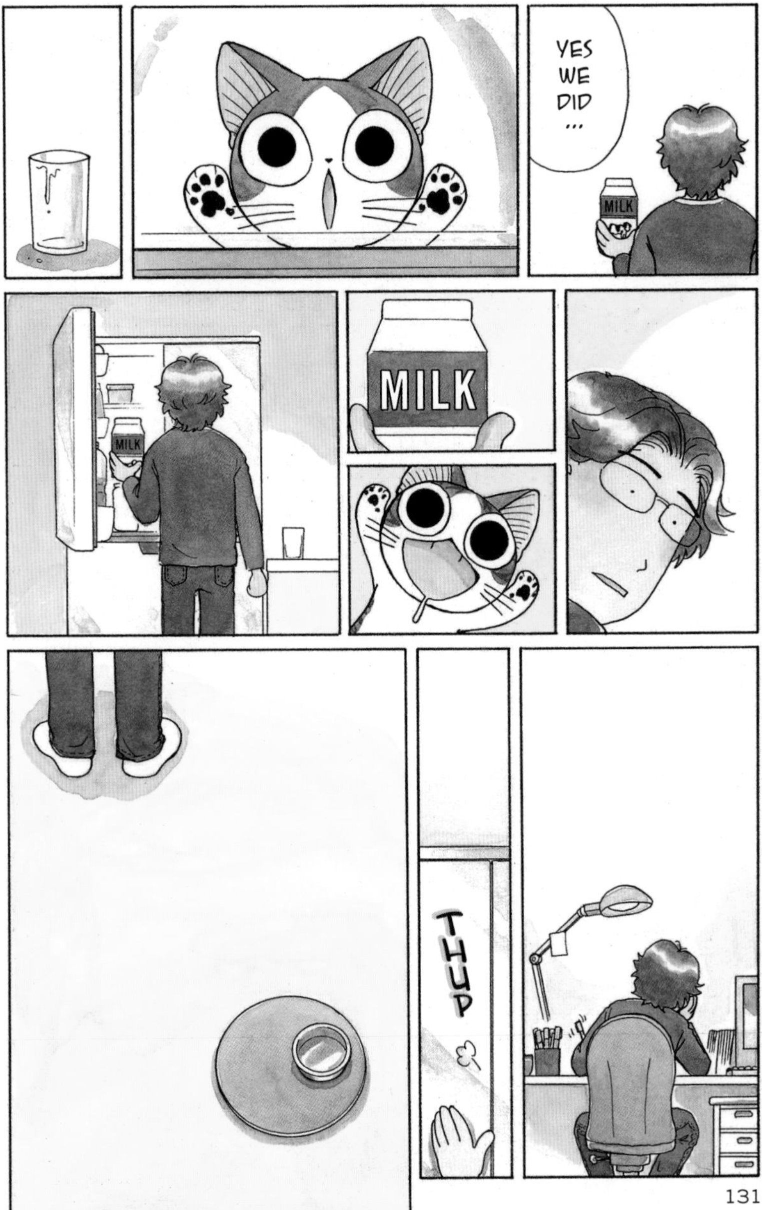
YES WE DID ...
MILK
MILK
MILK
THUP

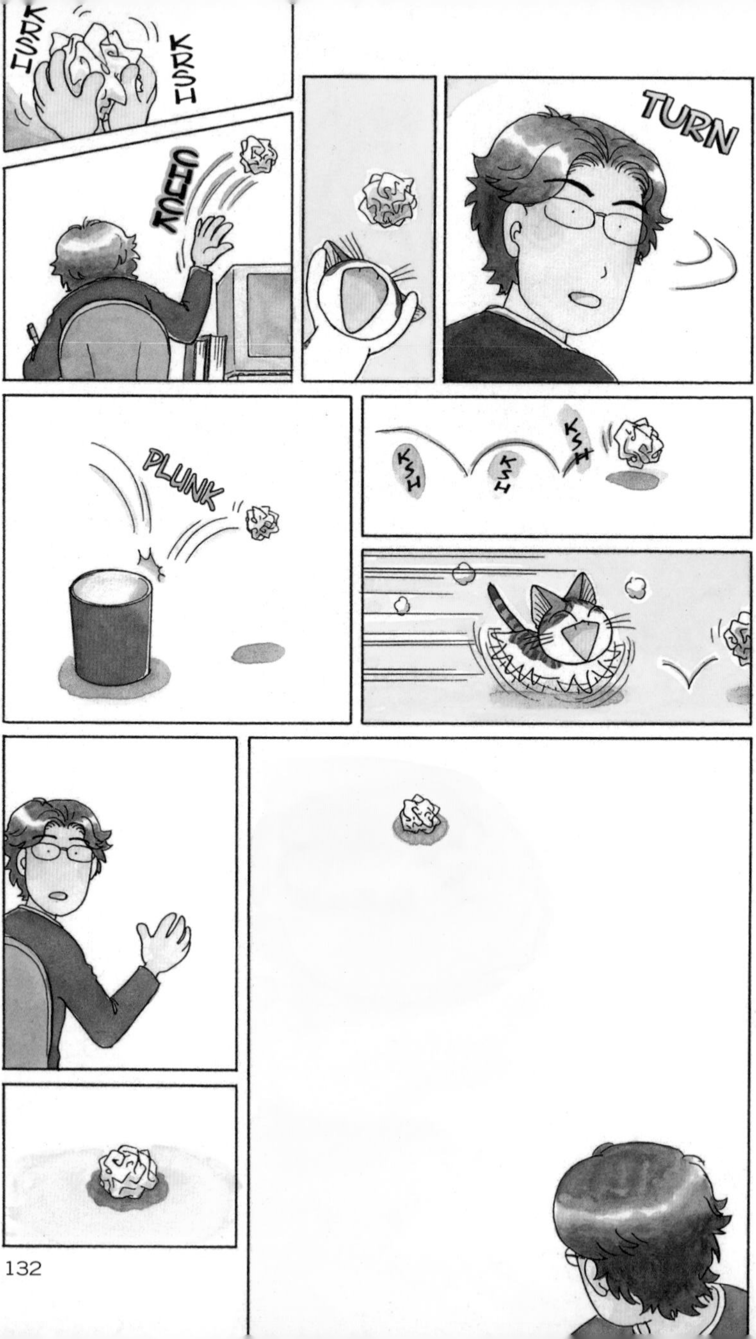
KRSH
KRSH
CHUCK
TURN
PLUNK
KSH
KSH
KSH

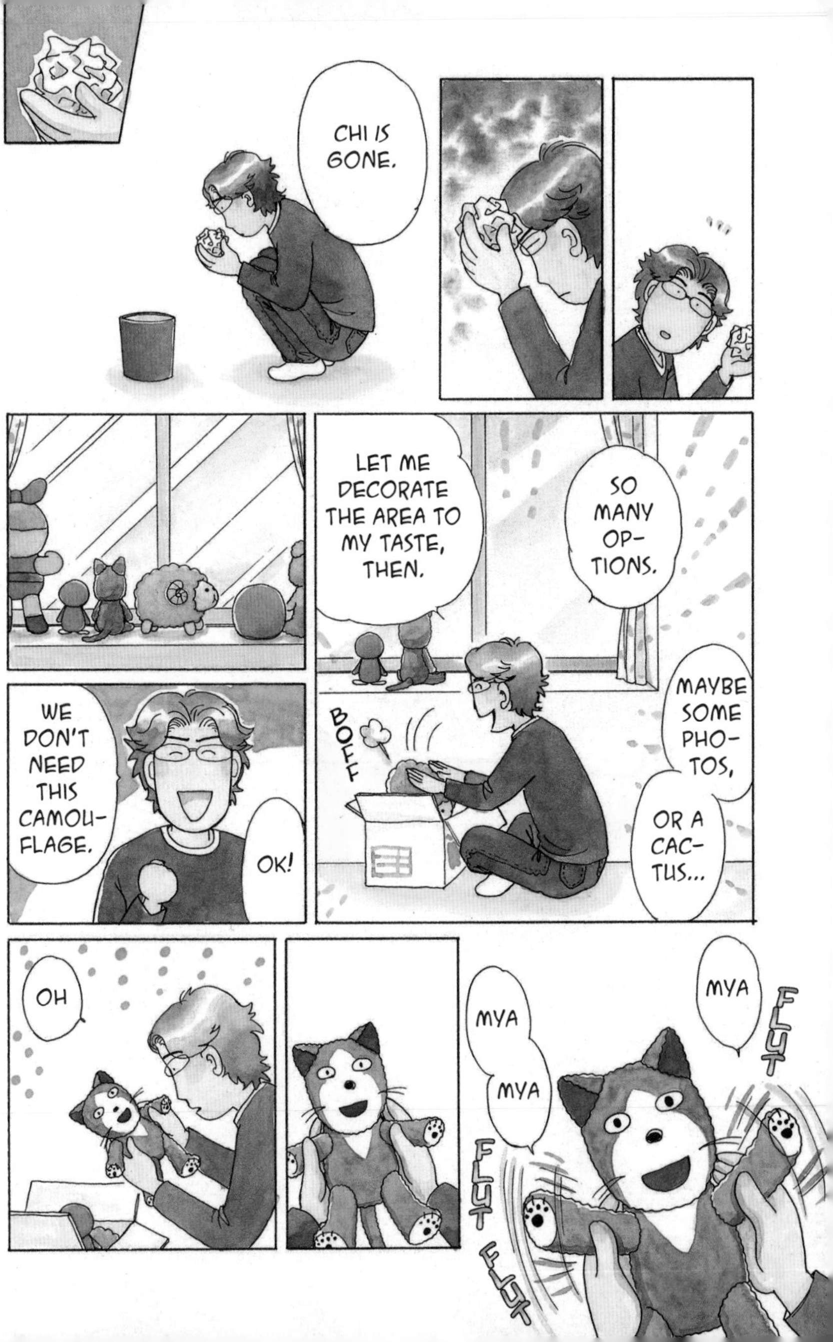
CHI IS GONE.
WE DON'T NEED THIS CAMOUFLAGE.
OK!
LET ME DECORATE THE AREA TO MY TASTE, THEN.
SO MANY OPTIONS.
BOFF
MAYBE SOME PHOTOS,
OR A CACTUS...
OH
MYA
MYA
MYA
FLUT
FLUT
FLUT

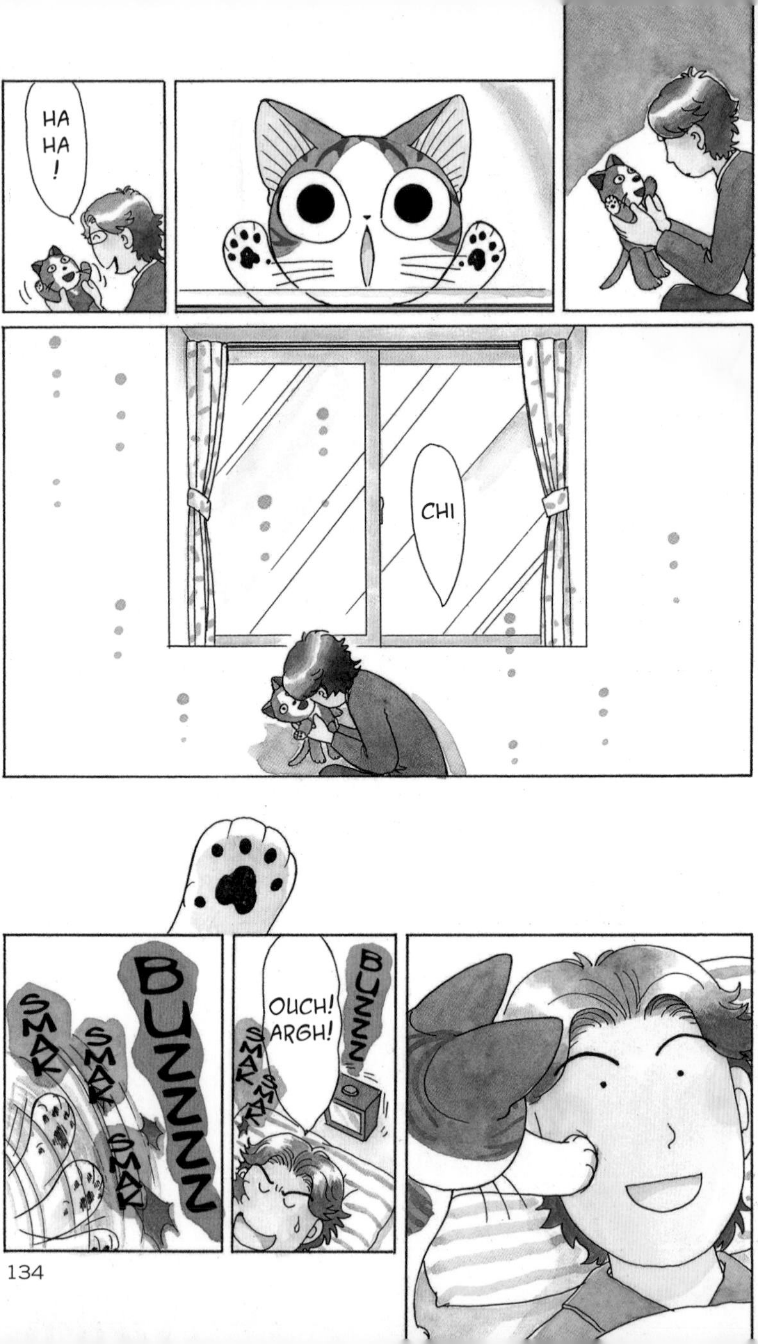
HA HA!
CHI
SMAK
SMAK
SMAK
BUZZZZ
OUCH! ARGH!
SMAK
SMAK
BUZZZ

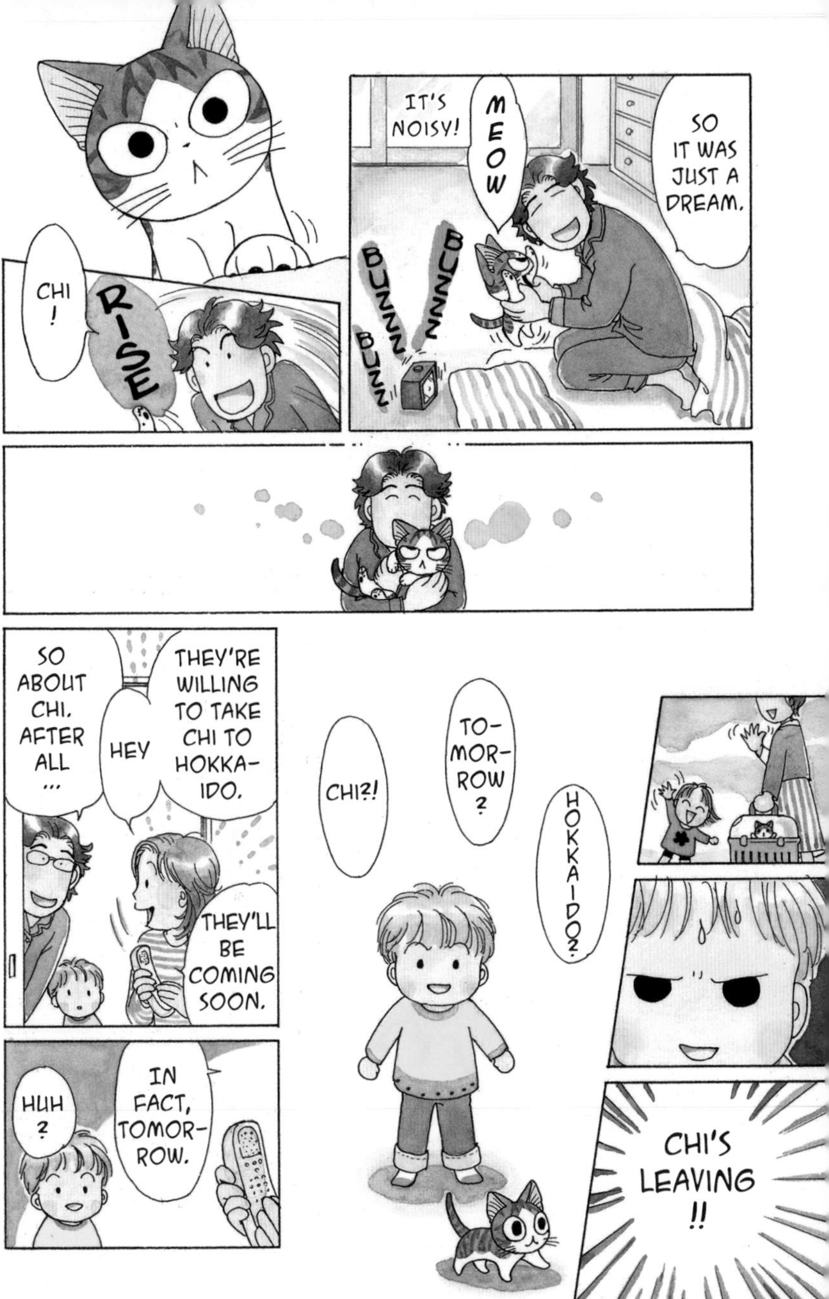
CHI!
RISE
IT'S NOISY!
MEOW
SO IT WAS JUST A DREAM.
BUZZZ
BUZZZ
BUZZ
SO ABOUT CHI, AFTER ALL...
HEY
THEY'RE WILLING TO TAKE CHI TO HOKKAIDO.
THEY'LL BE COMING SOON.
HUH?
IN FACT, TOMORROW.
CHI?!
TOMORROW?
HOKKAIDO?
CHI'S LEAVING!!

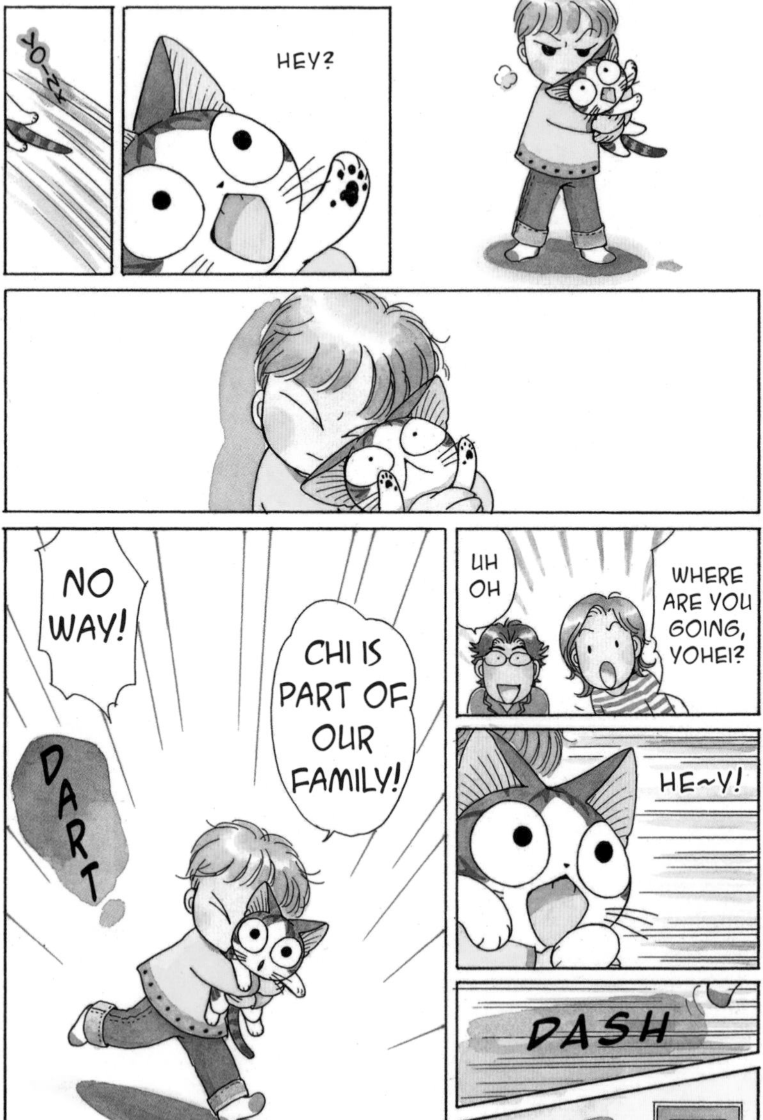
YO-ZY
HEY?
NO WAY!
CHI IS PART OF OUR FAMILY!
DART
UH OH
WHERE ARE YOU GOING, YOHEI?
HE~Y!
DASH
SLAM

the end

homemade 56: a cat runs away

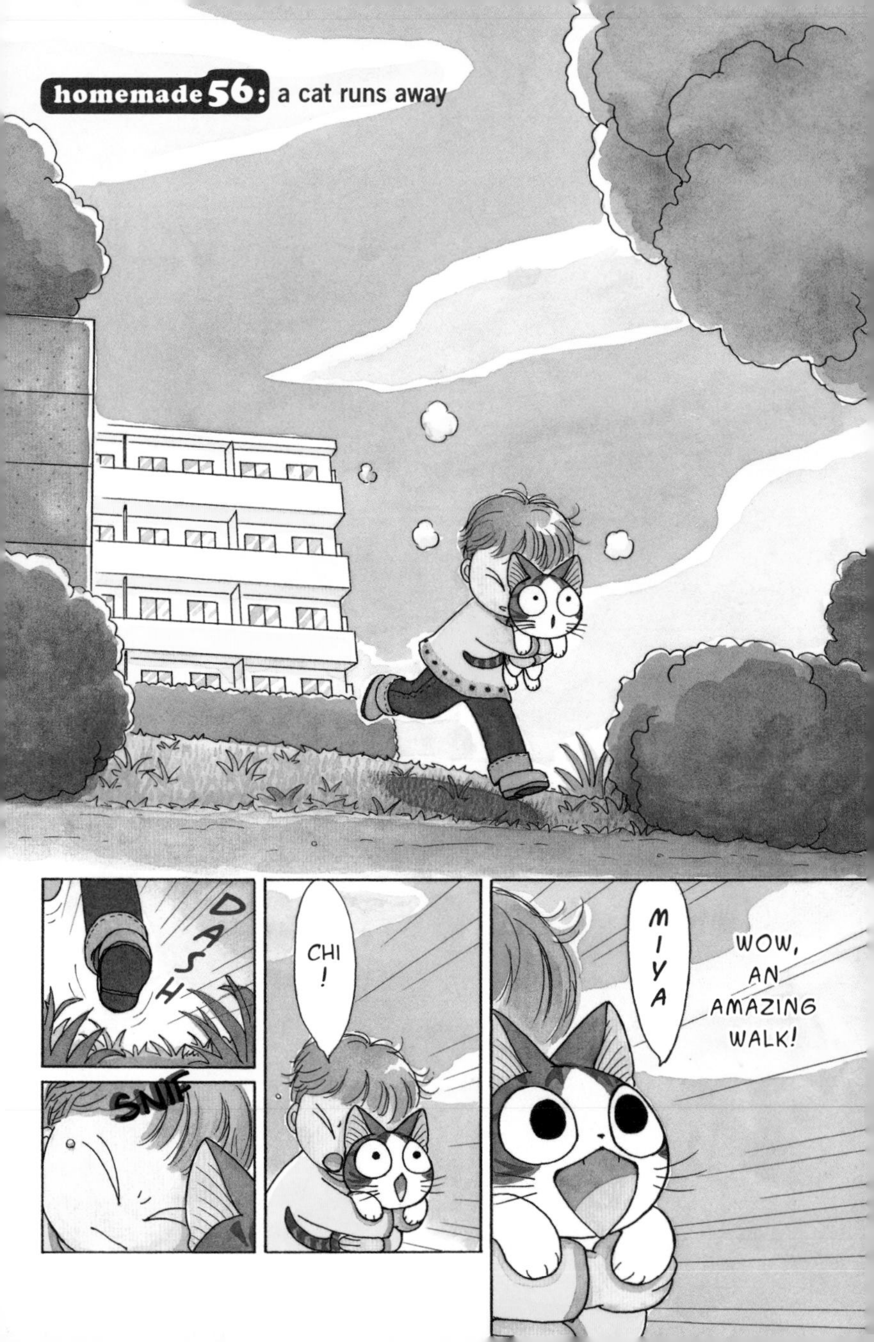
DASH
SNIF
CHI!
MIYA
WOW, AN AMAZING WALK!

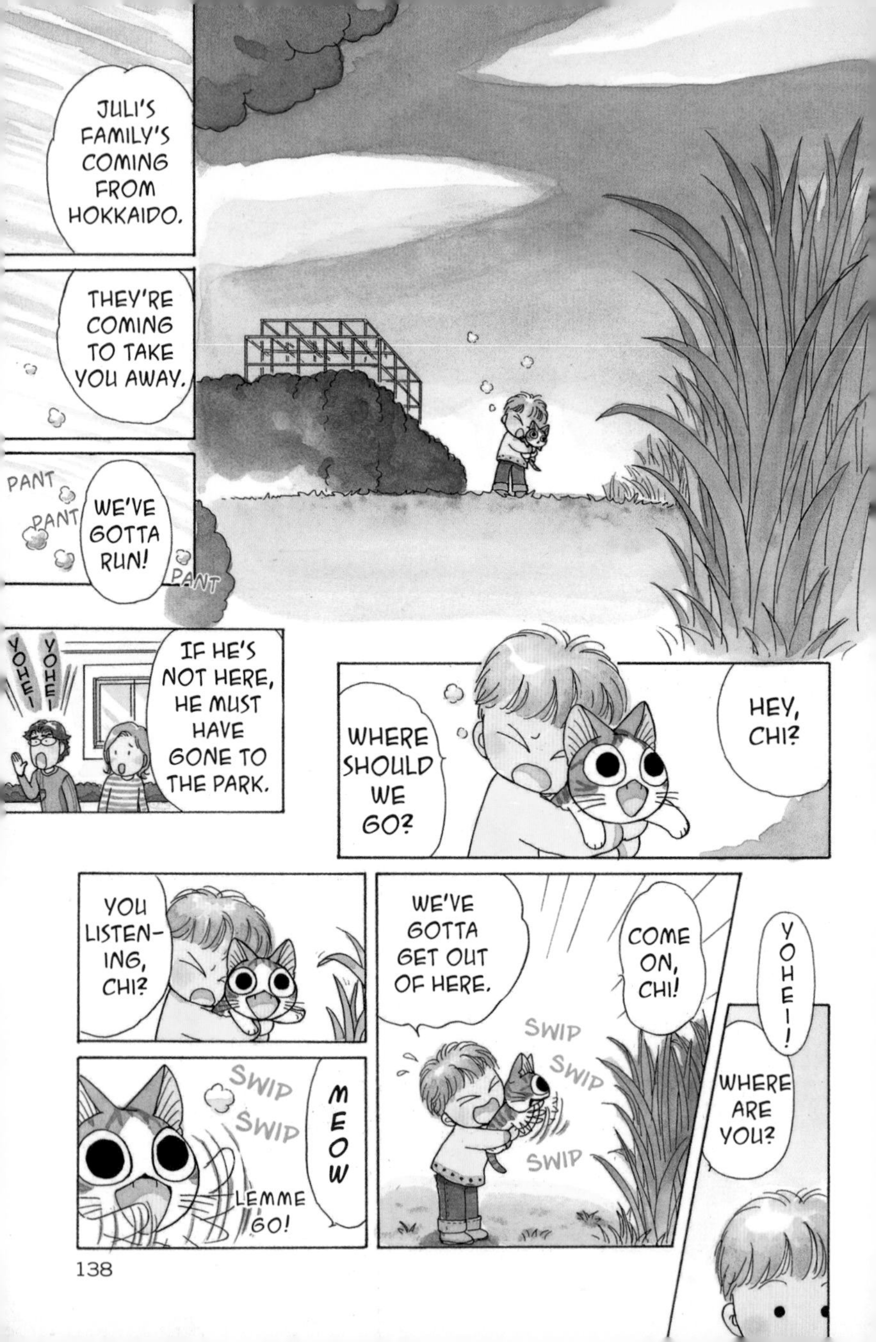
JULI'S FAMILY'S COMING FROM HOKKAIDO.
THEY'RE COMING TO TAKE YOU AWAY.
PANT
PANT
WE'VE GOTTA RUN!
PANT
YOHEI
YOHEI
IF HE'S NOT HERE, HE MUST HAVE GONE TO THE PARK.
WHERE SHOULD WE GO?
HEY, CHI?
YOU LISTEN-ING, CHI?
SWIP
SWIP
MEOW
LEMME GO!
WE'VE GOTTA GET OUT OF HERE.
COME ON, CHI!
SWIP
SWIP
SWIP
YOHEI!
WHERE ARE YOU?

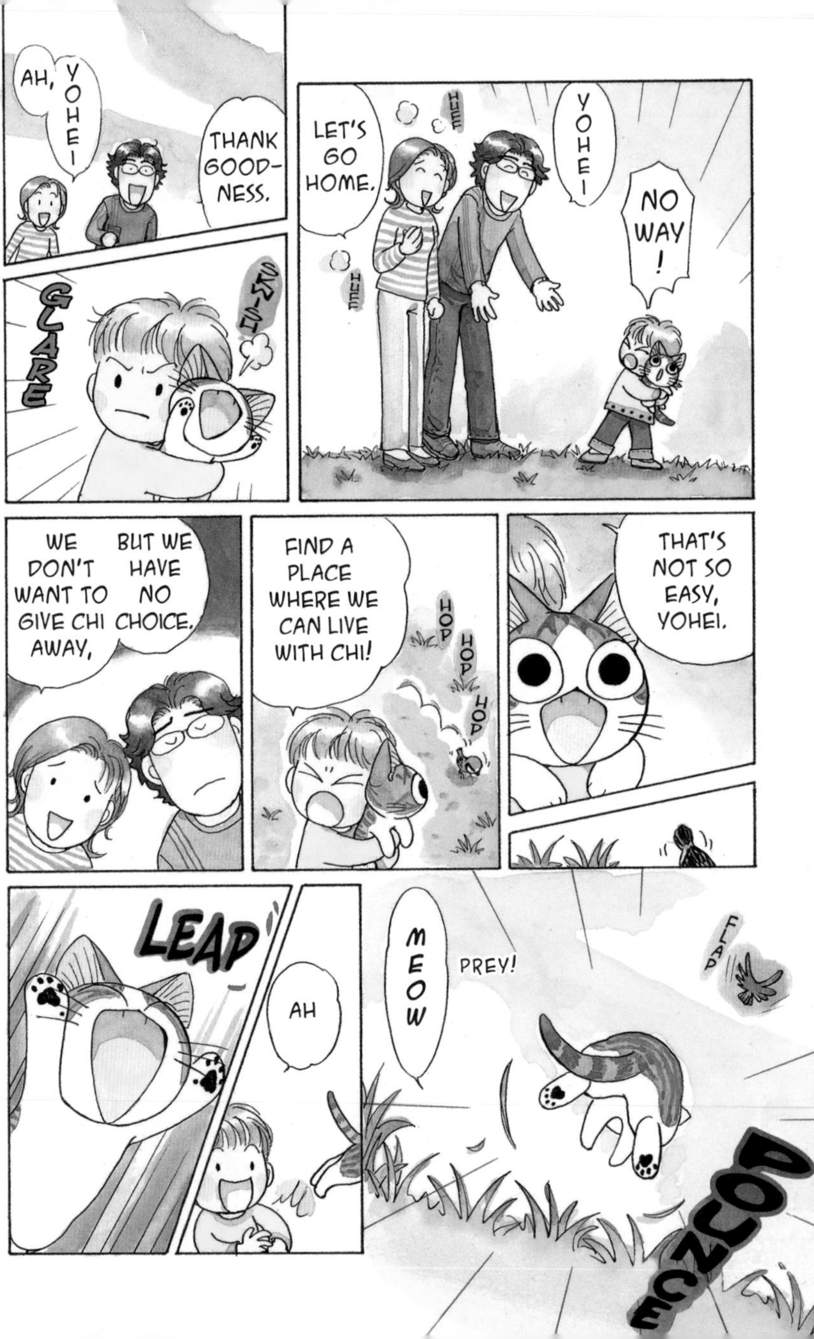

AH, YOHEI
THANK GOODNESS.
LET'S GO HOME.
HUFF
HUFF
YOHEI
NO WAY!
GLARE
SWISH
WE DON'T WANT TO GIVE CHI AWAY,
BUT WE HAVE NO CHOICE.
FIND A PLACE WHERE WE CAN LIVE WITH CHI!
HOP HOP HOP
THAT'S NOT SO EASY, YOHEI.
LEAP
AH
MEOW
PREY!
FLAP
POUNCE

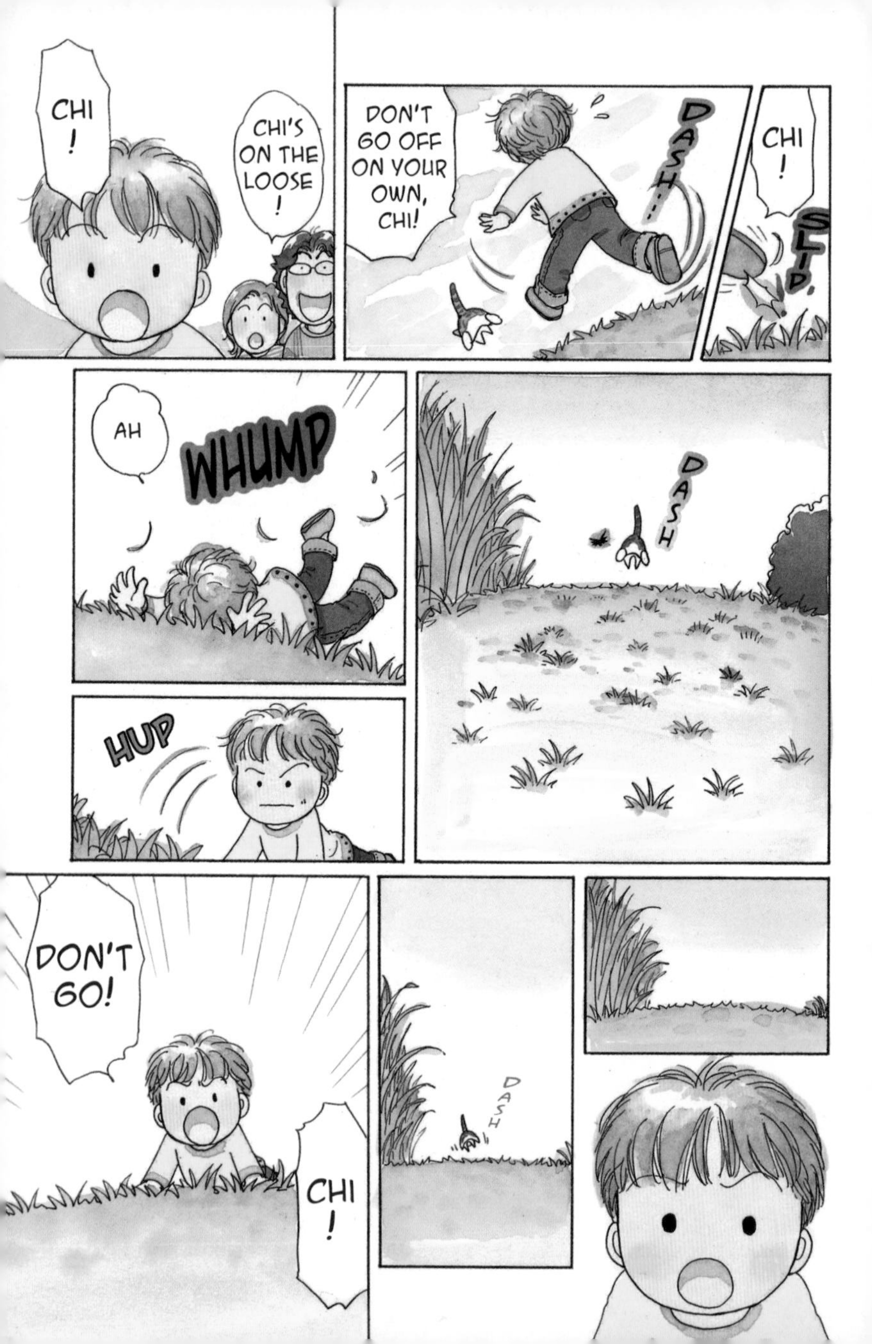

CHI!
CHI'S ON THE LOOSE!
DON'T GO OFF ON YOUR OWN, CHI!
DASH...
CHI!
SLID.
AH
WHUMP
DASH
HUP
DON'T GO!
CHI!
DASH

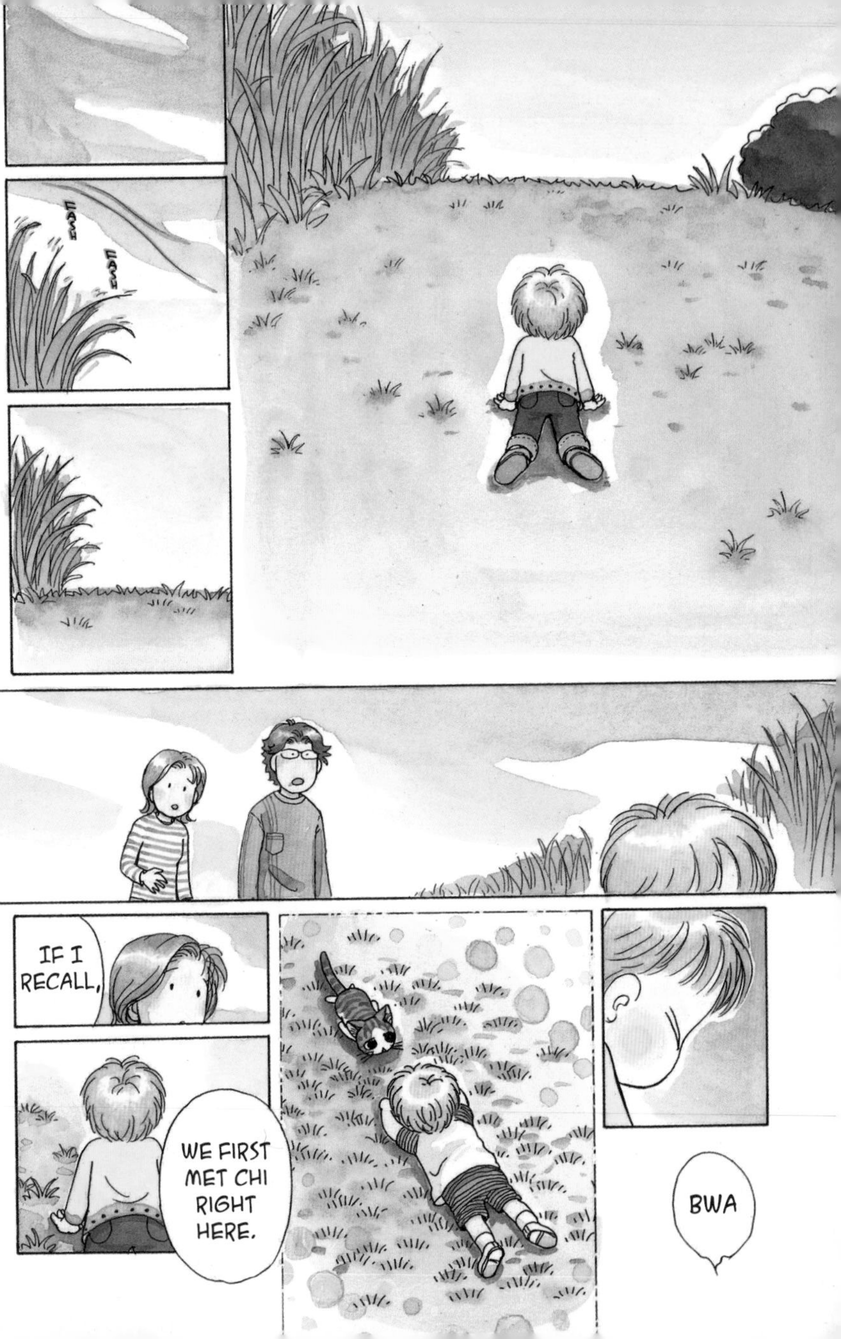

IF I RECALL,
WE FIRST MET CHI RIGHT HERE.
BWA

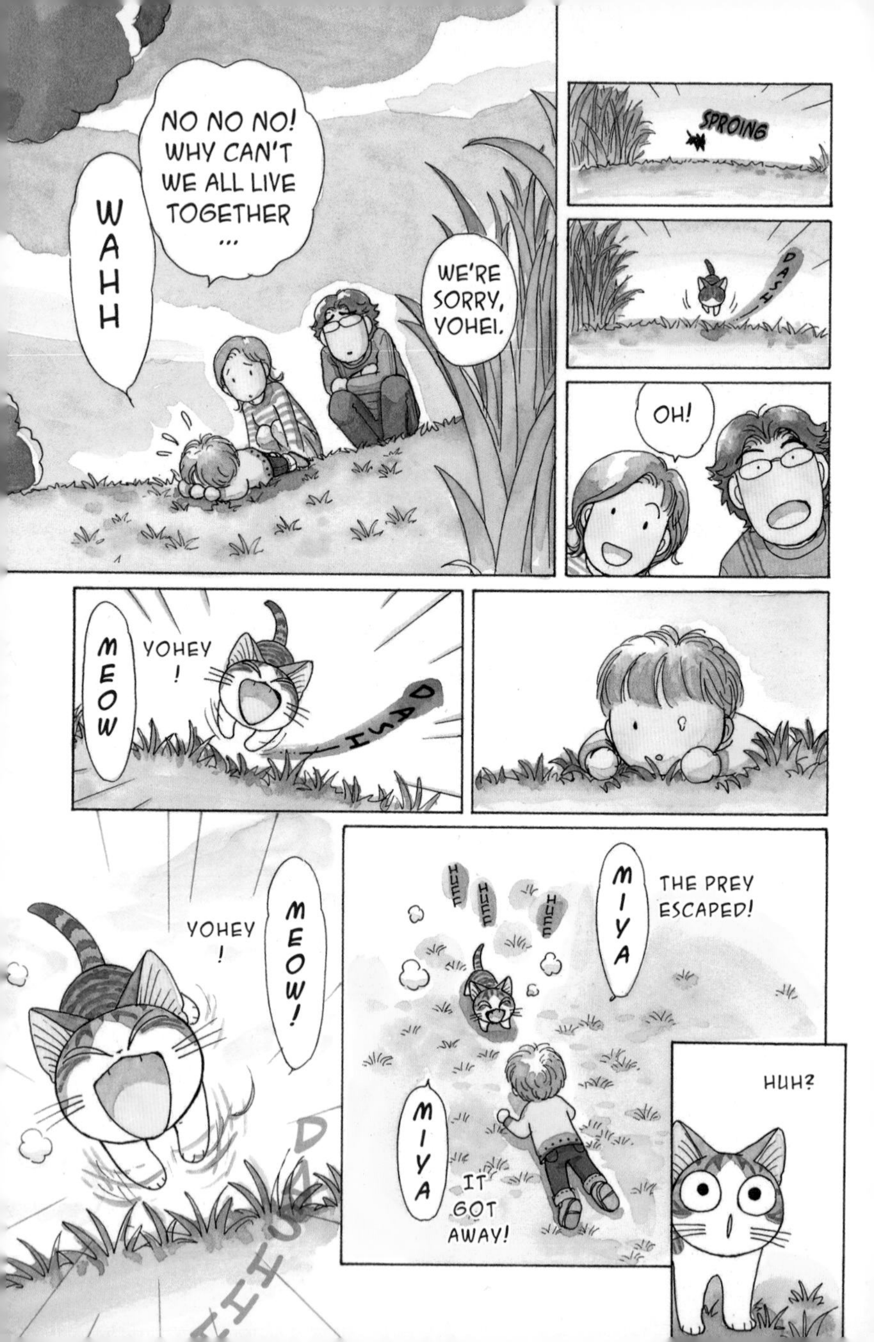
NO NO NO! WHY CAN'T WE ALL LIVE TOGETHER ...
WAHH
WE'RE SORRY, YOHEI.
SPROING
DASH
OH!
MEOW
YOHEY!
DASH
YOHEY!
MEOW!
DASH
HUFF
HUFF
HUFF
MIYA
THE PREY ESCAPED!
MIYA
IT GOT AWAY!
HUH?

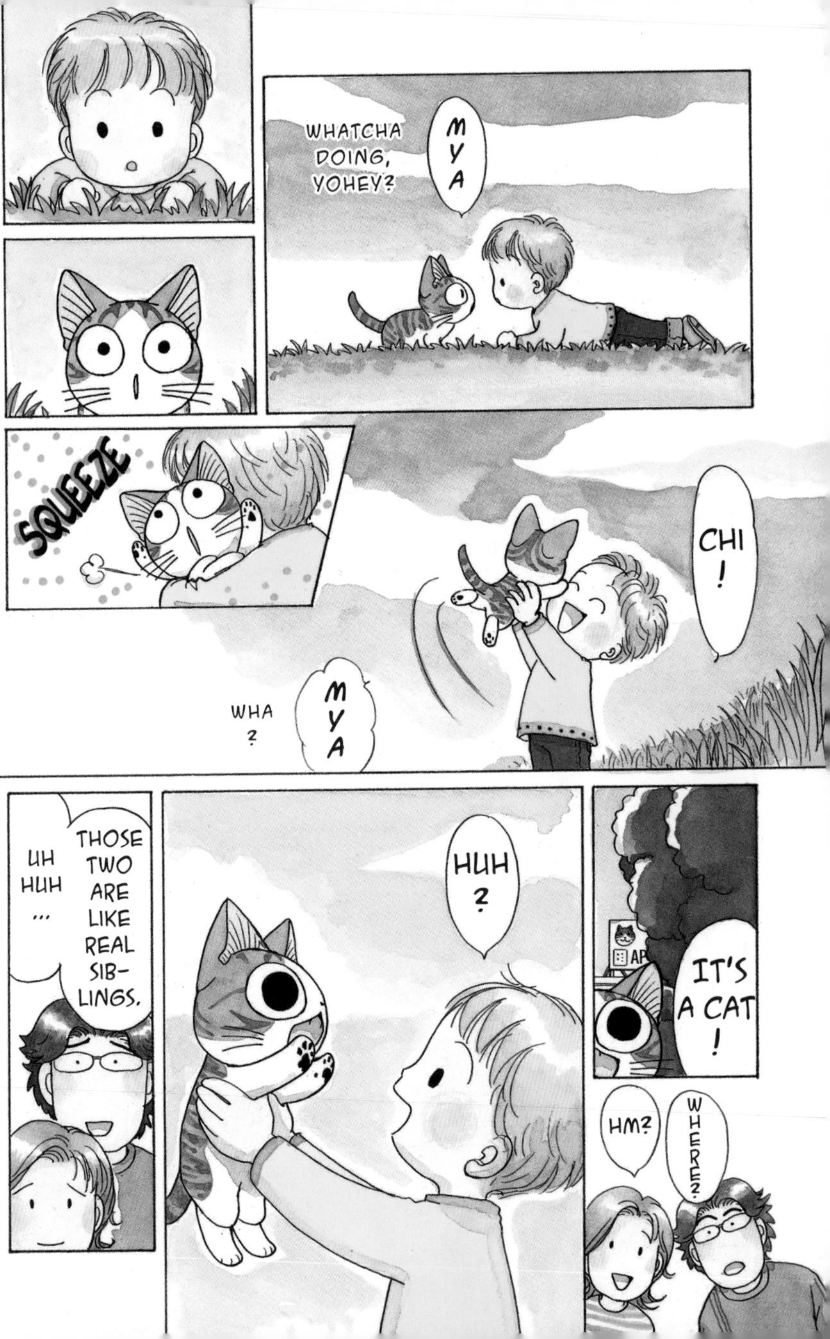
WHATCHA DOING, YOHEY?
MYA
SQUEEZE
CHI!
WHA?
MYA
THOSE TWO ARE LIKE REAL SIB- LINGS.
UH HUH ...
HUH?
IT'S A CAT!
HM?
WHERE?

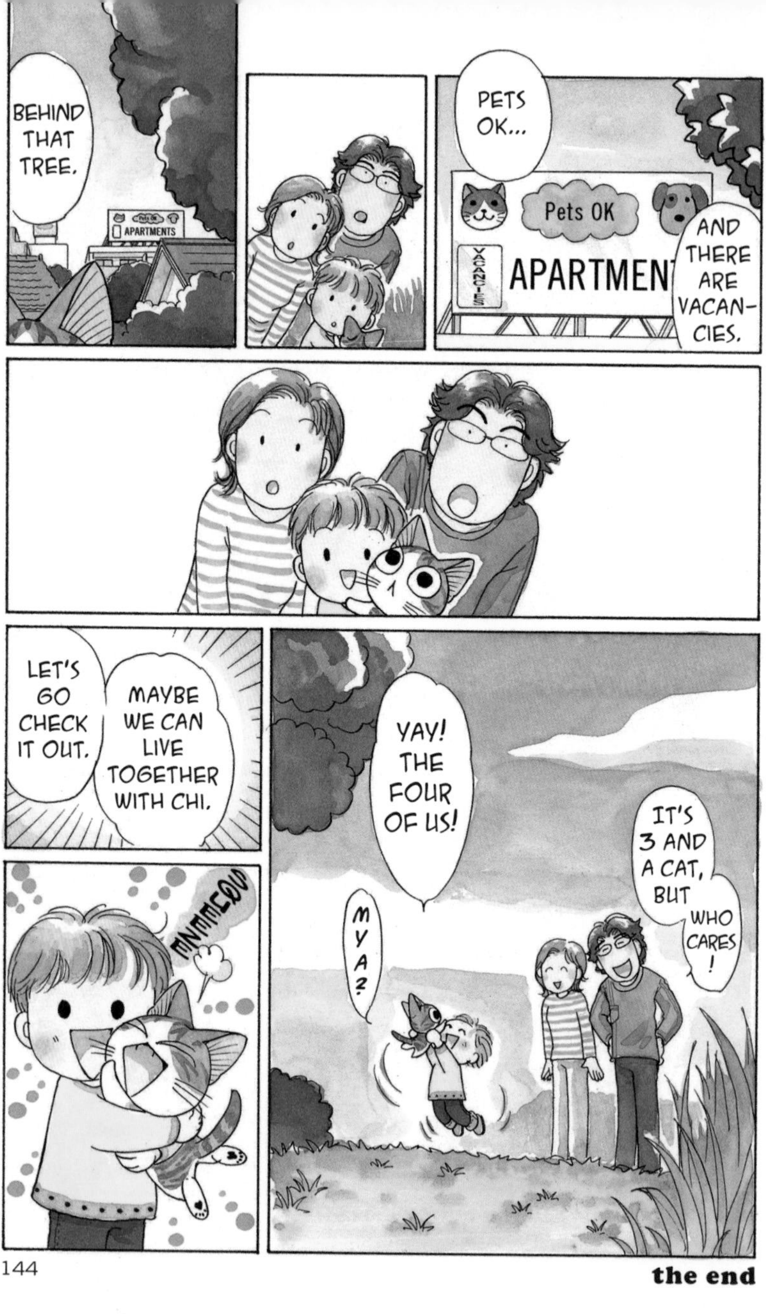
BEHIND THAT TREE.
Pets OK
APARTMENTS
PETS OK...
Pets OK
VACANCIES
APARTMENT
AND THERE ARE VACANCIES.
LET'S GO CHECK IT OUT.
MAYBE WE CAN LIVE TOGETHER WITH CHI.
YAY! THE FOUR OF US!
MYA?
IT'S 3 AND A CAT, BUT
WHO CARES!

the end

So how was
Chi's Sweet Home volume 3?

This is the volume where I leave Chi,
but I bet you're wondering
what'll happen to Chi
and the Yamadas.

Well, let's find out.

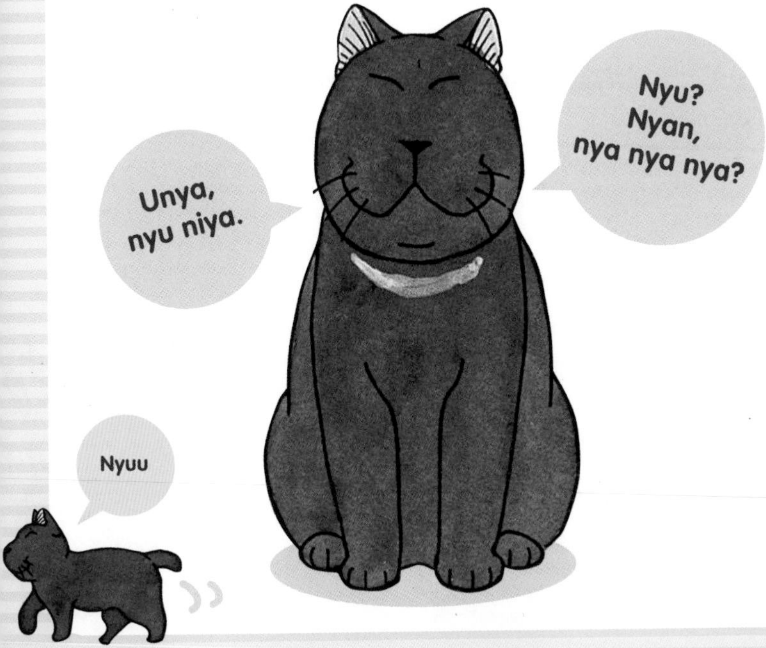
Unya, nyu niya.
Nyu? Nyan, nya nya nya?
Nyuu

1st Event

A Big Move

Will the pet-friendly apartment building they found by chance provide a new home? What sort of place will the Yamadas and their kitten be moving into?

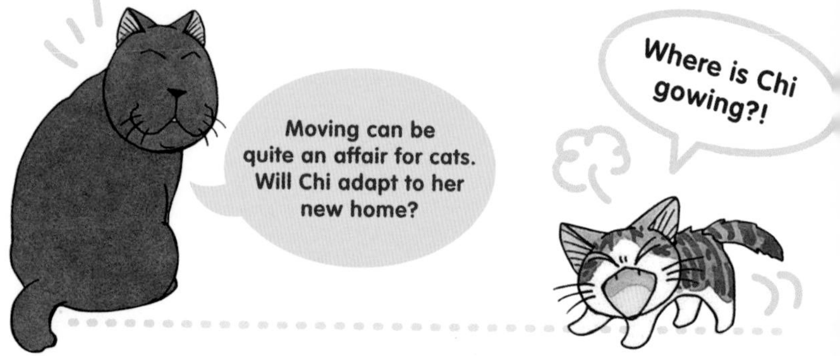
Moving can be quite an affair for cats. Will Chi adapt to her new home?
Where is Chi gowing?!

2nd Event

New Encounters?

There must be other pets living around Chi's new home. What sort of people and animals will we meet? Will Chi and Yohei be blessed with another encounter?

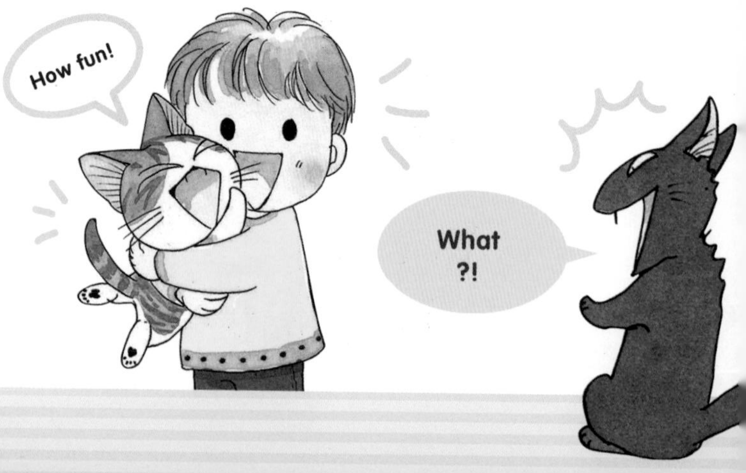
How fun!
What ?!

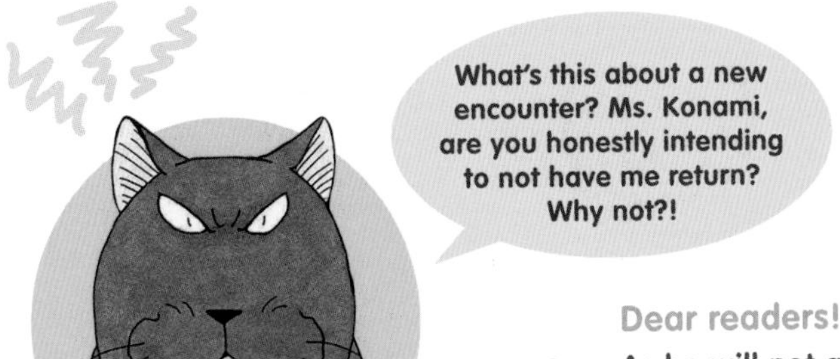
What's this about a new encounter? Ms. Konami, are you honestly intending to not have me return? Why not?!

Dear readers!

As he will not appear in the next volume, we await your messages of encouragement for the pitiful black cat.

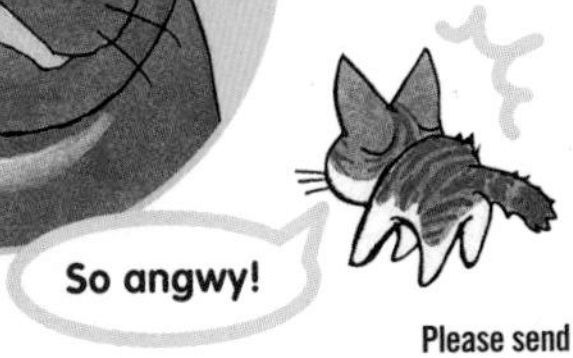
So angwy!

Please send your letters for him to our mailing address on the last page.

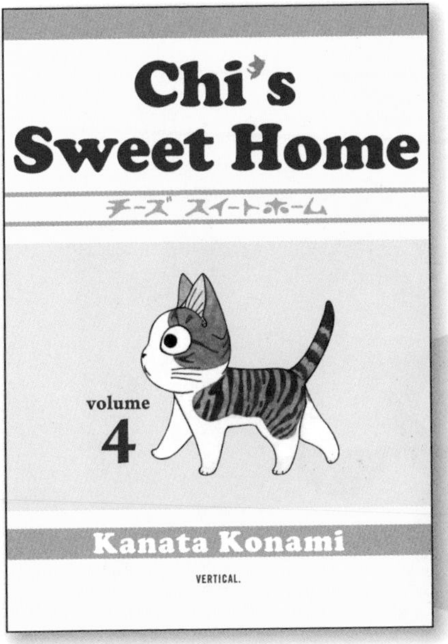
Chi's Sweet Home
チーズスイートホーム
volume 4
Kanata Konami
VERTICAL.

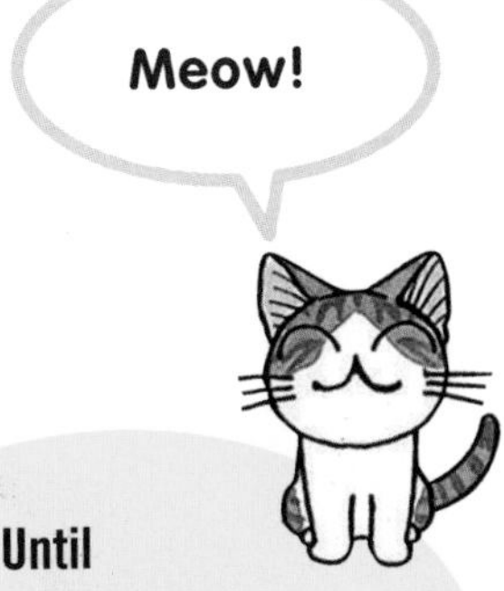
Meow!

Until Volume 4 of *Chi's Sweet Home*, on sale December 2010!

Meet our new friends!
They're easy to make!
The Cuter Book
ARANZI ARONZO
ARONZO
ARANZI ARONZO

CUTENESS RETURNS

Taking "kawaii" to new heights, Aranzi Aranzo's *The Cuter Book* doubles the doll count and quadruples the cute factor.

Full of character intros and patterns from the legendary Aranzi Aranzo!

40 designs, including special holiday mascots!

THE CUTER BOOK
$14.95 / $18.95 CND

Simply cute...
The best-selling book that launched the cute-it-yourself craze.

They're easy to make and easier to love.

THE CUTE BOOK
$12.95 / $16.00 CND

TWIN SPI

Space has never seemed so close and yet so far!

"It's easy to see why the series was a smash hit in its native land…
Each page contains more genuine emotion than an entire space fleet's
worth of similarly themed stories." —*Publishers Weekly*

Volume 1: 978-1-934287-84-2
Volume 2: 978-1-934287-86-6
Volume 3: 978-1-934287-90-3
$10.95/$12.99 each

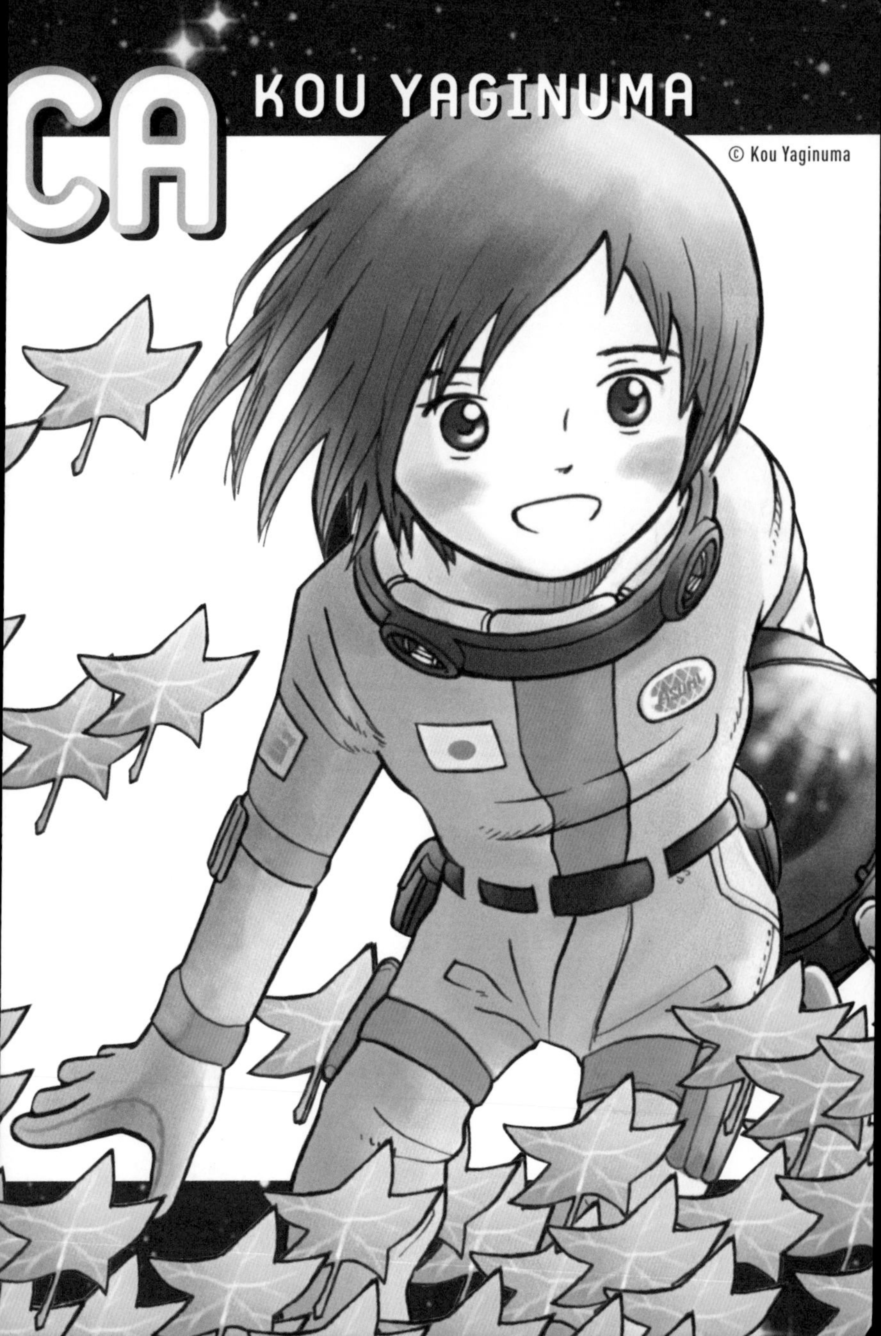
CA
KOU YAGINUMA
© Kou Yaginuma

Chi's Sweet Home, volume 3

Translation - Ed Chavez
Production - Hiroko Mizuno

First published in Japan in 2006 by Kodansha, Ltd., Tokyo
Publication for this English edition arranged through Kodansha, Ltd., Tokyo
English language version produced by Vertical, Inc.

Translation provided by Vertical, Inc., 2010
Published by Vertical, Inc., New York

Originally published in Japanese as *Chiizu Suiito Houmu* by Kodansha, Ltd., 2005-2006
Chiizu Suiito Houmu first serialized in *Morning*, Kodansha, Ltd., 2004-

Kuro-tan illustrated by Risa Ito, 2005

This is a work of fiction.

ISBN: 978-1-934287-91-0

Manufactured in China

First Edition

Vertical, Inc.
1185 Avenue of the Americas, 32nd Floor
New York, NY 10036
www.vertical-inc.com

Special thanks to Risa Ito, K. Kitamoto, & Y. Tanahashi